Innovation, Technology, and Knowledge Management

Series Editor
Elias G. Carayannis
George Washington University
Washington, DC, USA

More information about this series at http://www.springer.com/series/8124

Lihong Zhou • José Miguel Baptista Nunes

Knowledge Sharing in Chinese Hospitals

Identifying Sharing Barriers in Traditional Chinese and Western Medicine Collaboration

Lihong Zhou
School of Information Management
Wuhan University
Wuhan
Hubei, China

José Miguel Baptista Nunes
Information School
The University of Sheffield
Sheffield
South Yorkshire, UK

ISSN 2197-5698	ISSN 2197-5701 (electronic)
ISBN 978-3-662-45161-8	ISBN 978-3-662-45162-5 (eBook)
DOI 10.1007/978-3-662-45162-5
Springer Heidelberg New York Dordrecht London

Library of Congress Control Number: 2014953825

© Springer-Verlag Berlin Heidelberg 2015

This work is subject to copyright. All rights are reserved by the Publisher, whether the whole or part of the material is concerned, specifically the rights of translation, reprinting, reuse of illustrations, recitation, broadcasting, reproduction on microfilms or in any other physical way, and transmission or information storage and retrieval, electronic adaptation, computer software, or by similar or dissimilar methodology now known or hereafter developed. Exempted from this legal reservation are brief excerpts in connection with reviews or scholarly analysis or material supplied specifically for the purpose of being entered and executed on a computer system, for exclusive use by the purchaser of the work. Duplication of this publication or parts thereof is permitted only under the provisions of the Copyright Law of the Publisher's location, in its current version, and permission for use must always be obtained from Springer. Permissions for use may be obtained through RightsLink at the Copyright Clearance Center. Violations are liable to prosecution under the respective Copyright Law.

The use of general descriptive names, registered names, trademarks, service marks, etc. in this publication does not imply, even in the absence of a specific statement, that such names are exempt from the relevant protective laws and regulations and therefore free for general use.

While the advice and information in this book are believed to be true and accurate at the date of publication, neither the authors nor the editors nor the publisher can accept any legal responsibility for any errors or omissions that may be made. The publisher makes no warranty, express or implied, with respect to the material contained herein.

Printed on acid-free paper

Springer is part of Springer Science+Business Media (www.springer.com)

Series Foreword

The Springer book series *Innovation, Technology, and Knowledge Management* was launched in March 2008 as a forum and intellectual, scholarly "podium" for global/local, transdisciplinary, transsectoral, public–private, and leading/"bleeding" edge ideas, theories, and perspectives on these topics.

The book series is accompanied by the Springer *Journal of the Knowledge Economy*, which was launched in 2009 with the same editorial leadership.

The series showcases provocative views that diverge from the current "conventional wisdom" that are properly grounded in theory and practice, and that consider the concepts of **robust competitiveness**,[1] **sustainable entrepreneurship**,[2] and **democratic capitalism**,[3] central to its philosophy and objectives. More specifically,

---

[1] We define *sustainable entrepreneurship* as the creation of viable, profitable, and scalable firms. Such firms engender the formation of self-replicating and mutually enhancing innovation networks and knowledge clusters (innovation ecosystems), leading toward robust competitiveness (E. G. Carayannis, *International Journal of Innovation and Regional Development* 1(3), 235–254, 2009).

[2] We understand *robust competitiveness* to be a state of economic being and becoming that avails systematic and defensible "unfair advantages" to the entities that are part of the economy. Such competitiveness is built on mutually complementary and reinforcing low-, medium-, and high-technology and public and private sector entities (government agencies, private firms, universities, and nongovernmental organizations) (E. G. Carayannis, *International Journal of Innovation and Regional Development* 1(3), 235–254, 2009).

[3] The concepts of *robust competitiveness and sustainable entrepreneurship* are pillars of a regime that we call "*democratic capitalism*" (as opposed to "popular or casino capitalism"), in which real opportunities for education and economic prosperity are available to all, especially but not only younger people. These are the direct derivatives of a collection of topdown policies as well as bottom-up initiatives (including strong research and development policies and funding, but going beyond these to include the development of innovation networks and knowledge

the aim of this series is to highlight emerging research and practice at the dynamic intersection of these fields, where individuals, organizations, industries, regions, and nations are harnessing creativity and invention to achieve and sustain growth.

Books that are part of the series explore the impact of innovation at the "macro" (economies, markets), "meso" (industries, firms), and "micro" levels (teams, individuals), drawing from such related disciplines as finance, organizational psychology, research and development, science policy, information systems, and strategy, with the underlying theme that for innovation to be useful it must involve the sharing and application of knowledge.

Some of the key anchoring concepts of the series are outlined in the figure below and the definitions that follow (all definitions are from E. G. Carayannis and D. F. J. Campbell, *International Journal of Technology Management*, 46, 3–4, 2009).

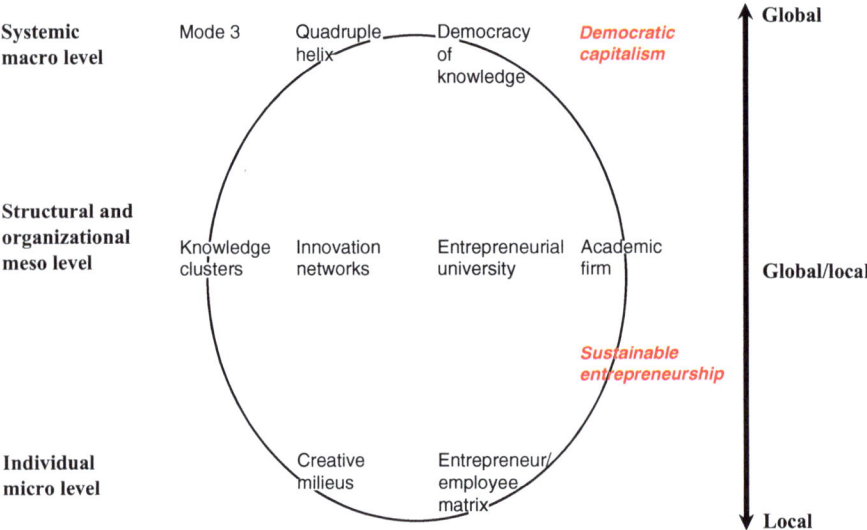

Conceptual profile of the series *Innovation, Technology*, and *Knowledge Management*

- The "Mode 3" Systems Approach for Knowledge Creation, Diffusion, and Use: "Mode 3" is a multilateral, multinodal, multimodal, and multilevel systems approach to the conceptualization, design, and management of real and virtual, "knowledge-stock" and "knowledge-flow," modalities that catalyze, accelerate, and support the creation, diffusion, sharing, absorption, and use of cospecialized knowledge assets. "Mode 3" is based on a system-theoretic perspective of

clusters across regions and sectors) (E. G. Carayannis and A. Kaloudis, *Japan Economic Currents*, pp. 6–10 January 2009).

socioeconomic, political, technological, and cultural trends and conditions that shape the coevolution of knowledge with the "knowledge-based and knowledge-driven, global/local economy and society."
- Quadruple Helix: Quadruple helix, in this context, means to add to the triple helix of government, university, and industry a "fourth helix" that we identify as the "media-based and culture-based public." This fourth helix associates with "media," "creative industries," "culture," "values," "life styles," "art," and perhaps also the notion of the "creative class."
- Innovation Networks: Innovation networks are real and virtual infrastructures and infratechnologies that serve to nurture creativity, trigger invention, and catalyze innovation in a public and/or private domain context (for instance, government– university–industry public–private research and technology development coopetitive partnerships).
- Knowledge Clusters: Knowledge clusters are agglomerations of cospecialized, mutually complementary, and reinforcing knowledge assets in the form of "knowledge stocks" and "knowledge flows" that exhibit self-organizing, learning- driven, dynamically adaptive competences, and trends in the context of an open systems perspective.
- Twenty-First Century Innovation Ecosystem: A twenty-first century innovation ecosystem is a multilevel, multimodal, multinodal, and multiagent system of systems. The constituent systems consist of innovation metanetworks (networks of innovation networks and knowledge clusters) and knowledge metaclusters (clusters of innovation networks and knowledge clusters) as building blocks and organized in a self-referential or chaotic fractal knowledge and innovation architecture,[4] which in turn constitute agglomerations of human, social, intellectual, and financial capital stocks and flows as well as cultural and technological artifacts and modalities, continually coevolving, cospecializing, and cooperating. These innovation networks and knowledge clusters also form, reform, and dissolve within diverse institutional, political, technological, and socioeconomic domains, including government, university, industry, and nongovernmental organizations and involving information and communication technologies, biotechnologies, advanced materials, nanotechnologies, and next-Generation energy technologies.

Who is this book series published for? The book series addresses a diversity of audiences in different settings:

1. *Academic communities*: Academic communities worldwide represent a core group of readers. This follows from the theoretical/conceptual interest of the book series to influence academic discourses in the fields of knowledge, also carried by the claim of a certain saturation of academia with the current concepts and the postulate of a window of opportunity for new or at least additional concepts. Thus, it represents a key challenge for the series to exercise a certain impact on discourses in academia. In principle, all academic communities that

---

[4] E. G. Carayannis, *Strategic Management of Technological Learning*, CRC Press, 2000.

are interested in knowledge (knowledge and innovation) could be tackled by the book series. The interdisciplinary (transdisciplinary) nature of the book series underscores that the scope of the book series is not limited a priori to a specific basket of disciplines. From a radical viewpoint, one could create the hypothesis that there is no discipline where knowledge is of no importance.
2. *Decision makers—private/academic entrepreneurs and public (governmental, subgovernmental)* actors: Two different groups of decision makers are being addressed simultaneously: (1) private entrepreneurs (firms, commercial firms, academic firms) and academic entrepreneurs (universities), interested in optimizing knowledge management and in developing heterogeneously composed knowledge-based research networks; and (2) public (governmental, subgovernmental) actors that are interested in optimizing and further developing their policies and policy strategies that target knowledge and innovation. One purpose of public *knowledge and innovation policy* is to enhance the performance and competitiveness of advanced economies.
3. *Decision makers in general*: Decision makers are systematically being supplied with crucial information, for how to optimize knowledge-referring and knowledge- enhancing decision-making. The nature of this "crucial information" is conceptual as well as empirical (case-study-based). Empirical information highlights practical examples and points toward practical solutions (perhaps remedies), conceptual information offers the advantage of further driving and further-carrying tools of understanding. Different groups of addressed decision makers could be decision makers in private firms and multinational corporations, responsible for the knowledge portfolio of companies; knowledge and knowledge management consultants; globalization experts, focusing on the internationalization of research and development, science and technology, and innovation; experts in university/business research networks; and political scientists, economists, and business professionals.
4. *Interested global readership*: Finally, the Springer book series addresses a whole global readership, composed of members who are generally interested in knowledge and innovation. The global readership could partially coincide with the communities as described above ("academic communities," "decision makers"), but could also refer to other constituencies and groups.

Elias G. Carayannis
Series Editor

Contents

1 Introduction 1
  1.1 Research Background 1
      1.1.1 Patient-Centred Care 3
      1.1.2 Sharing of Patient Knowledge 4
      1.1.3 The Research Context 5
  1.2 Research Questions and Objectives 5
  1.3 An Overview of Contents 6

2 TCM and WM Collaboration in Chinese Healthcare Organisations 9
  2.1 Development and Current Situation of TCM 9
  2.2 Development and Current Situation of WM 11
  2.3 Differences Between TCM and WM 12
  2.4 The Structure of the Chinese Health System 13
  2.5 Patient-Centred Approach in Chinese Healthcare Organisations ... 15
      2.5.1 Patients at the Centre of Healthcare 15
      2.5.2 The Role of Hospital Management 16
      2.5.3 The Role of Healthcare Professionals 17
  2.6 Summary and Discussion 17

3 Knowledge Sharing in Healthcare Sectors 19
  3.1 Definition of Knowledge 19
      3.1.1 Construction of Knowledge 20
      3.1.2 Taxonomies of Knowledge 22
  3.2 Definition of Patient Knowledge 23
      3.2.1 Explicit Patient Knowledge 23
      3.2.2 Tacit Patient Knowledge 24
  3.3 KS in Healthcare Organisations 25
      3.3.1 Definition of KS in Healthcare Organisations 25
      3.3.2 The Demand for KS in Patient-Centred Health Services ... 26
      3.3.3 KS in Chinese Healthcare Organisations 28

	3.4	KS Models	29
		3.4.1 SECI Model	30
		3.4.2 Practice-Based KS Model	31
		3.4.3 KM Model for Primary Care	32
		3.4.4 Six-C KM Model	34
	3.5	KS Barriers	35
	3.6	Conclusion	37

4 Research Paradigm and Methodology 39
   4.1 Research Philosophy 39
       4.1.1 Philosophical Assumptions 39
       4.1.2 Research Approach 41
       4.1.3 Research Paradigms 42
   4.2 Research Methodology 44
       4.2.1 The Selection of Research Methodology 44
       4.2.2 GT 45
       4.2.3 A Combined Approach of Case-Study and GT 50
   4.3 Conclusion 52

5 Research Design 53
   5.1 Case-Study 53
       5.1.1 Case-Study Site 53
       5.1.2 Obtaining Access 55
   5.2 Four Main Research Stages 56
   5.3 Data Collection 57
       5.3.1 Data Collection Method 57
       5.3.2 Theoretical Sampling Strategy 58
       5.3.3 Supporting Tools for Data Collection 60
       5.3.4 Data Analysis 62
       5.3.5 Research Stages 67
   5.4 Research Ethics 80
   5.5 Conclusion 81

6 Research Findings 83
   6.1 Introduction to the Research Findings 83
       6.1.1 Collaboration and Complementarity of Neurosurgical and TCM Medical Teams 84
       6.1.2 The Position of the Patient 85
       6.1.3 KS Processes in Interprofessional Collaboration 86
       6.1.4 The Evolution of Research Findings 87
       6.1.5 Section Summary 92
   6.2 Contextual Influences 93
       6.2.1 Political Influences 93
       6.2.2 Economical Influences 98

		6.2.3	Social Influences	101
		6.2.4	Section Summary	106
	6.3	Philosophical Issues		106
		6.3.1	Philosophical Conflicts	108
		6.3.2	Professional Conflicts	114
		6.3.3	Section Summary	121
	6.4	Chinese Healthcare Education		121
		6.4.1	Lack of Interprofessional Education in Healthcare HE	123
		6.4.2	External Influences on Healthcare HE	131
		6.4.3	Section Summary	134
	6.5	Interprofessional Training		135
		6.5.1	Existing Professional Training Structure	135
		6.5.2	Absence of Interprofessional Training in Neurosurgery Department	139
		6.5.3	Absence of Interprofessional Training in TCM Department	142
		6.5.4	Section Summary	144
	6.6	Hospital Management		145
		6.6.1	Management Bias Against TCM	145
		6.6.2	External Influences on Hospital Management	152
		6.6.3	Section Summary	154

7 Discussion ... 157
7.1 Integration of Findings ... 157
7.1.1 Philosophical Tensions ... 158
7.1.2 Professional Tensions ... 159
7.2 Comparison with Existing Models ... 160
7.2.1 Detailed Model Comparison ... 160
7.2.2 General Model Comparison ... 167
7.3 Implication of Findings for the Reality of Practice ... 174
7.3.1 Communication and Collaboration Issues ... 175
7.3.2 Education and Professional Training ... 178
7.3.3 Hospital Management ... 179
7.3.4 External Influences on KS ... 180
7.4 Contribution of Findings to the Body of Knowledge in the Field ... 182
7.4.1 Health Informatics ... 182
7.4.2 Knowledge Management and Sharing ... 183
7.5 Conclusion ... 183

8 Conclusion ... 185
8.1 Summary of Research Findings ... 185
8.2 Responding Research Questions ... 187
8.3 Practical Implications ... 187
8.3.1 Internal Actions ... 188
8.3.2 External Actions ... 188

8.4 Limitations of This Study and Mitigation Strategy Adopted 189
8.5 Future Works 190

Appendices 193

References 211

Chapter 1
Introduction

1.1 Research Background

> At this moment of entering the medical institution, I would like to swear a solemn oath:
> I am willing to devote myself to medicine, to my beloved motherland, and to the people.
> I will comply with the medical ethics; respect my teachers and their disciplines; study assiduously and tirelessly; develop all medical skills.
> I determine to dedicate all my efforts to fight against human illnesses, and to maintain the sanctity and honour of medicine, life-saving, painstaking, and persistent.
> I will devote myself to the practice of medicine in the land of China and to the well-being of humanity.
> Ministry of Education of the People's Republic of China (1991), Official Document, No. 106

In 1950, immediately after the establishment of the People's Republic of China (PRC), and as advocated by the first communist president Chairman Mao Zedong, the First National Healthcare Conference approved the creation of a national healthcare system, based on the provision of two very different types of medicine, namely Traditional Chinese Medicine (TCM) and Western Medicine (WM) (National Healthcare Conference 1950; cited in Hillier and Jewell 1983).

TCM has been a consistent element of Chinese culture (Wong et al. 1993), and was developed as the result of the accumulation of experiences and medical practices for over 2300 years (Cheng 2000). Hyatt (1978) asserts that TCM is not just "folk" medicine, but a highly developed art and science. However, TCM lost the dominant position it had held for thousands of years over the Chinese public health system to WM at the beginning of the twentieth century. WM, based on the scientific paradigm and evidence-based practice, was developed in Europe and North America after the industrial revolution, and is largely considered as the main component of today's Chinese healthcare system, despite its coexistence with TCM (Chi 1994).

The political decision for the TCM and WM collaboration was particularly important to the Chinese communist government. Taylor (2004) points out that, after the establishment of PRC, the Chinese communist government used TCM as a strategic tool to distinguish the new communist China from its superstitious and feudal past as well as to illustrate the Chinese cultural heritage. Therefore, in 1954, two main strategies were formulated, not only to bridge the gap between the two very distinctive professional communities, but also to explore possible areas of collaboration. Firstly, a number of TCM universities were established all over the country to provide formalised TCM education and to conduct systematic and scientific research on both TCM and its collaboration with WM. Secondly, a nation-wide search was conducted to select 2000 good WM professionals, who were pulled off from their jobs for full-time study of TCM and to explore methods of collaboration (Taylor 2004). These initial political decisions encouraged the two medical communities to work together and created the conditions for a complementary relationship that still exists today.

Nonetheless, the coexistence and the complementary relationship between TCM and WM communities were not always harmonious and stable. Not long after the formulation of the complementary relationship and the establishment of TCM specialised higher education (HE), TCM was put under stress during the "Great Cultural Revolution" (1966–1976), since the government at that time considered TCM as a *feudal* product of the old China, needing to be eliminated (Chen 1999; Fruehauf 1999). In this period of time, not only was the number of Chinese Traditional Medicine Colleges dramatically decreased from 21 to 11, but also the practitioners of TCM were criticised as *feudalists* and some were even persecuted (Fruehauf 1999). In contrast, during this crisis for TCM, WM reinforced its dominant position over the Chinese healthcare system and services.

Mao Zedong's death in 1976 brought an end to the Great Cultural Revolution as well as the crisis of TCM (Hesketh and Zhu 1997). The position of TCM was reinstated by the Official Document no. 52 issued by the central government in 1978 (Lv 2005). According to this author, the official document emphasised two points, namely: equality in the support for Western medicine and traditional medicine, and equal development of the two types of medicine. Since then, the official political statements have consistently declared that TCM and WM are equally supported, despite the dominance of WM (Liu 2004). Again, a recent public statement made by Zhu Chen, the Minister for Health, restated that the Chinese government equally supported both TCM and WM in the national healthcare system (Cai and Ju 2010).

Many researchers (e.g. Fruehauf 1999; Taylor 2004; Hyatt 1978) assert that the political decision was very successful, since it created a complementary relationship between the two types of professionals working in collaboration against a number of diseases deemed to be untreatable by WM alone (Taylor 2004, p. 103).

In any case, the complementary relationship and the collaboration of the two types of healthcare professionals should be patient-centred. Every individual Chinese healthcare professional is required to swear a medical oath (as shown at the beginning of this chapter) when becoming a medical student and is expected to follow it throughout their career. This oath does not only repeat the dedication to the motherland, but also stresses the devotion to the people and the well-being of humanity, which indicates that the healthcare services should be focused around patient needs and interests.

In fact, in 2006, by the request of the central government, patient-centred healthcare was introduced in all healthcare facilities and was required to be adopted by all healthcare professionals. However, some of these policies, movements and statements are made more for political purposes, and in this case their implementation does not necessarily benefit the patient. In fact, this politically inspired collaboration and complementarity does not guarantee that the interests of the patient are always protected and placed at the centre of the collaborative processes. If the benefits to the patient are not very well protected by these political decisions, then there is a contradiction to the patient-centred care advocated by the Chinese central government.

In order to ensure the patient-centeredness in the TCM and WM collaboration, it is essential for healthcare professionals to communicate and share knowledge with each other in order to look after the needs, requirements and benefits of the patient (Steward 2001; Maizes et al. 2009). Nonetheless, and in practice, the two types of healthcare professionals do not necessarily communicate and share knowledge (Liu 2005). In truth, there are barriers impeding the processes of sharing knowledge (Sun 2003; Liu 2005).

This book reports on a research project and aims at identifying knowledge sharing barriers in the patient-centred collaboration of TCM and WM healthcare professionals in the context of Chinese healthcare organisations. Ultimately the intention behind the project was to seek understanding of these barriers. In order to comprehend the nature of the problem, the following sections discuss definitions of the base concepts involved, namely: patient-centred care, knowledge sharing and the research context. The book then uses these basic concepts to develop a theory of the barriers.

1.1.1 Patient-Centred Care

Ethical conduct of medical practices has always been considered as one of the most essential ground rules for healthcare professionals (Holm 1997). Thus, the patient-centred approach is often adopted as the guiding principle for healthcare professionals to enact their ethical rules, concepts, and senses (McGrath et al. 2006). This is probably one of the reasons why the patient-centred approach is currently prevailing and has been implemented in a number of countries in Western Europe and North America, as well as in China.

According to Maizes et al. (2009), patient-centred care is defined as follows:

> Care that informs and involves patients in medical decision making and self-management, coordinates and integrates medical care, provides physical comfort and emotional support, understands the patients' concept of illness and their cultural beliefs, and understands and applies principles of disease prevention and behavioural change appropriate to diverse populations. (Maizes et al. 2009, pp. 277–278)

In 2006, the Chinese central government announced that the patient-centred approach must be taken as the most essential guideline and principle for healthcare professionals and organisations (Zhong 2009). The adoption of the patient-centred approach determines that the position of the patient must be maintained at the centre of all medical procedures, and demands that the patient's rights, benefits and requirements must be ensured in the TCM and WM collaboration. Therefore, effective communication and adequate knowledge sharing between TCM and WM healthcare professionals is the centrepiece of the implementation of patient-centred care in China (Maizes et al. 2009).

1.1.2 Sharing of Patient Knowledge

For nearly all types of organisations, Knowledge sharing (KS) is an effective strategy for building competitive advantages (McEvily 2000). In the healthcare environment, it is a universal perception that appropriate KS, based on good practices of knowledge creation, storage, transfer and utilisation, are fundamental to resolve daily medical problems challenging healthcare professionals, and, more importantly, can substantially improve the quality of healthcare services (Abidi 2007; Nicolini et al. 2008). KS in the context of healthcare can be defined as follows:

> Healthcare knowledge sharing can be characterised as the explication and dissemination of context-sensitive healthcare knowledge by and for healthcare stakeholders through a collaborative communication medium in order to advance the knowledge quotient of the participating healthcare stakeholders. (Abidi 2007, p. 69)

In this book, and to further develop this definition according to the needs of this research, KS can be defined as the exchange of patient knowledge between WM and TCM healthcare professionals through collaborative communication channels, aims to share knowledge about individual patients, to provide the best possible healthcare services to patients, to improve the quality of patient care, and to achieve patient satisfaction.

Summarising propositions from a number of authors, patient knowledge can be defined by the following typology:

- Technical Knowledge includes identification of patient conditions and problems, reasons and objectives of patient care, patient background, agreement to treatment strategy, and explicit patient requirements and needs (Smith 1996).
- Ethical and Emotional Knowledge is about ethically dealing with patient feelings, emotions, and psychological status; approaches to communicating with, persuading and managing individual patients; and maintaining trusting and collaborative professional-patient relationships (Fennessy and Burstein 2007).
- Social and Behavioural Knowledge is concerned with anticipating how others will behave, perception of patients' implicit requirements, behaviours and reactions, and expectations (Fennessy and Burstein 2007).

Among the three types of patient knowledge, the sharing of technical knowledge is the least problematic, since technical knowledge is easier to share and is usually recorded explicitly in the patient records. Moreover, the two types of healthcare professionals have adopted two entirely different therapeutic systems and each other's philosophical beliefs and technical insights do not seem to matter in the complementary provision of medical service (Guo 2006; Yang 2005).

Comparably, the ethical and emotional knowledge, as well as the social and behavioural knowledge consist of experiences and perceptions of individual healthcare professionals, which are accumulated through direct dealing and interacting with individual patients. Therefore, when compared with the technical knowledge, these two types of tacit patient knowledge are more difficult and more important to share among healthcare professionals. Thus, the research project reported in this book focuses on the sharing of ethical and emotional knowledge and social and behavioural knowledge in the patient-centred interprofessional collaboration of TCM and WM healthcare professionals.

1.1.3 The Research Context

The collaboration of the two types of healthcare professionals and the integration of their practices was imposed by political decision. Furthermore, the two very distinctive medical professional communities were asked (if not forced) to operate not only in the national healthcare system, but also in the same hospital, and sometimes even in the same building. This high-level policy making required that hospitals in China operate based on complementary treatments of the two professional practices, which were assumed to be beneficial to the patient.

However, these two counterparts are not necessarily coexisting harmoniously and communicating with each other unconditionally (Wang 2010; Guo 2010). TCM and WM healthcare professionals work side by side every day and a large number of compound treatments are provided to patients. But the two professional groups have different professional practices based on different beliefs, conceptual bases, methods and techniques. Consequently, there are significant KS barriers hindering the best provision of patient care and sharing patient knowledge (Liu 2005). Thus, there is a need to identify KS barriers inhibiting the interaction of patient knowledge between TCM and WM healthcare professionals, in order to not only improve the communication and KS between the two types of healthcare practitioners, but also promote the quality of healthcare services to patient in Chinese hospitals. This conundrum and resulting professional tensions led to the research project presented in this book.

1.2 Research Questions and Objectives

According to the research aim stated above, the following main research question was formulated:

> What are the barriers to sharing patient knowledge between healthcare professionals from traditional and Western medicine in their patient-centred interprofessional collaborations?

This main research question focuses on the research orientation and can be broken down into the following questions:

1. What are the barriers that hinder the sharing of patient knowledge between TCM and WM healthcare professionals?
2. What are the relationships between these barriers?

In order to answer these research questions, the following twelve research objectives are established:

1. Conduct a literature review about the research context, focusing on TCM and WM in Chinese healthcare organisations. The purpose for this literature review is to have a general understanding about the research context and to develop contextual sensitivity.
2. Conduct a literature review on knowledge management (KM) and KS in the healthcare environment, not only to enhance the theoretical sensitivity, but also to locate an appropriate theoretical framework to guide the remaining research stages.
3. Determine the research approach, overarching methodology, and tools and techniques for data collection and analysis.
4. Establish an appropriate research design.
5. Identify an appropriate, adequate and accessible site for the data collection.
6. Collect data using defined data collection tools and techniques at the selected research site.
7. Analyse data to identify individual barriers to sharing patient knowledge.
8. Analyse data to organise these KS barriers into categories and sub-categories.
9. Analyse data to determine relationships between categories, sub-categories, and KS barriers.
10. Conceptualise the research findings in order to initiate a theory and thus answer the research questions.
11. Contribute knowledge to KS in the context of healthcare sectors and KS in Chinese healthcare organisations in particular.

The definition of research objectives is extremely important, since these objectives underpin crucial stages throughout the entire research project which are described and discussed in this book. Moreover, the research objectives are the foundation for the selection of the research methodology discussed in Chap. 4 and shed important light on the research design discussed in Chap. 5.

1.3 An Overview of Contents

In order to present all research details and the progression of theory clearly, this book uses seven chapters to explain the research processes and findings.

The next chapter, Chap. 2, reviews existing literature on the research context. To be more specific, this chapter reviews the backgrounds and current developments of

1.3 An Overview of Contents

TCM and WM in Chinese healthcare organisations. This chapter also discusses the implementation of the patient-centred approach in Chinese hospitals.

The third chapter is also a literature review chapter, which is designed to enhance the theoretical sensitivity. This chapter defines patient knowledge, and reviews definitions, theories, and models of KS in the healthcare environment.

Chapter 4 presents and discusses the research methodology and design of this research project. More specifically, this chapter consists of three main components: research philosophy, research methodology, and research design.

Chapter 5 is dedicated to discussing the research findings. To be more specific, this chapter discusses five main categories which emerged from the data analysis, namely contextual influences, philosophical issues, Chinese healthcare education, interprofessional training, and hospital management.

After the presentation of research findings, Chap. 6 is the discussion chapter, which aims at conceptualising the research findings, comparing the emerging research model with existing models of KM and KS, identifying implication of findings for the reality of practice, and contribution to knowledge.

The final chapter concludes the book and sums up this project. This chapter also points out orientations for future research.

Chapter 2
TCM and WM Collaboration in Chinese Healthcare Organisations

This chapter describes and discusses the context of this research project. To be more specific, this chapter aims to (1) provide a perspective on the context; and (2) enhance the contextual sensitivity, which is essential to the researchers in order to understand, contextualise, and interpret informants' responses. To achieve these two aims, this chapter discusses five contextual issues: the development and current situation of TCM, the development and current situation of WM, differences between TCM and WM, the structure of the Chinese healthcare system, and the patient-centred approach in Chinese healthcare organisations.

2.1 Development and Current Situation of TCM

According to Hyatt (1978), the origin of Traditional Chinese Medicine (TCM) is usually related to three ancient emperors in Chinese history: Fu Hsi, Shen Nung, and Huang Ti. Fu Hsi, the first Chinese emperor, who began his reign in 2852 BC, is recorded as the formulator of TCM. Fu Hsi was the author of the book I-Ching (Book of Changes), the first book in Chinese history, which contains some fundamental theories such as Yin-Yang and Ba-Gua, which are the cornerstones of Chinese philosophy and Chinese medicine (Ma 2009). Shen Nung, the second emperor, is known as the father of agriculture and herbal medicine. His contribution, the book Shen Nung Pen Ts'ao (Shen Nung's Herbal), based on his own experimentation and research on native plants, is the very first reference to herbalism in China (Hyatt 1978). The third emperor, Huang Ti, is credited with the invention of wheeled vehicles (chariots), ships, the planetarium, cloth clothing, currency, musical notation, and so on. He wrote the book Huang Ti Nei Ching (The Yellow Emperor's Classic of Internal Medicine), which was the most important and the earliest extensive work on TCM (Xu 2009). However, TCM was most probably developed by the collective knowledge and efforts of Chinese people, rather than these three legendary emperors alone.

The Han Dynasty, which flourished at the same time as the Roman Empire, represents the emergence of China as a world power. All kinds of scientific developments were cultivated and stimulated, including medical studies. In fact, the basic principles of TCM were fostered under the Han Dynasty (Hyatt 1978).

India was the first country historically to influence Chinese medicine, in the golden age of Buddhism, which was brought into China by Buddhist missionaries in the first and second centuries (Hyatt 1978). However, the influence of the Indian medical system was not well accepted by Chinese people, though it was not completely unsuccessful (Chi 1994). In fact, there seem to have been a number of foreign influences in Chinese medicine. For instance, the critically important theory of Wu Hsing (five elements), both in Chinese culture and medicine, originated in Greece and was transmitted to China by Indian influence (Hyatt 1978). As Buddhism became gradually accepted, these concepts also became widespread (Chi 1994). Beside Buddhism, Taoism was the other religion that had profound effects on Chinese medicine, from the formative years directly to the golden age of the Tang Dynasty (Hyatt 1978). Chinese medicine steadily developed and took a dominant position in the health care system until the end of the Qing Dynasty, the last dynasty in Chinese history, when Western Medicine entered China (Li and Liu 1992).

TCM dominated the Chinese healthcare system until the early twentieth century. Due to a loss of confidence in Chinese civilisation and its values after a series of defeats and humiliations by Western powers, the entire official health care system turned into modern WM, long before the establishment of the People's Republic of China (Chi 1994).

TCM was reintroduced into the health system after 1949 by the communist party, mostly for political purposes. As discussed in Chap. 1, the Chinese government used TCM as a strategic tool to distinguish the new communist China from its superstitious and feudal past as well as to illustrate the Chinese cultural heritage. Since then, TCM specialist hospitals, universities and institutions have been set up in various cities in mainland China (Hyatt 1978). The development of and researches on TCM were greatly improved by the new Chinese government. In 1954, both Traditional Chinese and Western medical communities were asked to collaborate in a study of integration of the two distinct types of medicine, which was unexpectedly successful (Hyatt 1978). The first mutual understanding between TCM and WM practitioners led to suggestions for the modernising (or developing) of TCM and the emergence of the Integration of Chinese and Western Medicine in the same healthcare system.

The Integration of Chinese and Western Medicine represents a new scientific medical system—distinctively Chinese—incorporating contemporary scientific methods and knowledge into the study, collation and exploration TCM in order to enrich current medical and scientific research (Yan 2006). Yan (2006) proposes that the basic purpose of research into the integration of TCM and WM is to combine advantages from both medicines and at the same time minimise apparent disadvantages. Even though many TCM professionals and researchers protest that it is virtually impossible to integrate the two very distinctive types of medical philosophy and methodology (Liu 2003), the movement towards TCM and WM integration has reinforced the coexistence of TCM and WM in the Chinese healthcare system.

It is important to note that some authors regard the modernisation of Chinese medicine and the Integration of Chinese and Western medicine as rather different. Lv (2005) states that the modernising of TCM is the development of traditional theories and methods and would occur even independently from integration with WM; however, the integrating process has accelerated the speed of modernisation. To support this statement, a number of research studies (e.g. Taylor 2004; Tian 2003; Fruehauf 1999) point out that the Integration of Chinese and Western medicine is one of the products, or one of the divisions, of the modernisation of Chinese medicine.

The definition of Traditional Chinese Medicine (TCM) widely used by current healthcare professionals and academics is: a modernised Chinese medicine, which includes not only the traditional views of TCM based on the accumulation of subjective understandings of healing throughout Chinese history, but also theories, concepts and practices that are newly developed nowadays on the basis of scientific investigation and exploration of ancient understandings (Li 2009). On the other hand, TCM is no longer just a medicine from the past but is also a medicine of the present as well as a functional medicine that plays an indispensable role in current Chinese medical care together with WM.

2.2 Development and Current Situation of WM

In contrast to TCM's basis in culture, religion and long experience, WM employs a scientific attitude in diagnosis and treatments (Dally 2003). Unschuld (1985) claims that achievements from intensive and evidence-based scientific research have brought WM to an unchallengeable dominant position in world health care.

In China, WM was first presented in the seventeenth century, to Emperor Kang Hsi (1661–1722) of the Qing Dynasty. However, the emperor considered it to be too revolutionary and a potential threat to the harmony of Chinese civilisation and, therefore, ordered its suppression (Hyatt 1978).

Modern WM was only successfully introduced and widely used at the end of the Qing Dynasty when it finally won its dominance in the Chinese public health care system (Chi 1994). The expansion of Western medical knowledge during the period from the 1840s to the 1940s had an immediate impact on Chinese healthcare theories and practices. Chinese considered modern WM as one of the new Western scientific wonders and viewed it as a sign of modernity and a vehicle to lift China from its feudal and antiquated practices (Unschuld 1985).

Despite its very high popularity and demand, WM remained a privilege of the upper classes, and access was very difficult for the common Chinese people (Chen 1989). Moreover, there was very little research and development in WM before the institution of the People's Republic of China. WM was fed mostly from advances made abroad and transferred from health practices developed in the West In the period immediately after the foundation of the current Chinese regime, major developments in WM were mainly due to the reorganisation during the 1960s of the Higher Education (HE) systems and an institutional structure for teaching and research in WM (Chen 1989). At the same time, the Chinese healthcare system was being built on the basis of an extensive network of hospitals and clinics, many of which actually provided both WM and TCM practices (Hillier and Jewell 1983).

In the late 1970s, China entered a new era in its history with a national policy reformation in order to propel economic development (Chen 1989). In this era, the Chinese healthcare system developed into a systematic structured healthcare organisation covering both urban and rural areas. Remarkably, WM and TCM became inseparably integrated into this structure with the basic intention of uniting the "old-style doctor" and those trained in modern methods, as suggested in the First National Healthcare Conference in 1950 (Hillier and Jewell 1983). At this point, it is worthwhile to recall that, as explained in Chap. 1, the coexistence of WM and TCM was politically decided and enforced.

Nowadays, TCM and WM healthcare professionals collaborate with each other and provide healthcare services on the basis of a complementary relationship, in which WM takes the primary position, being complemented by TCM as an alternative healthcare therapy. Although the TCM and WM collaboration has been proven beneficial to patients (Taylor 2004), the collaborative health service provision could be very complicated, because the two types of healthcare professionals adopt very different philosophical perspectives, theoretical foundations, and diagnosis and treatment methods.

2.3 Differences Between TCM and WM

The main difference of Chinese traditional medicine in relation to its Western counterpart is its adoption of a holistic concept of healing, which emphasises the integrity of the human body as a whole and its close relationship with the environment (Cheng 2000). In contrast, WM doctors are more interested in localised diseases or illnesses and the corresponding part of the human body. WM practitioners aim at healing that specific part of the human body rather the more general problems of the patients (Dally 2003).

Moreover, TCM and WM have entirely different conceptual systems. For TCM doctors, the Yin-Yang theory[1] is an ancient Chinese belief and way of understanding the universe and is the most essential theoretical foundation to the practice of TCM (Cheng 2000). In contrast to TCM, which is based on Chinese ancient beliefs, WM is based on scientific paradigms and evidence-based research and is a combination of modern science and the art of healing (Warrell et al. 2005).

---

[1] Yin and Yang are "opposite but complementary qualities" (Maciocia 1989, p. 1). Yin represents inner and negative principles, such as cold, darkness, or passiveness. On the other hand, Yang stands for outer and positive principles, such as heat, light, stimulation, dominance, and dynamic potential (Eisenberg and Kaptchuk 2002). Cheng (2000) further points out that Yin and Yang are believed to be two interchangeable qualities of the human body. Therefore, the balance of Yin and Yang is the key factor of human health, and diseases result from imbalance.

Furthermore, the two types of healthcare methodology have completely different diagnosis methods. TCM doctors follow the ancient theory of Bian-zheng (distinguishing patterns) (Cheng 2000), which can be generally defined as "the process of identifying the basic disharmony that underlies all clinical manifestation" (Maciocia 1989, p. 175). To support the processes of Bian-zheng, TCM doctors apply four diagnosis methods to patients, namely: inspection, listening and smelling, inquiry, and palpation (Wang et al. 2004). Liu (2003) further points out that the TCM diagnosis mainly relies on the doctors' professional experiences and personal understandings of Bian-zheng. In this case, it is very common for different TCM doctors to produce totally different diagnoses of the same patient (Liu 2003). In contrast, WM professionals investigate the problems of patients and make decisions based on the identification of accurate medical evidence and the employment of modern diagnostic technologies, such as x-rays, laboratory tests, and computed tomography (CT) (Fitzgerald 1990).

Additionally, TCM and WM professionals have very different treatment approaches to dealing with patient problems. In the TCM methodology, there are four main categories of treatments: herbal medicine (oral intake and external use); heat therapy (moxibustion and cupping); massage (oriental massage, Gua Sha and magnets); and acupuncture (Sherman et al. 2005). These methods used by TCM doctors are often considered as too unusual by those WM healthcare professionals who are following the doctrine of modern medical science. To them, patient treatments can be simply divided into two categories, namely: medication and surgery (Goldman and Ausiello 2008).

Finally, both TCM and WM approaches have different advantages and can be used for different purposes and different patient conditions. It is widely accepted in China that WM is more effective in the acute stage of many diseases and works much faster than TCM in treating these acute diseases (Ma 1999). However, it is also acknowledged that WM creates more adverse side effects (Kaptchuk 2000). Nevertheless, healing herbs, acupuncture, massage and other health methods from TCM may sometimes be perceived to be more appropriate in long-term health promotion, prevention, treatment, and rehabilitation. Moreover, TCM may be used as a last resort, when Western medicine is either too toxic or unable to provide any further expected benefit (Chen 1989).

Liu (2003) asserts that WM is a *hard science*, whereas TCM is *an empirical [soft] science*. Even though the two approaches are entirely different, the integration of the two healing beliefs into the Chinese healthcare system constitutes a unique therapeutic plurality, which is believed to be beneficial to patients, and which is only presented in the structure of the Chinese healthcare system.

2.4 The Structure of the Chinese Health System

As discussed in Chap. 1, and even though the structure of the Chinese healthcare system was a political decision, the inclusive and fully integrated healthcare system may have its unique advantages. These advantages are maximised by current healthcare practices at multiple levels and distributed through the Chinese healthcare systems. According to "A Health Situation Assessment of the People's Republic of China", reported by the UN (2005), the Chinese healthcare system has a dual urban-rural structure, encompassing both medical and preventive care. However, sub-structures for urban and rural sectors are rather different.

In the urban area, hospitals are the centre of patient care services and are organised into a three-layered structure. Third level hospitals are run directly by the central authorities, with more than 500 beds providing tertiary care. These hospitals are usually equipped with advanced medical staff and equipment. Second level hospitals have 100–500 beds and provide full healthcare services to a district or a clearly defined set of communities. First level hospitals provide the most basic healthcare services of prevention, sanitation and essential medical services for a particular community. Guo et al. (2007) state that in the large majority of these hospitals, from the highest third level to the lowest basic community clinics, a combination of TCM and WM services is offered.

The rural health service system includes three levels: county level, township level and village level. County level facilities are hospitals, TCM clinics, and maternity and children's hospitals. Basic healthcare centres and village clinics provide the health services at both township and village levels. Hyatt (1978) asserts that TCM is more widely used in rural sectors than in the urban sectors. This may be due to the fact that the majority of the rural Chinese population can explain and understand their illness in Traditional Chinese medical concepts rather than in WM ones (Lam 2001). Another more pragmatic reason may be related to the fact that in general TCM services are cheaper than WM (Zhang et al. 2007). Moreover, poverty is a critical problem in Chinese rural environments (Beach 2001) and TCM becomes a primary instrument in fighting against many of the poverty-related diseases (Tao 2005). In support of this, a survey undertaken by Zhang et al. (2007) on township level health services in 2005 found that 73.1% (84 out of 132) of registered health practitioners are certified to practice TCM, 90% (317 out of 352) of clinics have specialised TCM services, and 34% (14985 out of 44063) of patient treatments were exclusively through TCM.

At the national level, according to official statistics gathered by the National Bureau of Statistics of China in 2005, 3792 (4.64%) out of a total number of 81,742 health service organisations or clinics are exclusively dedicated to TCM services. Out of 4,929,481 healthcare professionals, 465,703 (9.45%) are TCM healthcare providers.

It is clear that the current framework for the Chinese healthcare system tries to integrate the TCM and WM communities and health service professionals. The provision of healthcare services in different levels and types of healthcare organisations should be based on the collaboration of TCM and WM healthcare professionals aiming at serving the centre of patient.

2.5 Patient-Centred Approach in Chinese Healthcare Organisations

The patient-centred healthcare approach is a fundamental requirement for Chinese healthcare organisations and a basic guideline for healthcare practices. This approach has been widely recognised as an essential principle in improving healthcare services, guiding the behaviour of healthcare professionals, and developing a harmonious doctor-patient relationship (Zhong 2009).

In fact, the concept of patient-centred healthcare is not new in China. As discussed by Yao (2009), in ancient China, medical practices were referred to as "仁术 (ren-shu)". This term consists of two characters: "仁" means benevolence, which is the ultimate aim for healthcare practices; "术" refers to the actions of medical treatment and care. Additionally, Yao (2009) claims that thousands of years ago Confucius advised that benevolence and patient orientation are fundamental rules for a healthcare professional.

As explained in Chap. 1, in 2006 the Chinese government decided to install patient-centred healthcare into the healthcare system (Zhong 2009). Thus, the patient-centred approach is politically required to be employed as the ultimate principle which must be followed by all healthcare professionals and healthcare organisations (Hu 2009).

The patient-centred approach has been intensely discussed by many Chinese health and hospital management researchers. In more detail, the current discussions on this approach are mostly around the three main actors involved, namely, patients, healthcare professionals, and hospital managers.

2.5.1 Patients at the Centre of Healthcare

In the traditional healthcare approach, healthcare professionals have almost complete power over the patients (Li et al. 2009). Very differently, in the patient-centred approach, patients are at the centre of healthcare practices and are the empowered party. In this case, patients have the liberty to select whatever medical methods they consider appropriate (Yao 2009).

In more detail, Li et al. (2009) provide a definition of patient rights in Chinese healthcare organisations:

- Patients have the right to be fully informed.
- Patients have the right to choose medical methods.
- Patients have the right to be treated equally to other patients.
- Patients have the right to protect their personality, dignity, privacy, and emotions.

However, in reality, the interests of the patient are probably not very well protected. Cao and Sun (2009) conducted a study which included 20 medical departments and 260 in-patients from a public hospital in North China. Findings of this study show that 18.2% of the patients did not understand the purpose of specific treatments;

14.6% of the patients were not informed about laboratory test results; and 2.2% of the patients did not even know their medical conditions (Cao and Sun 2009). Additionally, these authors state that health professionals only provide information when patients ask them to do so. These results indicate that healthcare professionals still hold the decisive power over patients, who are probably not at the centre and whose rights might not be very well protected.

2.5.2 The Role of Hospital Management

Successful implementation of the patient-centred approach depends to a certain extent on the attention and support of hospital management (Zhong 2009). Liu (2009) and Hu (2009) assert that hospital management must motivate all healthcare professionals to follow this approach, and must integrate this approach into all regulations and protocols, definitions of professional behaviour, and aims and objectives for all hospital operations.

Furthermore, hospital management needs to reform the traditional information management strategies, which currently only aim at assisting the administration and running of the hospital. Information management in a patient-centred hospital environment should be patient-oriented, and should aim at managing patient information and knowledge, such as patient medical information, medical history, personal requirements, and expectations (Zhang and Cang 2009).

However, many studies (e.g. Zhong 2009; Yao 2009; Zhang and Cang 2009) claim that the patient-centred approach has not been truly implemented, due to hospital management prioritising the pursuit of financial income and profitability. In order to understand this problem, the Chinese context must be explained.

As discussed in Wang (2008), in 1978, the Chinese central government decided to implement a market economy policy, which resulted in a significant market reformation from the planned economy[2] (the communist economic system that was adopted by the PRC for the first 30 years) into the socialist market economy[3]. The market economy policy substantially boosted the Chinese economy and has been widely recognised as one of the most important decisions in the Chinese economic reformation since 1978.

However, this national policy is not flawless (Wang 2008). Hsiao (1995) and Shao (2007) claim that under the market economy policy, the central government

---

[2] Under a planned economy system as defined by the Chinese Government (2012), "industrial production, agricultural production, and the stocking and selling of goods in commercial departments were all controlled by state plan. The variety, quantity and prices in every sphere of the economy were fixed by state planners."

[3] According to Qian and Wu (2000), the goal for the Chinese "socialist market economy" is to achieve the transformation to a market economy. The word "socialist" is an adjective to show special Chinese characteristics and to distinguish the system from the "market socialism" advocated by some Eastern European reformers in the 1970s and 1980s. The Chinese Government (2012) states that the socialist market economic system has now taken shape and will become comparatively mature in 2020.

significantly reduced funds and financial support to healthcare organisations and health services. Therefore, hospitals are relying on themselves to support all hospital expenses, include paying tax, updating medical equipment, and providing salaries for healthcare professionals. In these conditions, hospital management is pressed to give more attention to controlling costs and maximising income, but has very little concern about the patient's interests and needs (Zhong 2009). This author also points out that, to many hospital managers, patients can be seen as service consumers, whilst healthcare professionals are tools for hospital management to use in pursuing higher financial profits, rather than saving lives and curing patients.

2.5.3 The Role of Healthcare Professionals

Healthcare professionals are the ones who apply patient-centred care to patients (Yao 2009). The centre of the discussion that emerges from the current literature focuses on the dialogue between healthcare professionals and patients, in which healthcare professionals are obliged to keep patients and their relatives fully informed (Ju 2009). Additionally, Huang and Huang (2009) state that healthcare professionals not only need to communicate with patients in a polite and respectful way, but also need to respect the requirements, needs, and social and cultural backgrounds of patients in communication, treatment and periods of interment in hospital.

However, Ju (2009) claims that healthcare professionals do not take communication with patients very seriously. She points out that 30% of nurses did not know how to talk to patients and relatives; 33.3% of nurses choose to ignore patient requirements when they are difficult to achieve; and, finally, 80% of medical accidents resulted from lack of communication. These figures show that healthcare professionals are probably not following the patient-centred approach.

Similarly, Yao (2009) demonstrates the results of a research project conducted by the Chinese Ministry of Health and aimed at evaluating the implementation of patient-centred care in six Chinese provinces. Astonishingly, only 54.11% of healthcare professionals admitted that they were following the patient-centred approach; 46.3% of professionals considered technical skills were the centre of healthcare; 31.34% of them admitted that they were practising medicine for their own benefit (e.g. salary, bonus, career progressions); and 22.56% of them claimed that care should be centred on the development of the hospital. Clearly, the implementation of the patient-centred approach was unsuccessful.

2.6 Summary and Discussion

Despite the significant differences between TCM and WM, the two approaches have been successfully integrated into the current Chinese healthcare structure and form a complementary relationship, in which WM takes the primary position, complemented by TCM. As perceived, the collaboration of the two very different types of healthcare professionals could be very beneficial to patients and should be centred on patients.

All healthcare professionals and healthcare organisations in China are expected to follow the patient-centred healthcare approach. Certainly, TCM and WM healthcare professionals should protect the benefits, requirements, and rights of patients consistently and unconditionally throughout all collaboration stages and processes.

However, the review of literature shows that the patient-centred approach has probably not been successfully adopted and fully implemented in Chinese healthcare services. The rigours and requirements of the patient-centred approach are not fully satisfied by healthcare professionals. Moreover, it is reported that patients are unaware of the patient-centred approach and are almost unable to maintain their rights and requirements when receiving medical services. Additionally, and very disappointingly, the literature review has not found any materials reporting how the central role of the patient is maintained in the collaboration of TCM and WM healthcare professionals.

Furthermore, although, as explained in Chap. 1, the interaction of patient knowledge between healthcare professionals is one of the most essential requirements of patient-centred care, communication and KS between healthcare practitioners in Chinese hospitals are not well reported in existing literature. Thus, despite the recognition of communication problems in TCM and WM collaboration, there is a very limited body of literature discussing these problems and reporting the barriers to communication.

Therefore, at the beginning of this research project, and due to the lack of existing explanatory theory and studies, it is essential to review literature about the definition of knowledge and the definition and models of KS in the healthcare environment, the reality of KS implementation in Chinese healthcare organisations, and KS barriers identified by research studies conducted in the past. Reviewing these issues has allowed the researchers to acquire a relatively good understanding of the theory around KS, establish the necessary background for the exploration of KS barriers, and enhance theoretical sensitivity. These issues are discussed in the following chapter, Chap. 3.

Chapter 3
Knowledge Sharing in Healthcare Sectors

In order to achieve the main aim of this research project, which is to identify KS barriers between TCM and WM healthcare professionals in the Chinese healthcare environment, it is fundamental to review existing KS and KM literature relating to the healthcare environment. This exercise of literature review has three main purposes: (1) to enhance theoretical sensitivity, which is crucial to the collection and analysis of data and the conceptualisation of research findings; (2) to locate appropriate theoretical frameworks to guide the remaining research stages; (3) to draw indications for the selection of research methodology and for the research design.

In order to achieve these purposes, five areas of concern were reviewed: definition of knowledge, definition of patient knowledge, KS in healthcare organisations, KS models, and KS barriers. These areas are introduced and discussed in detail in this chapter.

3.1 Definition of Knowledge

Knowledge has always been valued as the vital element in any society throughout the history of human civilisation. However, never have societies accessed, produced and consumed so much knowledge as today (Chen et al. 2009). Therefore, it has never been so vitally important as in today's knowledge society to access and share information in organisational settings (Mertins et al. 2003).

Nonetheless, and interestingly, there is still no unified definition of knowledge. This debate dates back to ancient Greece, when Plato made probably the very first attempt to define knowledge, as true and justified belief (Welbourne 2001; Chen et al. 2009). This definition has evolved into our modern understanding, in which Plato's definition is criticised as an "absolute, static and non-human view of knowledge […] fails to address the relative, dynamic and humanistic view of knowledge" (Nonaka et al. 2000, p. 7).

Until now, it is still rather difficult to define knowledge accurately, and currently there are numerous descriptions and definitions for this term (Mertins et al. 2003). According to the existing literature, the current debate on knowledge is mostly around two main issues, the construction of knowledge and the taxonomies of knowledge. These two issues are introduced and discussed in the following two Sects. (3.1.1 and 3.1.2).

3.1.1 Construction of Knowledge

There are two schools of understanding about the construction of knowledge: an objectivist epistemology of knowledge, and a practice-based epistemology of knowledge.

Objectivist Epistemology of Knowledge
The objectivist epistemology of knowledge is rooted in the positivism of the mid nineteenth century (Stenmark 2002). It views knowledge as an object and as an absolute and universal truth. Alavi and Leidner (2001) add that, in this perspective, knowledge is something that can be stored and manipulated and is separated from the knower. From this epistemological stance, knowledge is defined by distinguishing data, information, and knowledge (Alavi and Leidner 2001):

> Data is raw numbers and facts, information is processed data, and knowledge is authenticated [processed and verified] information. (Alavi and Leidner 2001, p. 109)

Moreover, and based on this definition, several researchers (e.g. Petrides 2002; Hussain et al. 2004; Mohamed 2008) assert a progressive continuum from data, through information, to knowledge. This continuum is always represented in a hierarchical diagram as shown in Fig. 3.1.

The continuum starts from data. Data become information when they are analysed and placed in a context relevant to the recipient (Stenmark 2002). Then, information is processed [authenticated] into knowledge "when it is interpreted by individuals and given a context and anchored in the beliefs and commitments of individuals" (Nonaka et al. 2000, p. 7).

Furthermore, it needs to be emphasised that there are two basic assumptions underlying this continuum diagram (Sheffield 2008). Firstly, knowledge is objective and is universal. Secondly, the object of knowledge is evolved from two more fundamental objects (data and information) from lower in the hierarchy.

However, the data—information—knowledge continuum diagram is rather reductionist, simplistic, and even misleading. Stenmark (2002) lists three main problems about this diagram. Firstly, this diagram should not be linear, with equal distances between the three elements, which imply the same amount of effort when converting data to information and information to knowledge. Secondly, this diagram shows that data could be converted into information, which then could be

3.1 Definition of Knowledge

Fig. 3.1 The data—information—knowledge continuum diagram. (Adopted from Stenmark 2002, p. 18)

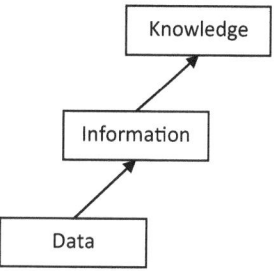

transformed into knowledge, but not the other way around; however, this may not be correct. In fact, Tuomi (1999) points out that knowledge should exist before information can be formulated and even should exist before data can be measured or collected to form information. Nevertheless, Stenmark (2002) argues that Tuomi (1999) is also not right, since "it is not the one way or the other way" (Stenmark 2002, p. 18). In fact, data, information, and knowledge are interconnected in more complicated ways. Finally, although knowledge is at the top end of the continuum, it does not mean that knowledge is more valuable than information, which in turn may not be more important than data.

Nevertheless, although the objectivist view has been adopted by a number of KM and KS research studies, this view is challenged by the practice-based epistemology of knowledge (Cook and Brown 1999; Alavi and Leidner 2001; Stenmark 2002; Chen et al. 2009).

Practice-Based Epistemology of Knowledge
In the practice-based perspective, knowledge is created, shared, and acquired through interactions with the social and physical world rather than being transferred as an object (Chen et al. 2009). Knowledge in this perspective is described as "a state or fact of knowing", in which the knowing is a condition of knowledge obtained from experience or study (Alavi and Leidner 2001, p. 110).

Stenmark (2002) further argues that this school of understanding is rooted in the critique of the positivism and quantitative approach to science. Knowledge cannot be viewed as an object and cannot be defined universally. In truth, it can only be defined, obtained and shared through practice, through the activities of people and the interactions between individuals (Stenmark 2002).

Finally, and although the differences between these two epistemological perspectives are significant, Stenmark (2002, p. 17) argues that the construction of knowledge is perhaps "a little bit of both".

In this research project, the practice-based epistemological perspective is adopted. This is because, as explained in Chap. 1, patient knowledge is considered as the core for this study, and is accumulated through processes of dealing and interacting with individual patients, and shared between TCM and WM healthcare professionals during collaborative practices of providing medical care to patients.

3.1.2 Taxonomies of Knowledge

As in the debate on the construction of knowledge, there are several very different definitions for the taxonomies of knowledge. For instance, Blackler (1995) defines five different types of knowledge: embrained, embodied, embedded, encultured, and encoded; Choo (2000) identifies three types of knowledge: explicit, tacit, and culture knowledge; Boisot (1995) categorises knowledge into proprietary, public, personal, and commonsense knowledge; Cook and Brown (1999) propose explicit, tacit, group, and individual knowledge. Nonetheless, the commonly agreed definition, widely used in the knowledge management field, is provided by Nonaka (1994), who divides knowledge into two forms: tacit and explicit knowledge.

Tacit Knowledge

All knowledge is either tacit or rooted in tacit knowledge (Polanyi 1966). This type of knowledge is defined thus:

> Tacit knowledge is highly personal and hard to formalize, making it difficult to communicate or to share with others. Subjective insights, intuitions, and hunches fall into this category of knowledge. Furthermore, tacit knowledge is deeply rooted in an individual's action and experience, as well as in the ideals, values, or emotions he or she embraces. (Nonaka and Takeuchi 1995, p. 8)

To be more concise, Salmador and Bueno (2007) state that tacit knowledge comprises values, ideas, customs, routines, emotions and experiences. This type of knowledge is embedded in people's heads and is 'spoken understanding' rather than written down in a document or recorded in a database (Servin 2005).

Explicit Knowledge

Very different from tacit knowledge, explicit knowledge can be externalised and formalised, and is much easier to share with others. Explicit knowledge is defined thus:

> […] it is a view of knowledge as necessarily "explicit"-something formal and systematic. Explicit knowledge can be expressed in words and numbers, and easily communicated and shared in the form of hard data, scientific formulae, codified procedures, or universal principles. (Nonaka and Takeuchi 1995, p. 8)

Explicit knowledge can be expressed in language, data, instruction manuals and other documents and records. It is easier to share and transmit from individual to individual, as well as from organisation to organisation (Salmador and Bueno 2007). Moreover, Servin (2005) further divides explicit knowledge into structured explicit knowledge (such as documents, databases and spreadsheets) and unstructured explicit knowledge (such as e-mails, images, training courses, and audio and video archives).

Despite the great differences, tacit and explicit knowledge are complementary to each other, as discussed by Nonaka et al. (2000, p. 8): "Explicit knowledge without tacit insight quickly loses its meaning. Written speech is possible only after internal speech is well developed." Both types of knowledge are fundamental to KM and KS. In fact, Nonaka and Takeuchi (1995) stress that continuous transfer of knowledge between tacit and explicit becomes a constant job in KM.

Nevertheless, the definition, construction, and taxonomy of knowledge discussed here always need to be embedded in models of knowledge management adopting either objectivist or practice-based epistemological views of knowledge. Nonetheless, the explicit-tacit knowledge taxonomy is used in this study to define patient knowledge shared between TCM and WM healthcare professionals. Finally, and based on this knowledge taxonomy, definitions of both explicit and tacit patient knowledge used in this research are presented and discussed in the following section, Sect. 3.2.

3.2 Definition of Patient Knowledge

Steward (2001, p. 444) emphasises that "definitions of patient-centred care seek to make the implicit in patient care explicit". This implies, as pointed out by this author, that healthcare professionals need to explicitly identify knowledge about individual patients, including patient background, and implicit and explicit requirements and expectations.

However, patient knowledge has not been very clearly defined and is usually generally treated as a type of healthcare knowledge. Therefore, the following two Sects. (3.2.1 and 3.2.2) define explicit and tacit patient knowledge by reviewing existing literature on healthcare knowledge.

3.2.1 Explicit Patient Knowledge

There are three types of explicit healthcare knowledge identified by the Department of Health UK and reported in the official government document "Information for Health: An Information Strategy for the Modern NHS" (Department of Health 1998). These three types of explicit knowledge are: (a) knowledge about patients; (b) medical knowledge; and (c) knowledge to underpin clinical practice evaluation, planning and research, clinical governance, and continuing professional development. However, this definition is very concise and too simplified for the needs of this research project.

A much more inclusive definition is developed by Smith (1996), based on Gorman (1995)'s work on the information needed by physicians. The Smith (1996)'s definition of explicit healthcare knowledge is presented in Table 3.1.

Analysing Table 3.1, and synthesising and refocusing the definition into the context of patient-centred healthcare, explicit patient knowledge consists mostly of one type of knowledge, which can be recorded explicitly and used for diagnosing and treating patients from a pure medical technical perspective. Therefore, this type of knowledge has been defined for the purpose of this research as technical knowledge. The definition of technical knowledge is shown in Chap. 1 and also presented here:

Table 3.1 Categories of information needed by doctors. (Based on Smith 1996, p. 1063)

Type of healthcare information	Source
On particular patient	Patient; patient's family, referring doctor, rest of health team, patient record, laboratory data
Data on health and sickness within local population	Public health departments
Medical knowledge	Textbooks, journals, electronic databases, many other sources
Local information on doctors available for referral, etc	Local sources
Information on local social influences and expectations	Local sources
Information on scientific, political, legal, social, management, and ethical changes that will affect both how medicine is practiced in a society and how doctors will interact with individual patients	Diverse sources: local, national, and international

Technical Knowledge includes identification of patient conditions and problems, reasons and objectives of patient care, patient background, agreement to treatment strategy, and explicit patient requirements and needs.

As discussed in Chap. 1, technical knowledge can be acquired by consulting and interacting with patients. Moreover, technical knowledge is relatively easily located, shared and stored, and is usually kept in the patient records.

3.2.2 Tacit Patient Knowledge

When compared with explicit knowledge, up to 80 % of organisational knowledge is in the tacit form (Eardley and Czerwinski 2007). Moreover, these authors further point out that the percentage of tacit knowledge is probably even higher in healthcare organisations (for example in NHS England). Therefore, managing tacit knowledge in the healthcare environment is probably more important than managing explicit knowledge (Srikantaiah and Koeing 2000; Bouthillier and Shearer 2005; Gabbay and le May 2004).

Fennessy and Burstein (2007, p. 30) propose four types of tacit knowledge needed by healthcare professionals as shown in Table 3.2.

Table 3.2 Categories of healthcare tacit knowledge. (Based on Fennessy and Burstein 2007, p. 30)

Types of tacit knowledge	Descriptions
Empirical knowledge	Usually owned by professionals, such as physiology
Process knowledge	About how to get things done and how the health process operates
Control knowledge	About dealing with feelings and emotions, designed to be used in ethical ways
Knowledge of people	Concerned with anticipating how others will behave

Further developing the definition presented in Table 3.2, and according to the aim of this research project, there are two main types of tacit patient knowledge that are identified in the literature and then articulated and defined in this study, namely ethical and emotional knowledge, and social and behavioural knowledge. The two types of tacit patient knowledge are defined in Chap. 1 and repeated here:

- Ethical and Emotional Knowledge is about ethically dealing with patient feelings, emotions, and psychological status; approaches to communicating with, persuading and managing individual patients; and maintaining trusting and collaborative professional-patient relationships.
- Social and Behavioural Knowledge is concerned with anticipating how others will behave, perception of patients' implicit requirements, behaviours and reactions, and expectations.

Also, as discussed in Chap. 1, since the ethical and emotional knowledge and social and behavioural knowledge are very difficult to share and are critically important to the provision of patient-centred health services, this project only focuses on the sharing of both types of tacit patient knowledge between TCM and WM healthcare professionals in their patient-centred collaborations.

3.3 KS in Healthcare Organisations

The value of knowledge increases during the processes of sharing (Sawhney and Prandelli 2000). It has been widely recognised that KS is an effective strategy to establish competitive advantages for all types of organisations, including those in the healthcare sectors (McEvily 2000).

This section defines KS in the context of healthcare organisations, discusses the demand for KS in health services, and describes the current situation of KS in Chinese healthcare organisations.

3.3.1 Definition of KS in Healthcare Organisations

KS can be simply understood as the behaviour of making knowledge available to others (Ipe 2004). Lee (2001) proposes that KS is the activity of transferring or disseminating both explicit and tacit knowledge between people, groups, or organisations. Moreover, Al-Hawamdeh (2003) defines KS in more detail:

> Knowledge sharing, in its broadest sense, refers to the communication of all types of knowledge, which includes explicit knowledge or information, the 'know-how' and 'know-'who' which are types of knowledge that can be documented and captured as information, and tacit knowledge in the form of skills and competencies. (Al-Hawamdeh 2003, p. 81)

However, despite the fact that these definitions have accurately defined KS, they have done so in a very broad organisational context and can be evaluated as too general for this research project. Consequently, it is necessary to define KS in healthcare organisations.

Ryu et al. (2003) provide a definition of KS in the healthcare setting:

> Knowledge sharing in healthcare is the degree to which physicians actually share their knowledge with their colleagues for professional tasks. (Ryu et al. 2003, p. 114)

Nevertheless, this definition is too simplistic and too vague to define the processes and activities of KS.

A much more comprehensive and accurate definition for KS in the healthcare context is provided by Abidi (2007):

> Healthcare knowledge sharing can be characterised as the explication and dissemination of context-sensitive healthcare knowledge by and for healthcare stakeholders through a collaborative communication medium in order to advance the knowledge quotient of the participating healthcare stakeholders. (Abidi 2007, p. 69)

This definition implies five key factors in healthcare knowledge sharing:

1. what to share: context-sensitive healthcare knowledge, which includes both explicit and tacit knowledge;
2. how to share: explication and dissemination;
3. who it may concern: healthcare stakeholders;
4. communication channel: collaborative communication media;
5. why to share: advancing the knowledge quotient.

According to the above factors, KS adopted by this research project can be defined as the interaction of ethical and emotional knowledge and social and behavioural knowledge about individual patients between WM and TCM healthcare professionals through collaborative communication channels, in order to provide the best possible healthcare services to patients, to improve the quality of patient care, and to achieve patient satisfaction.

Moreover, as reported by a number of studies identified in the literature, there are clear and important demands for KS in the patient-centred healthcare environment. These demands are described and discussed in Sect. 3.3.2.

3.3.2 *The Demand for KS in Patient-Centred Health Services*

The patient-centred approach, as discussed in Chap. 2, has been widely adopted in a number of countries and often employed as the guiding principle for healthcare professionals to enact their ethical rules, concepts, and senses (McGrath et al. 2006). The patient-centred approach requires healthcare providers to interact and share knowledge with one another continuously (Van Beveren 2003; D'Amour and Oandasan 2005; Delva et al. 2008; Maizes et al. 2009), in order to "reconcile their

3.3 KS in Healthcare Organisations

differences and their sometimes opposing views" (D'Amour and Oandasan 2005, p. 9). In fact, KS has been widely recognised as a necessary foundation to the provision of patient care, as there are those who advocate that KS has a greater potential to improve the healthcare of patients than any drug or technology likely to be developed in this decade (Brice and Gray 2003).

According to the existing literature, there are three main problems existing in the healthcare environment which urgently need to be resolved by the implementation of KS, namely: overload of healthcare information, disconnection between medical research and the reality of health practice, and prevention of repeating medical errors.

The demand for effective KS in the patient-centred healthcare environment is due to overload of healthcare information (Pavia 2001). As indicated by Abidi (2007), the domain of medical knowledge has been expanded to a degree that the human mind cannot manage. Dwivedi et al. (2007) add that, since 1996, the National Library of Medicine's Medline database has included 4500 journals in 30 languages. Until 2002, Medline contained 11.7 million citations, and, on average, about 400,000 new entries were being added per year. Dwivedi et al. (2007) claim that it would take 1000 years to get up to date with the new literature added every year. Therefore, due to the unmanageable amount of healthcare information and knowledge, it is often the case that "those who [healthcare professionals] complain about the information overload are the same people who complain about never being adequately informed" (Gray 1998, p. 832). More dangerously, some knowledge in doctors' heads is either out of date, or wrong (Smith 1996), since it is very difficult for health practitioners to find the right knowledge for their needs.

The improvement of patient services is impeded by serious disconnections between the worlds of medical research and health practices (Lomas 2007). Therefore, Lomas (2007) and Andrew et al. (2001) emphasise that it is extremely important to connect the two worlds by establishing KS strategies.

Finally, KS is critical in ensuring patient safety by preventing medical errors from being repeated. De Brún (2007) claims that healthcare organisations need to establish KS strategies and processes to store and share lessons and experiences learnt from previous errors. Only by sharing these lessons can the same errors be prevented from recurring.

As discussed above, and since KS is considered to be critically important to health services and very beneficial to patient care, concepts of KS have been widely adopted in hospitals. However, and according to the aim of this research project, these problems and demands for KS are mostly reported in research studies conducted in Western countries. Thus, it is necessary to review literature reporting implementation, processes and problems existing in KS within the context of Chinese healthcare organisations.

3.3.3 KS in Chinese Healthcare Organisations

Although KS is a relatively new concept to Chinese healthcare organisations, it has been credited as extremely important to the quality of health services (Song et al. 2006; Chen et al. 2009; Chen 2009; Zhang and Li 2006; Yang et al. 2006). Moreover, and in truth, KS in China has an additional expectation, which is to be a tool to gain a competitive edge and to enhance profitability[1] (Yan 2009; Li and Wang 2008; Du and Sun, 2005; Li et al. 2008).

According to the existing literature, there are five main strategies which have been commonly used for the establishment of KS in Chinese hospitals. These strategies are synthesised as follows:

1. Changing hierarchical hospital structure: most Chinese hospitals have highly hierarchical organisational structures (Rong et al. 2005). As reported by these authors, some Chinese hospitals have attempted to abandon the traditional structure and were adopting a two-layer structure consisting of the hospital management and medical departments. This is because, as explained by Bian et al. (2008), this structure encourages the collaboration of medical departments, and intra- and inter-departmental communication.
2. Establishing KS culture: many hospitals have attempted to cultivate an organisational culture to encourage KS and value sharing behaviours (Zhang and Li 2005; Yang 2009; Bian et al. 2008; Rong et al. 2005).
3. Building a learning organisation: a number of professional training strategies, such as lectures, seminars, and online courses, have been adopted as common approaches in Chinese hospitals. In addition, many studies advocate building apprenticeship and mentorship relationships between experienced and relatively junior professionals (e.g. Rong et al. 2005; Cheng 2008, 2009; Bian et al. 2008). For instance, Chen (2009) highly values the apprenticeship type of training. She claims that only in this approach can the accumulated experiences of senior professionals be shared with junior professionals.
4. Implementing information and knowledge systems: a number of existing Chinese literature propose that the information and knowledge systems are an essential platform for KS (Yang 2009; Zhou and Liu 2007; Guo 2005; Du and Sun 2005). Zhou and Liu (2007) report a case study in which an information system was evaluated as capable of increasing communication and KS between medical departments and between professional teams. Additionally, Yan (2009) and Yang et al. (2006) claim that a large number of hospitals are implementing some kind of information system. In order to support learning and KS, many of them have purchased online knowledge bases.

---

[1] As introduced in Sect. 2.5.2, due to the implementation of the market economy policy, the central government significantly reduced funds and financial support to healthcare organisations. Therefore, hospitals need to compete with each other, and are relying on profits made from patient services to support all hospital expenses, including paying tax, updating medical equipment, and providing salaries for healthcare professionals. In these circumstances, hospital managements are pressed to use strategies (such as KS) to maximise incomes.

5. Using hospital libraries: currently, the hospital library is the main source for professionals seeking medical knowledge. In this case, effective management and use of the hospital library can increase the sharing of professional knowledge (Liu et al. 2007). However, as discussed by Li and Li (2006), Liu et al. (2006), and Cao and Wei (2006), hospital libraries mainly focus on providing explicit professional knowledge, whereas tacit knowledge is ineffectively managed and very often overlooked.

Chinese hospitals are making efforts to manage knowledge, but KS cannot be considered to have been very well implemented (Yang 2009). Li et al. (2008) and Yan (2009) point out that KS in Chinese hospitals is generally at a beginning stage. Many hospitals are still experimenting with new KS strategies and exploring necessary KS tools.

Li et al. (2008) propose a possible explanation for the slow development. They point out that many hospital managers employ a very short-term view, in which they put more resources and attention into increasing the financial income, purchasing new hi-tech medical equipment, and constructing new buildings. KS, therefore, is very often not prioritised (Li et al. 2008; Yan 2009).

It is very important to note that the findings of the literature review show that KS in Chinese healthcare organisations has not been very well investigated. Also, the literature review reveals that potential KS problems have been neither adequately identified and reported nor studied in depth. In fact, the majority of existing studies on KM and KS in Chinese hospitals are conceptual works without empirical data collected in the real hospital environments (e.g. Bian et al. 2008; Zhang and Li 2005; Yang 2009). Therefore, the lack of an existing body of knowledge about KS in Chinese hospitals points to two important indications for this research project: firstly, it is very difficult to establish a base theory to guide data collection and to frame data analysis; secondly, this study needs to adopt an inductive approach, and aims to develop a theory, which should be grounded in the data collected in the context of Chinese hospitals.

3.4 KS Models

Based on the definition of patient knowledge and the discussion on KS in Chinese hospitals in Sects. 3.2 and 3.3, this section reviews and discusses four KS models, which are evaluated as fundamental for this project. Firstly, the SECI model is introduced and discussed. This model, developed by Nonaka and Takeuchi (1995), is one of the most frequently cited works in the field of KM (Grant 2007). Secondly, Cook and Brown (1999)'s practice-based KS model is reviewed. It needs to be noted that both of these models are based upon the practice-based view of knowledge. Very different, and derived from the objectivist view of knowledge, de Lusignan et al. (2002)'s model is described and discussed. Finally, concerning the Chinese healthcare environment, a model named after the initials of its components, the Six-C Model (Li 2005), is presented.

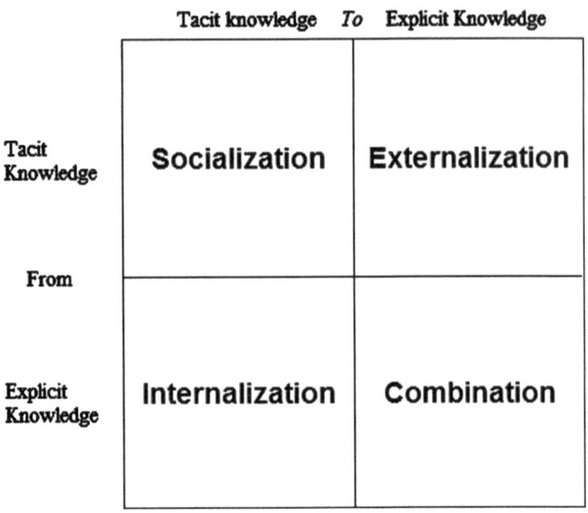

Fig. 3.2 Four modes of knowledge conversion. (Adopted from Nonaka and Takeuchi 1995, p. 62)

	Tacit knowledge *To* Explicit Knowledge	
Tacit Knowledge (From)	Socialization	Externalization
Explicit Knowledge	Internalization	Combination

3.4.1 SECI Model

SECI stands for socialisation, externalisation, combination, and internalisation, which are claimed by Nonaka and Takeuchi (1995) to be the four stages of knowledge conversion between the tacit and explicit knowledge forms. It is believed that, through these four stages, both forms of knowledge are shared between individuals (Sharif et al. 2005).

As shown in Fig. 3.2, these four stages can be explained as follows (Nonaka and Tacheuchi 1995; Choo 1998; Nonaka et al. 2000; Vasconcelos 2008):

- Socialisation: from tacit to tacit. A process of creating new tacit knowledge through social interaction to share knowledge and experience. This type of knowledge conversion usually takes place in informal non-work social meetings. Socialisation can also occur in the traditional master-apprentice type of learning, in which apprentices learn the craft of their masters through observation, imitation and practice.
- Externalisation: from tacit to explicit. A process of articulating tacit knowledge into explicit knowledge, through storytelling and the use of metaphors, analogies, and models.
- Combination: from explicit to explicit. A process of creating new explicit knowledge by combining or merging explicit knowledge, which is gathered from both inside and outside the organisation.
- Internalisation: from explicit to tacit. A process of internalising explicit knowledge into personal tacit knowledge. In this process, explicit knowledge is internalised to become part of individuals' tacit knowledge in forms of shared mental models and know-how.

These four modes of conversion cannot be taken as independent, as in fact they are highly inter-dependent. Each mode relies on, contributes to and benefits from other modes (Alavi and Leidner 2001). Additionally, Nonaka and Takeuchi (1995) propose that the continuation of the four modes of knowledge conversion should be viewed in a spiral, in which knowledge is continuously transformed, amplified, created and shared (Vasconcelos 2008).

To contextualise this model, Nonaka and Takeuchi (1995) raise an example of designing a bread-making machine at Matsushita. Vasconcelos (2008) provides a very good synthesis and explanation of this example:

> A product development engineer at this company suggested that the development team learned about the process of kneading dough, by observing what the bakery team at the Osaka International Hotel, renowned by baking the best bread in Osaka, did. She joined the team as an apprentice and as she learned to make bread, noticed that the head baker used a particular technique of stretching the dough while kneading it (socialisation). She then translated this technique into what the design team at Matsushita should do, using the expression "twisting stretch" (externalisation). The team codified this knowledge and integrated it with their knowledge about bread making machine design through processes and through the development of prototypes (combination). Finally, the team internalised processes and principles about bread-making machine design (internalisation). (Vasconcelos 2008, p. 430)

Nevertheless, and despite the fact that Nonaka and Takeuchi's study (1995) is one of the most frequently cited works in KM (Grant 2007), the SECI model is blindly used as a spine in an increasing number of KM research studies and business activities without necessarily questioning the construction of this model with sufficient supporting empirical evidences (Gourlay 2003). Moreover, Vasconcelos (2008) comments that this model is very controversial, since it is particularly difficult to define how tacit knowledge can be transferred between individuals. Furthermore, this model ignores the contextual influences involved in the social interactions (Vasconcelos 2008). Because of these criticisms, and despite the fact that the SECI model is very interesting and influential in the field of knowledge management, this project has carefully decided to reject this model.

3.4.2 Practice-Based KS Model

Very different from Nonaka and Takeuchi, the practice-based KS model developed by Cook and Brown (1999, p. 381) defines the activity of KS as "the generative dance between knowledge and knowing", in which knowledge is something people possess and knowing is something people do (Matsuo and Easterby-Smith 2008).

Moreover, the practice-based model stresses knowing as a tool for the processes of knowledge acquisition through interactions between the individual and the world (Cook and Brown 1999; Matsuo and Easterby-Smith 2008; Vasconcelos 2008). This model stresses that the generation of knowledge is in the individual's own hands (Vasconcelos 2008). On this very point, Cook and Brown (1999, p. 397) question the SECI model, claiming that "it is not possible, under any circumstances, for tacit knowledge to become explicit (or vice versa)". To support this argument, Matsuo and Easterby-Smith (2008) raise a very interesting example: an individual can only learn to drive a car by direct experience. The learning processes can be supplemented by reading textbooks and attending lectures, which, however, cannot be substituted for the direct experience.

Further challenging the SECI model, the example of the bread-making machine used by Nonaka and Takeuchi (1995) is interpreted very differently by Cook and Brown (1999). They explain that this example exemplifies the interaction between what is known and knowing by drawing both simultaneously, rather than asserting that conversions took place from tacit to explicit and explicit to tacit (Vasconcelos 2008).

In addition, Cook and Brown (1999) support their point of view by offering another example of three flute companies in Boston. This case study is concisely summarised by Vasconcelos (2008):

> These flute workshops, based in Boston, produce world-class flutes using very skilled craftsmanship. Each flute is produced by a specific team and each flute maker is responsible by only one part of the flute. Each part is developed by a flute maker until it meets a standard of quality, after which it is handed in to the next flute maker, who assesses the work in terms his or hers own set of standards. If the part does not "feel right" it is returned for further work. Each component is validated by the next stage and this work and is often assessed by eye or by hand. (Vasconcelos 2008, p. 431)

This example shows that tacit knowledge was produced through the interactions between the flute makers and the flute-making processes during flute production. Furthermore, it shows that tacit knowledge cannot be, at least, fully converted into explicit (Vasconcelos 2008).

However, without going deeper into a discussion of the different points of view adopted by the two KS models, the criticism raised by Cook and Brown (1999) against the SECI model is irrelevant to this project. It is because, as discussed above, the SECI model is not going to be used in this project.

Also, this practice-based KS model is evaluated as inappropriate for use in this research project. The main reason is that Cook and Brown (2009, p. 381) define "four distinct and coequal forms of knowledge", namely, explicit, tacit, individual and group. This definition conflicts with the explicit-tacit taxonomy of knowledge employed by this project and adopted by the majority of research studies in the field of knowledge management, as confirmed by an extensive literature review.

Finally, both this practice-based KS model and the SECI model which has already been discussed are not related to the healthcare environment. The next Sect. (3.4.3) discusses a healthcare KM model developed by de Lusignan et al. (2002).

3.4.3 KM Model for Primary Care

For the healthcare environment, de Lusignan et al. (2002) have developed a model for managing knowledge in primary care. This model is shown in Fig. 3.3.

3.4 KS Models

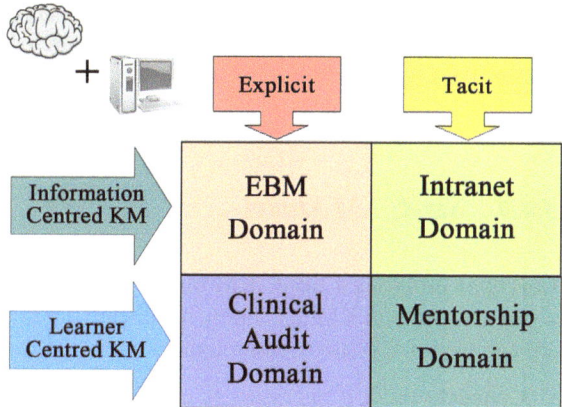

Fig. 3.3 Model for knowledge management in primary care. (Adopted from de Lusignan et al. 2002, p. 301)

As shown in Fig. 3.3, the x-axis of this model represents explicit and tacit forms of knowledge. The y-axis includes two main KM approaches, namely, information-centred approach and learner-centred approach. The information-centred approach focuses on disseminating existing knowledge, whereas the learner-centred approach aims at encouraging learning (de Lusignan et al. 2002).

Furthermore, the four elements formulate a two-by-two matrix consisting of four domains of KM activities, which are introduced as follows:

- Evidence-Based Medicine (EBM)[2] Domain: concerned with using information and communication technologies to share explicit knowledge.
- Intranet Domain: using online informal activities and communities of practice to support KS and learning. This approach could be very effective for sharing tacit knowledge.
- Clinical Audit Domain[3]: clinical audit "is used to improve aspects of care in a wide variety of topics. It is also used in association with changes in systems of care, or to confirm that current practice meets the expected level of performance" (NHS 2002). By continuous evaluation, individual healthcare professionals are encouraged and motivated to improve their practice of medicine, in order to achieve the expected level of performance.
- Mentorship Domain: focuses on the sharing of tacit knowledge from experienced to less experienced healthcare professionals.

However, even though this model is very interesting, it is heavily IT-centred. Hence, this model is very difficult to use in this study, because hospitals in China usually do not have such comprehensive IT infrastructures as those that have been imple-

---

[2] Evidence-Based Medicine is defined as "the process of systematically finding, appraising and using contemporaneous research findings as the basis for clinical decisions" (Rosenberg and Donald 1995, p. 1122).

[3] According to the National Health Service (NHS) in the UK, clinical audit is defined as "a quality improvement process that seeks to improve patient care and outcomes through systematic review of care against explicit criteria and the implementation of change" (NHS 2002).

mented and utilised in hospitals in the West, where this KM model was developed. Finally, in accordance with the aim of this research project, and to relate the discussion to the context of Chinese healthcare, Li's (2005) Six-C KM model is introduced and discussed next.

3.4.4 Six-C KM Model

Li (2005) proposes a Six-C KM model which consists of six key determinants to achieve successful KM in Chinese healthcare organisations. These six determinants are connectivity, content, community, culture, cooperation, and commerce:

- Connectivity: it is necessary to establish ICT infrastructure aimed at supporting the creation, storage, transfer and utilisation of knowledge. Moreover, the ICT infrastructure provides very good communication channels to connect individual healthcare professionals and those geographically distributed medical departments.
- Content: it is extremely important to identify different types of knowledge according to the local context and patient requirements. Only on the basis of this identification can KM strategies be established.
- Community: for the purpose of KM, both formal and informal communities need to be established to enhance face-to-face communication between healthcare professionals.
- Culture: successful KM needs to be facilitated by a compatible organisational culture, which must be carefully cultivated, monitored, and controlled in accordance with KM strategies and changes of hospital environment.
- Collaboration: KM demands collaborations, not just inside the hospital environment, between individual healthcare professionals, medical professional teams, and medical departments, but also outside the hospital environment, in alliances with other hospitals, research institutions, and universities.
- Commerce: in order to achieve the successful KM, it is necessary to develop specific motivational and incentive strategies.

This KM model includes six critical factors for the establishment of KM in Chinese healthcare organisations and is compatible to the Chinese healthcare environment, as claimed by Li (2005). The factor "collaboration" is of particular interest to this project, which investigates KS in TCM and WM collaboration. Nevertheless, it is argued here that the determinants included in this model are in no way different to the ones identified in the West. In fact, none of these critical factors reflects any Chinese characteristics and conditions. Moreover, Li (2005) provides no empirical evidence to support or to justify his processes of model development. Therefore, there are concerns about the validity of this model, and it has therefore been decided not to use this model in this research project.

Therefore, to summarise the discussion about the four KS models selected and presented, none of them can provide complete explanations on the processes of KS and problems in communication between TCM and WM healthcare professionals in Chinese hospitals. This suggests that new models for this context need to be formed inductively. This book aims at contributing with such a model for KS barriers.

3.5 KS Barriers

Despite the great importance of sharing knowledge, it is well reported that the processes of KS are often impeded by different types of barriers. Because this project aims at identifying barriers to sharing patient knowledge in the collaboration of WM and TCM healthcare professionals, this section reviews KS barriers reported in the existing literature for two purposes: (1) to identify an appropriate theoretical framework to guide the remaining research stages; (2) to enhance the theoretical sensitivity.

For business organisations, a very inclusive framework of KS barriers has been developed by Riege (2005), based on an extensive and systematic review of literature. This study not only identifies a large number of KS barriers, but also categorises these barriers into three dimensions: individual barriers, organisational barriers, and technological barriers. Nonetheless, it is perceived that this framework can provide very few theoretical indications to this research project, since Riege's (2005) framework was developed for business organisations. This type of organisation aims at maximising business profits. It is very different from healthcare organisations, which mostly aim at providing satisfactory and safe healthcare services to patients. Therefore, KS barriers in Chinese healthcare organisations are probably very different from the ones identified by Riege (2005)'s framework.

Moreover, some studies have investigated KS barriers in healthcare settings (e.g. Van Beveren 2003; Nicolini et al. 2008; Lin et al. 2008; De Brún 2007; Currie and Suhomlinova 2006; Currie et al. 2007). Probably, the most comprehensive framework was developed by Nicolini et al. (2008, p. 255), based on a broad review of literature including 178 articles relevant to KM in healthcare. Their framework includes seven barriers to successful healthcare knowledge management:

- over management and interference from the political sphere;
- clinical managerial conflict;
- professional barriers;
- lack of trust;
- poor quality relationships;
- insufficient technological skills;
- lack of strategic breadth and leadership.

Nevertheless, these barriers identified in Western healthcare organisations in the Western healthcare environment may not be present as barriers in Chinese healthcare organisations and are found in homogeneous medical groups, not in the context of collaboration between two heterogeneous medical groups which is the focus of this research study. Therefore, it was carefully decided not to include this framework

Table 3.3 Framework of knowledge flow barriers in healthcare organisations in Taiwan. (Based on Lin et al. 2008, p. 338)

ID	Knowledge flow barriers
1	The knowledge source wants to maintain his prestige
2	The knowledge source wants to maintain his competence
3	The knowledge receiver doubts whether the knowledge is updated
4	The knowledge receiver lacks absorptive capacity
5	The knowledge receiver lacks a positive attitude
6	The NIH syndrome
7	It is difficult to concretely express medical knowledge
8	The uncertain nature of medical knowledge
9	The complex nature of medical knowledge
10	It is difficult to standardize medical knowledge
11	The knowledge lacks evidence
12	Physicians lack time for knowledge flow
13	Poor relationships between the knowledge source and the knowledge receiver
14	Lack of communications between the knowledge source and the knowledge receiver
15	Knowledge sources/knowledge receiver don't know the other end of the knowledge flow
16	Lack of a knowledge sharing culture among peers
17	Lack of rewards and incentives towards knowledge flow
18	Lack of performance appraisal concerning knowledge flow
19	Lack of leadership for promoting knowledge flow
20	The large distance between the echelons of knowledge sources and receivers
21	Too many medical specialties
22	Lack of sufficient mechanisms of knowledge flows

as a theoretical foundation for this project. This is because, as discussed by some studies (e.g. Ford and Chan 2003; Tong and Mitra 2009), KS barriers are very often highly context-attached and become less significant once they are taken off from the original environment. For instance, Tong and Mitra (2009) point out that some Chinese cultural traits can be evaluated as KS barriers in Chinese organisations, such as hierarchy consciousness, fear of losing face, and sense of modesty, but would not necessarily be the same in the West. However, the search of the literature did not find any studies reporting on KS barriers in Chinese healthcare organisations.

Additionally, Lin et al. (2008) have developed a framework of knowledge flow barriers based on investigating seven hospitals located in different parts of Taiwan, where the social context might be similar to that of mainland China. This framework is shown in Table 3.3.

However, although the identification of knowledge flow barriers could be relevant to this project, it was decided not to adopt this framework for the exploration of KS barriers in this research. This decision was made for two main reasons. Firstly, although Lin et al. (2008) provide no clear information, it is presumed that all interview participants were from the biomedical discipline (WM in this research project). That is very different from this study, which investigates the interaction between two very distinctive types of healthcare professionals. Secondly, the validity and reliability of this framework are questioned. Lin and his colleagues attempt to study the knowledge flow. However, they not only fail to define clearly what knowledge flow is, but also use the terms 'knowledge flow', 'KS' and 'KM' interchangeably in their publication. Moreover, some of the barriers are questionable. For instance, barrier eight "the uncertain nature of medical knowledge" and barrier nine "the complex nature of medical knowledge" are very vaguely differentiated and could be repeating each other.

Consequently, on the basis of an extensive search of literature in both English and Chinese languages, it is concluded here that very few existing studies can provide insightful indications to this research project. Moreover, there are no conceptual frameworks that can be evaluated as sufficient to be adopted as the theoretical framework to guide the remaining research stages.

In this case, instead of deductively finding and testing an existing theory in the research context, it is more appropriate to inductively develop a theory, which is explainable and applicable to the KS problem in Chinese healthcare organisations. Moreover, as informed by the literature review, it is very difficult to form an in-depth and concrete theoretical foundation and to establish a theoretical framework to guide data collection and analysis and theory development in the remainder of the research. Therefore, it is more realistic to adopt a grounded approach, in which the theory would emerge from collected data.

3.6 Conclusion

This chapter reviews the definitions and concepts of knowledge, patient knowledge, KS and KM in the healthcare environment, KS models and KS barriers. This literature review was carried out for three purposes, namely: enhancing the contextual and theoretical sensitivity, locating appropriate theoretical frameworks to guide the remainder research stages, and drawing indications for the selection of research methodology and for the research design.

The existing literature was evaluated and shown to contain no sufficient theoretical foundation for this research project. However, the findings of the literature review provide three important indications for the research design:

1. The literature review shows that the KS problem between TCM and WM healthcare professionals investigated by this study has not been recognised and investigated either politically or academically. In fact, this project could be the first study to investigate this problematic phenomenon. Consequently, this research project is purely inductive in nature and aims at establishing a theory.
2. The literature review has not identified any sufficiently robust framework to be adopted as *a priori* framework to guide data collection and analysis. Thus, theory development is more likely to emerge from and be grounded in data.

3. There was a need to conduct a pilot study to confirm whether the KS problems anticipated did present themselves in the reality of practice of a Chinese hospital and to identify early results and insights to guide the remainder research stages.

These indications brought important clues and have been taken into consideration in the selection of research methodology and the research design, which are discussed in the next chapter, Chap. 4. Specifically, the next chapter underpins the underlying research philosophy of this project, explains and justifies the selection of Grounded Theory as the overarching research methodology, and finally thoroughly introduces and discusses processes of implementing Grounded Theory techniques and strategies into a single case-study research design.

Chapter 4
Research Paradigm and Methodology

This chapter presents the research methodology selected for the research project presented in the book. The selection of research methodology was guided by the main aim of this project, which is to identify KS barriers between TCM and WM healthcare professionals in their patient-centred collaboration. Furthermore, the selection of research methodology was decided after the literature review exercise and on the basis of the implications provided by the literature review.

In order to clearly present the research methodology employed in this research project, this chapter consists of two main sections, namely: research philosophy, and research methodology.

4.1 Research Philosophy

Philosophical stances are the most essential foundation for the selection of research methodology and the establishment of a suitable research design. This section explores the philosophical nature of this project from three perspectives: philosophical assumptions, research approaches, and research paradigms.

4.1.1 Philosophical Assumptions

The philosophical assumptions are one of the most important issues defining the nature of a research study. Bryman (2001) asserts that there are two fundamental philosophical assumptions in social science, namely, ontology and epistemology.

4.1.1.1 Ontology

Ontology can be simply understood as the study of "being" (Koepsell 1999, p. 217). Ontology is concerned with the nature of reality, or the nature of social entities (Saunders et al. 2007; Bryman 2001).

There are two ontological positions in terms of social science research, namely, objectivism and constructivism (Bryman 2001). Objectivism asserts that social phenomena and categories are separated from social actors (Bryman 2001). Very differently, constructivism claims that social phenomena and social actors are closely interrelated. In fact, social phenomena and their meanings are created, interpreted, and constantly changed by social actors (Bryman 2001). More specifically, Bryman and Bell (2003) point out two basic assumptions of social constructivism:

1. Social phenomena and categories are constructed through social interactions.
2. Social phenomena and categories are in a constant state of revision.

Therefore, according to the research question and the aim of this study, the constructivist ontological position was adopted, since the KS barriers that hinder the interaction of patient knowledge are created and continuously revised by TCM and WM healthcare professionals through their interactions.

4.1.1.2 Epistemology

Epistemology is "a branch of philosophy that investigates the possibility, origins, nature, and extent of human knowledge" (Ayyub 2001, p. 4). Epistemology concerns the study of knowledge and what is acceptable as valid knowledge in a field of study (Bryman 2001; Collins and Hussey 2003; Maylor and Blackmon 2005; Saunders et al. 2007). Bryman (2001) further specifies two main epistemological positions in social science:

- Positivism is derived from the philosophy of the natural sciences (Maylor and Blackmon 2005) and takes the view that "objective reality exists beyond the human mind" (Weber 2004, p. iv). Taking this epistemological position, positivist social science researchers adopt an objective worldview and advocate applying research methods from the natural sciences to study social reality and beyond (Bryman and Bell 2003). Furthermore, Remenyi et al. (1998) point out that the end product of positivist social research is generalised disciplines or laws, which can be very similar to results from physical and natural science research.
- Interpretivism adopts a contrasting position to positivism. The interpretivist epistemology considers that "knowledge of the world is intentionally constituted through a person's lived experience" (Weber 2004, p. iv). Interpretivist research-

4.1 Research Philosophy

ers respect the differences between people (Bryman and Bell 2003) and thus tend to investigate and capture subjective insights and meanings of social phenomena from the perspective of social actors (Saunders et al. 2007).

According to the research question and the aim of this project, the researchers need to identify individual KS barriers by capturing subjective insights, interpreting the meanings of discourse, and understanding the actions of individual TCM and WM healthcare professionals. Therefore, clearly, this research project needed to adopt an interpretivist epistemology.

4.1.2 Research Approach

Upon the basis of constructivist ontology and interpretivist epistemology, it is necessary to choose a suitable approach to answer the research question and to achieve the main aim.

In social science, there are generally two main approaches leading to the acquisition of new knowledge, namely deduction and induction.

4.1.2.1 Deduction

Deduction represents the commonest perspective on the relationship between theory and social research (Bryman 2001). According to Hyde (2000), the deductive approach consists of a series of theory testing processes, which begin with an established theory, and then verify whether the theory is applicable to specific instances. In this case, the deductive approach is also called a "top down" approach (Trochim 2006).

As shown in Fig. 4.1, deduction starts from identifying a theory that is of interest to the research topic. Then the theory is articulated into specific hypotheses, which are tested and verified by empirical evaluation and observation. As a result, a confirmation (or not) of the original theory is made (Trochim 2006; Bryman 2001). Moreover, deductive research projects usually adopt the objectivist ontological position and the positivist epistemological position (Bryman and Bell 2003).

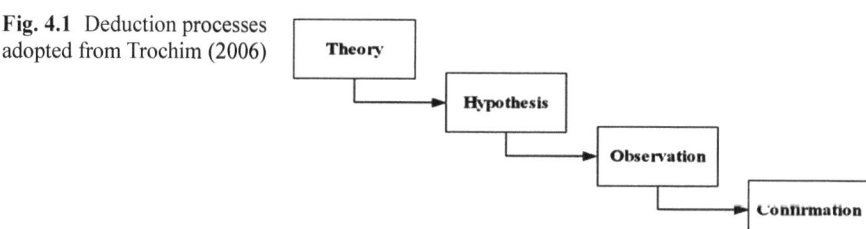

Fig. 4.1 Deduction processes adopted from Trochim (2006)

Fig. 4.2 Induction processes adopted from Trochim (2006)

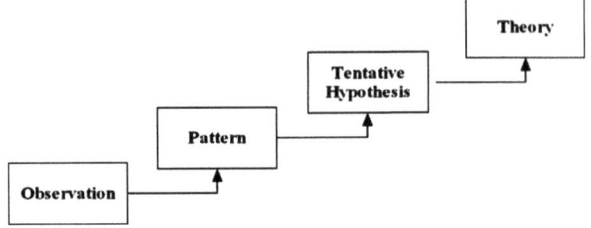

4.1.2.2 Induction

In contrast, induction is a "bottom up" approach and usually used for theory building (Trochim 2006). As shown in Fig. 4.2, the inductive approach begins with specific observation and evaluation in order to identify patterns and regularities, which are then articulated into tentative hypotheses. Finally, based on these hypotheses, general conclusions or theories are developed (Trochim 2006).

Additionally, Bryman (2001) points out that inductive researchers need to involve personal judgments and interpretations to evaluate the implications of research findings and to build a theory. Therefore, inductive research projects usually employ the constructivist ontology and the interpretivist epistemology (Gorman and Clayton 2005).

This project adopted the inductive approach for two clear reasons. Firstly, induction is compatible with the constructivist ontology and the interpretivist epistemology. Secondly, as shown in the literature review, there was no base theory to use in a deductive approach.

4.1.3 Research Paradigms

As discussed in Sects. 4.1.1 and 4.1.2, this research project adopted the constructivist ontology, the interpretivist epistemology and the inductive approach. On the basis of these philosophical foundations, it is essential to choose between two research paradigms, the quantitative paradigm and the qualitative paradigm.

4.1.3.1 Quantitative Paradigm

The quantitative paradigm attempts to understand a social phenomenon by interpreting numbers. More specifically, this paradigm emphasises quantification in processes of data collection and analysis (Bryman 2001). Moreover, Veal (2005) adds that the quantitative paradigm relies on numerical evidence to test a theory and to draw conclusions. Thus, in order to ensure the reliability of the results, it is important to collect data from a relatively large sample of people or organisations (Veal 2005).

Additionally, Bryman and Bell (2003) attribute three fundamental philosophical stances to the quantitative paradigm:

- It entails a deductive approach and aims at testing theories.
- It adopts the objectivist ontological position and views social reality as external.
- It adopts the positivist epistemological position and incorporates norms and models from the natural sciences.

Consequently, and according to all three philosophical stances, the quantitative paradigm is evidently not suitable for this project, which aims at developing a theory, rather than testing theories.

4.1.3.2 Qualitative Paradigm

By contrast to the stress which the quantitative paradigm places on quantification, qualitative research studies depend on the use of words (Bryman 2001). To be more specific, Gorman and Clayton (2005, p. 3) provide a comprehensive definition of qualitative research:

> Qualitative research is a process of enquiry that draws data from the context in which events occur, in an attempt to describe these occurrences, as means of determining the process in which events are embedded and the perspectives of those participating in the events, using induction to derive possible explanations based on observed phenomena. (Gorman and Clayton 2005, p. 3)

Also, Veal (2005) claims that qualitative research study does not usually need to include a large sample population, but tends to collect in-depth information from a relatively small group of people or organisations.

Bryman and Bell (2003) point out three fundamental philosophical stances to this paradigm:

- It predominately stresses an inductive research approach and aims at the generation of theories.
- It employs the constructivist ontological position and views social reality as being continuously changed by social actors.
- It rejects the practices and norms of the natural science model, as well as the positivist epistemology. Instead, it relies on qualitative researcher to interpret the social world as social actors.

In the light of the research question and the aim of this research, the qualitative approach is more appropriate to this project and is therefore adopted. This decision was made because of the following indicators:

1. This project is inductive in nature and aims at generating a theory.
2. This research adopts the constructivist ontological position and the interpretivist epistemological position.
3. The nature of this study requires the researchers to enter the research site and to capture and interpret meanings from discourses made by healthcare professionals.

4.2 Research Methodology

Discussion in Sect. 4.1 underpins the base philosophy for this research project, which is inductive, employs the constructivist ontology and the interpretivist epistemology, and adopts the qualitative approach to answer the research question and to achieve the research aim.

On the basis of the philosophical foundation, it is extremely important to choose a suitable research methodology to guide data collection and analysis, and processes of theory development.

This section uses three sub-sections to describe and discuss the selection of research methodology for this research project. These three sub-sections are: the selection of research methodology, grounded theory (GT), and a combined approach of case-study and GT.

4.2.1 The Selection of Research Methodology

For a research project, a research methodology needs to be carefully selected according to the research aim, the research question and the base research philosophy. Saunders et al. (2007) list seven research methodologies commonly used in information science research: experiment, survey, case study, action research, ethnography, grounded theory (GT) and historical research. Among these methods, many researchers (e.g. Saunders et al. 2007; Pickard 2007; Myers 1997) assert that action research, GT, case-study, ethnography, and historical research are qualitative research methodologies; these are therefore introduced below.

- Action research advocates addressing practical problems and contributing to general scientific theories at the same time (Elden and Chisholm 1993). Rapoport (1970) stresses that action research aims at pursuing actions to the practical concerns of people from within the human activity system, and in the meantime achieving the goals of social science. Therefore, because this research project did not intend to initiate any action, the action research methodology was considered as not appropriate for this study.
- Grounded Theory (GT) consists of a series of systematic procedures for data collection and analysis, and is particularly useful for theory development (Goulding 2007). In contrast to other qualitative research methodologies, a very basic condition of using GT is that researchers must conduct data collection and analysis without predefined knowledge about the field, which needs to be investigated (Saunders et al. 2007; Strauss and Corbin 1998). Therefore, in this research project, since the literature review conducted at the beginning of this project provided very limited predefined knowledge, this made GT a very appropriate and useful choice. At the same time, it was very difficult to use other methodologies, such as case study, which are better started with a concrete theoretical foundation or a priori specification of theoretical constructs (Eisenhardt 1989).

- Case-study is one of the most widely used methodologies in social science research (Orlikowski and Baroudi 1991; Alavi and Carlson 1992; Myers 1997). Yin (2003) points out two basic characteristics of the case-study methodology. Firstly, a case-study investigates contemporary phenomena. Secondly, a case-study highlights the contextual conditions and the connection between the social context and the social phenomenon. The case-study methodology was evaluated as not suitable for this project, since as discussed above this approach usually requires a theoretical foundation for the development of theory (Yin 2003). Nonetheless, this methodology could be used to provide a specific context setting (Gorman and Clayton 2005).
- Ethnographic research is one of the most in-depth research methods possible (Myers 1999). This methodology is usually adopted in the study of culture and is evaluated as very important in areas such as anthropology and sociology (Maylor and Blackmon 2005). Moreover, ethnographic researchers focus on the interpretation of behaviour or specific events in the everyday lives of social actors (Pickard 2007). This approach usually requires the researcher to engage into the research field and to spend a significant amount of time (at least a year) in the field (Pickard 2007), in order to gain deep understandings of the people, the organisation, and the context (Myers 1999). The ethnographic research methodology is not used in this research project, since the researchers are not healthcare professionals, and therefore it is almost impossible to investigate the everyday lives of social actors as part of the research context.
- Historical research provides perspectives and insights on historical phenomena (Mason et al. 1997). Yin (2003) claims that the historical methodology is a preferred strategy when there is no access or control. It largely relies on data that already exist in different forms (Pickard 2007). This methodology is clearly not suitable for this project. A very evident reason is that this study focuses on a contemporary social phenomenon.

When choosing a research methodology for a project, as Saunders et al. (2007) emphasise, no research strategies should be considered as superior or inferior to others. Every research strategy has its particular advantages and disadvantages (Yin 2003). In fact, the selection of an appropriate research methodology needs to be carefully decided according to the research question, the research objectives, the extent of existing knowledge, the amount of time and other related resources, and researchers' personal philosophical comprehensions (Saunders et al. 2007).

Therefore, after careful consideration, this research project reported in this book adopted GT as the overarching methodology.

4.2.2 GT

GT as a systematic and flexible approach to theory generation can be particularly useful in exploring insights for theory development. The GT approach is defined as:

A qualitative research method that uses a systematised set of procedures to develop and inductively derive grounded theory about a phenomenon. (Strauss and Corbin 1990, p. 24)

GT was first presented by Barney Glaser and Anselm Strauss in their book *The Discovery of Grounded Theory* published in 1967. The two co-founders, despite their very different backgrounds (Anselm Strauss was a qualitative researcher from the University of Chicago and Barney Glaser was a quantitative researcher from Columbia University), arrived at a belief that inductive theory generation needs to be grounded in data systematically collected and analysed (Corbin and Strauss 1990; Strauss and Corbin 1998; Pickard 2007).

4.2.2.1 Two Distinctive GT Approaches

After the initiation of GT, these two co-founders gained conflicting understandings of how to apply GT. These conflicts are clearly illustrated by their respective publications, namely, Strauss and Corbin's book *Basics of Qualitative Research*, published in 1990, and Glaser's book *Basics of Grounded Theory Analysis*, published in 1992. These two divisions of GT understanding were then developed into two systematic approaches, namely *Straussian* and *Glaserian* (Fernández 2004; Onions 2006). Straussian advocates using a more structured approach to collect and analyse data (Pickard 2007). However, the Straussian approach was criticised as having "moved too far from the original concepts" (Pickard 2007, p. 156), as "forcing data" and as "no longer a GT methodology" (Glaser 1992, p. 122). By contrast, the Glaserian approach advocates that the researcher should stand at a passive position, free from preconceptions, not forcing structure onto data, and trusting that theory will emerge (Rodon and Pastor 2007).

To differentiate the two approaches, Onions (2006) developed a table to demonstrate the key differences between the Glaserian and Straussian GT approaches As shown in Table 4.1, differences between the two approaches are various, yet subtle. If we compare the two approaches, the Straussian approach provides more pragmatic rigour and clearer techniques for researchers to handle processes of data collection and analysis. Therefore, the researchers of this project decided to follow the Straussian approach. More specifically, the application of this approach followed instructions from Strauss and Corbin's book *Basics of Qualitative Research: Techniques and Procedures for Developing Grounded Theory* (1998). This selection was supported by Rodon and Pastor (2007), who claim that novice researchers should adopt the Straussian approach, because "the Straussian version would help more in guiding the data analysis" (Rodon and Pastor 2007, p. 72).

Nevertheless, despite the decades of dispute between the two approaches, both Straussian and Glaserian researchers adopt an identical philosophical view, that theory should emerge from or be 'grounded' in the data (Van Niekerk and Roode 2009). Moghaddam (2006) adds that even though the two approaches have very distinctive paths to develop a theory, both Straussian and Glaserian have a conjugate with regard to the main processes of GT, namely: use of literature, theoretical sampling, coding processes, comparative analysis, and theoretical saturation.

Table 4.1 Key differences between Glaserian and Straussian GT approaches adopted from Onions (2006, pp. 8–9)

Glaserian	Straussian
Beginning with general wonderment (an empty mind)	Having a general idea of where to begin
Emerging theory, with neutral questions	Forcing the theory, with structured questions
Development of a conceptual theory	Conceptual description (description of situations)
Theoretical sensitivity (the ability to perceive variables and relationships) comes from immersion in the data	Theoretical sensitivity comes from methods and tools
The theory is grounded in the data	The theory is interpreted by an observer
The credibility of the theory, or verification, is derived from its grounding in the data	The credibility of the theory comes from the rigour of the method
A basic social process should be identified	Basic social processes need not be identified
The researcher is passive, exhibiting disciplined restraint	The researcher is active
Data reveals the theory	Data is structured to reveal the theory
Coding is less rigorous, a constant comparison of incident to incident, with neutral questions and categories and properties evolving. Take care not to 'over-conceptualise', identify key points	Coding is more rigorous and defined by technique. The nature of making comparisons varies with the coding technique. Labels are carefully crafted at the time. Codes are derived from 'micro-analysis which consists of analysis data word-by-word'
Two coding phases or types, simple (fracture the data then conceptually group it) and substantive (open or selective, to produce categories and properties)	Three types of coding, open (identifying, naming, categorising and describing phenomena), axial (the process of relating codes to each other) and selective (choosing a core category and relating other categories to that)
Regarded by some as the only 'true' GT method	Regarded by some as a form of qualitative data analysis

4.2.2.2 Use of Literature

In traditional inductive qualitative research, it is usual to review existing literature extensively at the beginning, in order to produce a priori theoretical framework, which is normally adopted as the theoretical foundation and the starting point for data collection and analysis (King 2010).

It is very different in GT projects, in which the literature review needs to be practised cautiously. In fact, Strauss and Corbin (1998, p. 49) advise that there is no need to review all the literature at the beginning, since early steeping in the literature may "constrain", "stifle", or even "paralyze" the researcher's analytical senses, and may possibly bring strong biases to the emerging theory. Consequently, Strauss and Corbin (1998) propose that GT researchers need to maintain an objective stance, which means to set aside his/her personal knowledge and experience, but to listen to the 'voice' from the data.

Nonetheless, as also discussed by Strauss and Corbin (1998), although familiarity with the relevant literature can block the analytical senses, it enhances the theoretical sensitivity of a researcher. Theoretical sensitivity is crucial for theory development, as it is the ability to capture subtle nuances in data, generate concepts from data, and relate them according to normal models of theory in general (Glaser 1978). Consequently, in this research project, a general review of literature was undertaken at the beginning, which provided background knowledge for the development of theory and enhanced the theoretical sensitivity. Moreover, an additional literature review which was carried out at the end of this project (after the emergence of theory) served to confirm the research findings and to identify where the literature is incorrect or overly simplistic (Strauss and Corbin 1998).

Additionally, instead of heavily relying on the a priori framework to frame and guide processes of data collection and analysis, GT encourages researchers to practise and direct data collection according to the analysis and the needs of theory development (Strauss and Corbin 1998). This strategy is called theoretical sampling.

4.2.2.3 Theoretical Sampling

Theoretical sampling is valued as a basic principle and a unique technique of GT. Theoretical sampling is defined as:

> Data gathering driven by concepts derived from the evolving theory and based on the concept of "making comparisons", whose purpose is to go to places, people, or events that will maximize opportunities to discover variation among concepts and to densify categories in terms of their properties and dimensions. (Strauss and Corbin 1998, p. 201)

The theoretical sampling strategy closely connects the processes of data collection and analysis. In fact, there is an ongoing interplay between the collection and analysis of data, in which the collection of data is driven by the analysis, which starts as soon as the first bit of data is gathered. On the basis of the data analysis, the researcher articulates and derives indications for further data collection (Corbin and Strauss 1990).

Therefore, Strauss and Corbin (1998) advocate that the GT researcher needs to enter the investigation site with an empty mind. In this case, by using the theoretical sampling strategy, the researcher can "maximize opportunities to compare events, incidents, or happenings to determine how a category varies in terms of its properties and dimensions" (Strauss and Corbin 1998, p. 202).

Nevertheless, it is very important to mention that Strauss and Corbin (1998) do not suggest that the researcher should be completely empty-minded. In fact, they claim that the researcher needs to decide whether to "develop a list of interview questions or areas for observation. […] Initial interview questions or areas of observation might be based on concepts derived from literature or experience or, better still, preliminary field work" (Strauss and Corbin 1998, p. 205). However, Strauss and Corbin (1998) warn that, because the predefined concepts are not grounded in the 'real' data, they must be considered as provisional, and discarded as soon as the data start to come in.

In order to ensure the final theory is truly grounded in data, this research project adopted the theoretical sampling strategy to direct the data collection and analysis.

4.2.2.4 Coding Processes

GT demands microanalysis of data, which means detailed line-by-line examination of data in order to identify incidents and concepts, to generate categories with properties and dimensions, and eventually to formulate a theory (Strauss and Corbin 1998). Strauss and Corbin (1998) advise that the microanalysis is practised by applying three types of coding to the data: open coding, axial coding, and selective coding.

- Open coding is "the analytic process through which concepts are identified and their properties and dimensions are discovered in data" (Strauss and Corbin 1998, p. 101). Open coding breaks data down into discrete fragments, closely and thoroughly examined for similarities and differences (Strauss and Corbin 1998). Through these processes, events, objects, actions and interactions which are identified as conceptually similar or related in meaning are grouped to form categories (Corbin and Strauss 1990).
- Axial coding is "the process of relating categories to their subcategories" (Strauss and Corbin 1998, p. 123). Axial coding interconnects properties, concepts and subcategories around the axis of a category (Strauss and Corbin 1998). Moreover, axial coding examines the axial interconnections against data (Corbin and Strauss 1990).
- Selective coding represents "the process of integrating and refining the theory" (Strauss and Corbin 1998, p. 143). In selective coding, "the major categories are finally integrated to form a larger theoretical scheme in which the research findings take the form of theory" (Strauss and Corbin 1998, p. 143). Moreover, poorly developed categories are identified and refined by practising the selective coding.

It needs to be noted that a misunderstanding could occur based on the introduction of the three types of coding. The practice of open, axial and selective coding seems sequential, structured and static. However, as explained by Pandit (1996), researchers do not need to strictly follow the sequence from open, through axial, to selective coding. In fact, as discussed by Strauss and Corbin (1998), the data analysis is flexible and free-flowing, in the sense that analysts move quickly back and forth between all three types of coding.

4.2.2.5 Comparative Analysis

Comparative analysis is a symbol of social science research and an essential feature of GT analysis. GT requires the researcher to adopt the comparative analysis technique throughout all data analysis and theory development processes. More specifically, Strauss and Corbin (1998) propose two fundamental types of comparison:

- The first type of comparison "pertains to the comparing of incident to incident or of object to object, looking for similarities and differences among their properties to classify them" (Strauss and Corbin 1998, p. 94). Goulding (2007) further explains that this type of comparison is mostly used when exercising open and axial coding.
- The second type is practised at an abstract level, as it compares "categories (abstract concepts) to similar or different concepts to bring out possible properties and dimensions when these are not evident to the analyst" (Strauss and Corbin 1998, p. 94). This type of comparative analysis is mostly used in axial and selective coding processes (Goulding 2007).

In order to support the practice of comparative analysis, this research project adopted three practical tools: a code definition list (which supports the comparison between individual open codes), a quotation list (which supports the comparison between individual quotations), and a concept map (which supports comparisons between properties, concepts, sub-categories, and categories). These tools are introduced in greater detail in Sect. 5.3.4 Data Analysis.

4.2.2.6 Theoretical Saturation

The theoretical saturation is extremely important as it is a sign for the completion of data gathering, theoretical sampling, and data analysis. Additionally, and more importantly, the theoretical saturation indicates the completion of theory generation.

Strauss and Corbin (1998, p. 212) formulate three essential rules which need to be used when determining whether the theoretical saturation has been achieved:

1. "No new or relevant data seem to emerge regarding a category."
2. "The category is well developed in terms of its properties and dimensions demonstrating variation."
3. "The relationships among categories are well established and validated."

In this study, according to the rules presented above, the theoretical saturation was considered as achieved when (1) no new open codes emerged from data; (2) properties and dimensions of individual categories are examined as explainable to the social phenomenon reflected from data; (3) the relationships between individual categories were examined and confirmed by checking with data.

4.2.3 A Combined Approach of Case-Study and GT

Despite the lengthy discussion of GT in Sect. 4.2.2, Pickard (2007, p. 155) criticises GT by stating "[it is] more about how data is collected and analysed than about the entire research design". Therefore, this author asserted that GT should be applied in a combined approach with other research methodologies, e.g. ethnography, case-study, action research, and historical research (Pickard 2007, p. 155).

4.2 Research Methodology

It is worthwhile to remind that Sect. 4.2.1 concludes that ethnography, action research, and historical research have been evaluated as inappropriate and thus excluded from this research project. Nonetheless, the case-study approach could be used to contextualise the application of GT. In fact, many researchers suggest that case-study and GT are not merely compatible with each other, but are really a combination that is ideal for establishing a valid and reliable inductive theory (e.g. Glaser and Strauss 1967; Glaser 1978; Eisenhardt 1989; Tellis 1997; Allan 2003; Pickard 2007). Fernández (2004) proposes three advantages of combining these two approaches, based on Eisenhardt (1989)'s work on the case-study approach.

1. Theory building by this method is likely to develop novel theory. This results from the contradiction and paradox in data, in that the use of the comparative method in reconciling these accounts often forces the analyst to think creatively.
2. The emerging theory can be further tested and expanded due to the close connection between the theory and the data.
3. The theory is likely to be empirically valid since the validation processes have been practised implicitly by constant comparison and constant data questioning.

Case-study is a common approach in social sciences which is used to explore and understand complex and localised human activity systems and social environments (Zhou et al. 2008). Some of the well-known studies in organisational research have been derived from this research approach (Bryman 2002).

There are various different definitions for the case-study approach, but probably the most widely cited one is provided by Yin (2003, p. 13), who defines the case-study approach thus:

"A case study is an empirical inquiry that:

- investigates a contemporary phenomenon within its real-life context, especially when
- the boundaries between phenomenon and context are not clearly evident."

The case-study is generally accepted as a qualitative research method and is an approach particularly suited to generating answers to 'why', 'how', and 'what' questions (Saunders et al. 2002). Furthermore, a qualitative case-study can be used for different purposes, namely, to provide description, theory testing, and theory generation (Eisenhardt 1989).

Case-study is a suitable approach to this project, as this study investigates a contemporary problematic situation existing in the current Chinese healthcare system. Moreover, this selection complies with the research question, which is a 'what' question, and the main aim of this project, which is to generate a theory.

However, it must be noted that there is a potential conflict in implementing GT and case study in one research project. Fernández (2004) mentions that Glaser (1998) highlights that utmost care must be taken to make sure techniques used in the case-study do not distort the natural emergence of theory grounded in data. On the other hand, Yin (1994) claims that "theory development prior to the collection of any case study data is an essential step in doing case studies" (Yin 1994, p. 28). This basic requirement, although is critically important to case-study research projects, contradicts one of the most essential principles of GT, which stresses that there should be no pre-conceived ideas or hypotheses before data collection (Allan 2003). Therefore, as Fernández (2004) points out, when combining GT and case-study, the researcher must clearly identify which methodology should be used as the main drive.

This potential conflict was carefully prevented in this study by employing GT as the overarching research methodology to guide the data collection and analysis. The case-study approach, on the other hand, aimed at contextualising the application of GT by providing a social context.

The actual application of the case-study method has two different forms of design, namely, single case design and multiple case design. Benbasat et al. (1987) explain the differences between the two:

- Single case design employs a single case to conduct in-depth investigation. This design is most useful for exploratory purposes and for initiating a theory.
- Multiple case design contains more than one single case. This design is desirable when the intention of the research is description, cross-case analysis, the extension of theory and to generalise research results.

According to the above discussion, and in the light of the research question and the aim of this project, a single case design was adopted. This decision was made for two reasons: firstly, considering China is one of the largest countries in the world, with a population exceeding 1.3 billion, it would be virtually impossible to generate a theory that would encompass the whole nation; secondly, since this project aims at generating a first set of insights on this problem, a single case design is better suited for the purposes of exploration and theory generation based on in-depth investigation. In the end, a public hospital in the city of Xiangyang, province of Hubei, was selected as the case-study site, which is discussed as part of the research design.

The design of this research project and the application of GT in the case-study selected is presented and discussed in Chap. 5.

4.3 Conclusion

This chapter presents and discusses the research methodology selected for this research project. Specifically, this study adopted a GT approach as the overarching research methodology. GT was applied in a social context by using a single case-study design, for which Xiangyang Central Hospital in the city of Xiangyang, Hubei province, was selected as the case-study site.

To conclude, this chapter explains and justifies the research methodology and techniques selected. The next chapter (Chap. 5) explains, describes and discusses the application of the methodology in the research context.

Chapter 5
Research Design

On the basis of the discussion focusing on research methodology in Chap. 4, this chapter presents and discusses research design.

Research design is defined as the "science (and art) of planning procedures for conducting studies so as to get the most valid findings" (Vogt 1993; cited in Collis and Hussey 2003, p. 113). Therefore, the research design is extremely important, as it provides a detailed action plan to direct the data collection and analysis.

The research design for this project is discussed in this chapter, which consists of four sections: case-study, data collection, data analysis and research stages.

5.1 Case-Study

As discussed in Sect. 4.2.3, this research project adopted a single case-study design to provide a social context to the application of GT. Therefore, it is essential to select a suitable and sufficient case-study site (a hospital in China) for an in-depth investigation.

5.1.1 Case-Study Site

This research project chose Xiangyang Central Hospital as the case-study site. According to the hospital website (www.xfszxyy.cn), this hospital was established in 1949 and currently has more than 2900 employees working in 33 different medical departments and is regarded as one of the top hospitals in Hubei. In 2014, about 1.3 million outpatients and 86,000 inpatients visited this hospital. A picture of the hospital is shown in Fig. 5.1.

The hospital is located in the city of Xiangyang, which is famous to Chinese people for its 2800 years of history. Moreover, Xiangyang has become a connecting point for Hubei, Henan, Sichuan and Shanxi provinces in terms of transportation and cultural and economic communication (Hubei Government 2014). According

Fig. 5.1 An overview of Xiangfan central hospital

Fig. 5.2 A picture of the north gate of Xiangyang city

to the website of Xiangyang City Council (www.xiangyang.gov.cn), Xiangyang is a medium-sized city in terms of both its geographical size (20,000 km^2) and its population (5.6 million people currently reside in the city). A picture of Xiangyang is shown in Fig. 5.2.

Xiangyang is located in the northwest region of Hubei province in central China with the Yangtze River flowing across the province. The geographic locations of Xiangyang and Hubei are illustrated in Fig. 5.3.

According to the website of Hubei Government (2014), Hubei consists of 13 cities, among which Wuhan, Jingzhou, Xiangyang and Yichang are famous Chinese historical, cultural, and industrial cities. Hubei province has six pillar industries: automobiles, iron and steel, electricity, building materials, textiles and clothing, and chemicals. Hubei has a population of 58 million, and is ranked 9th out of 34 provincial administrative districts, while its economy is ranked 12th.

It needs to be pointed out that Xiangyang Central Hospital was selected for two main reasons. Firstly, it provides both WM and TCM services to patients and has done so for several decades. Therefore, it was perceived that this case-study could provide rich and meaningful information that would help to achieve the research

Fig. 5.3 Geography of Hubei province

aim. Secondly, and very pragmatically, the researchers obtained guaranteed access to the informants and support for the project.

5.1.2 Obtaining Access

Obtaining access to the case-study site has always been considered as one of the crucial issues which determine the final success of qualitative research projects (Saunders et al. 2007). However, in this research project, securing access to the case-study site was difficult and challenging.

Initially, several attempts were made to contact healthcare professionals in hospitals in Wuhan, the capital of Hubei province. These contacts were not only unsuccessful but rather frustrating, with potential informants being interested neither in the project nor in being interviewed.

This failure made it clear that without using personal contacts it was virtually impossible to approach the potential interviewees. Personal contacts or relationships, i.e. *guan-xi*, are treated very seriously in China, as they define status and place in the social structure, as well as providing security, trust and a prescribed role for the individual in society (Hammond and Glenn 2004). Because the researchers were without *guan-xi*, it is not surprising that the researchers could not secure entry into the Wuhan hospitals as initially intended. Having reflected on this situation, the researchers then decided to approach Xiangyang Central hospital in the city of Xiangyang, also in the province of Hubei, the city of origin of the lead researcher, where the researcher had a few personal contacts.

It is also worthwhile to mention that the researchers witnessed how other Chinese cultural characteristics determined the degree of success in gaining access to Xiangyang Central Hospital. According to Hofstede (1994), China has a high power distance culture, in which subordinates are expected to be told what to do.

Moreover, due to the collectivist nature of the Chinese culture, subordinates and in-groups are usually dependent on power figures (Hofstede and Hofstede 2005). Therefore, if not asked by a senior health manager, medical professionals in China are not likely to readily volunteer or even agree to be interviewed. Consequently, without the participation of the senior manager to champion the research internally the participation of practitioners with lower professional standing and power cannot be guaranteed.

Therefore, the researchers established contacts with the deans of both the Neurosurgery Department and the TCM Department in Xiangyang Central Hospital. The leaders of these two departments have relatively high professional standing and influence within the hospital, and agreed to guarantee full cooperation and to champion the project within their respective departments. They also agreed to help identify appropriate informants in accordance with the research needs. Their staffs were briefed about the project during the routine weekly departmental meetings. Both deans encouraged their departmental practitioners to participate fully in the project. As a result, out of 46 interview participants, only one neurosurgical nurse refused to participate, claiming that she was "too shy".

5.2 Four Main Research Stages

Doing GT research requires the researchers to use personal experience to drive the data collection and analysis, to theorise about every incident in the field, and to react to any unexpected events which could endanger the whole piece of research. Therefore, in order to ensure a success, the application of GT was planned according to a four-stage design, as already mentioned in Chap. 1.

- The literature review consisted of two main components: the research context, focusing on TCM and WM in Chinese healthcare organisations, and the theoretical background, on KM and KS in a healthcare environment. The purpose of the literature review was to have a general understanding about the research context and the existing literature, and to enhance contextual and theoretical sensitivities. In fact, at the beginning of the project, it was expected that through the process of reviewing the literature a well-established framework could be identified, in order to guide the data collection and analysis and to be adopted as the starting point for theory development. However, the literature review could not find such a framework. This led to the choice of GT as the overarching research methodology.
- The pilot study aimed at confirming and exploring the communication and KS problems identified in the literature review. The pilot study also aimed at obtaining a better understanding of the current situation in Chinese healthcare institutions with regard to KS between TCM and WM practitioners, and providing emerging findings for the remainder of the research. Findings from this stage suggested that different departments in the hospital exhibit very different patterns

of KS behaviour in the two medical communities. The study also showed that very different levels of integration of complementary treatments may take place in different departments. This resulted in the decision to choose one specific department, namely the Department of Neurosurgery. This department has a proven history of using WM and TCM compound treatments for rehabilitating patients after craniotomies.
- The main study aimed at identifying KS barriers between the two communities when dealing with problems from neurosurgical patients. The exploration of barriers in this stage started on the basis of the pilot study findings and aimed at theoretical saturation. However, the findings indicated a need for further study on external contextual influences on KS.
- The follow-up study was the final stage of the field study and aimed at exploiting external influences on KS. Furthermore, it aimed at fully developing emerging categories and achieving theoretical saturation.

This four-stage design was considered as important to the final success of the project, since the gap between each two stages provided time and opportunities for the researchers to review any mistakes made when in the field, think over experiences gained from both successes and failures, and draw implications for the later research stages.

5.3 Data Collection

According to the four-stage research design discussed above, the researchers entered the case-study site on three different occasions to collect data. This section introduces and discusses data collection methods and tools in three sections: data collection method, sampling strategy, and supporting tools for data collection.

5.3.1 Data Collection Method

According to Bryman (2001) and Pickard (2007), qualitative research studies mainly employ three qualitative data collection methods, namely: observation, focus group, and interview. This project selected the interview as the data collection method, for the following reasons:

First of all, it was difficult to practise observation in this study, for two main reasons. On one hand, the researchers are not qualified to participate and thus cannot observe KS activities in medical practices. On the other hand, even without participation, it is virtually impossible to carry out the observation, as it could invade the privacy of the patient and violate ethical rules.

Secondly, it is very difficult to organise focus groups to involve both WM and TCM healthcare professionals, since these healthcare professionals usually have very varied and tight schedules. Moreover, focus groups are essentially to observe interaction in the group, and hence require at least two investigators, one to moderate the discussion and another to observe the interaction. Therefore, the focus group technique is not applicable to this project.

Finally, due to their effectiveness, interviews have been recognised as one of the most important data collection tools by a number of inductive qualitative researchers. Generally, there are three types of interviews: structured, semi-structured, and unstructured (Saunders et al. 2003; Bryman 2001):

- Structured interviews are based on a pre-designed and identical set of questions (Saunders et al. 2003). This technique has limited flexibility and no room for improvisation (Myers and Newman 2007).
- Semi-structured interviews are supported by an interview question list, which is pre-designed but incomplete. Therefore, the interviewer has sufficient space and flexibility to add/delete interview questions during the interview process when appropriate.
- Unstructured interviews are undertaken without a pre-determined list of interview questions, but the interviewer needs to have a clear orientation to conduct the interviews (Bryman 2001).

Also, nowadays, there is an increasing trend to use information and communication technology to conduct interviews via telephone, video links and the Internet, but the traditional face-to-face interview is still most widely used. Therefore, this study conducted interviews face-to-face with individual participants.

This research project employed semi-structured face-to-face interviews consisting of open-ended questions. This selection is based not only on the consideration that this method is easy to drive and compatible with both case-study and GT, but also on the belief that this technique is capable of gathering deep, meaningful, and reliable data.

5.3.2 Theoretical Sampling Strategy

As discussed in Sect. 4.2.2.3, the theoretical sampling strategy was adopted by this research project, and was used to inform the researchers "where to go to obtain the data necessary to further the development of the evolving theory" (Strauss and Corbin 1998, p. 201).

To be more specific, the theoretical sampling strategy guided the data collection in the case-study site and pointed to the inclusion of 46 interview participants in a total number of 49 interviews. The demographic profile of the participants is illustrated in Table 5.1.

As reflected in Table 5.1, the theoretical sampling strategy was practised in the pilot study, the main study, and the follow-up study:

- The pilot study: To achieve the aim of the pilot study as mentioned in Section "Aim", a total of seven healthcare professionals and workers were purposively approached and interviewed. These participants were two WM doctors,

5.3 Data Collection

Table 5.1 Demographic profile of participants ($N=46$)

Gender	Number of participants			
	Pilot study	Main study	Follow-up study	Total
Male	6	13	7	26
Female	1	12	10	23
Professional position				
Senior neurosurgeons	1	2	1	4
Junior and middle-level meurosurgeons	0	9	1	10
Neurosurgical nurses	1	8	3	12
Senior TCM doctors	1	5	2	8
Junior and middle-level TCM doctors	1	1	0	2
Orthopaedics doctor	1	0	0	1
Chief hospital manager	1	0	0	1
Hospital ICT manager	1	0	0	1
TCM educator	0	0	1	1
Healthcare politician in local government	0	0	1	1
Patient relatives/carers	0	0	8	8

one WM nurse, two TCM doctors, one ICT manager and one hospital administrator. These interviewees were purposively selected before travelling to the case-study site and for the purpose of gaining insights not only from the perspective of medical professionals, but also from a technical perspective provided by a ICT manager and from a management perspective by interviewing a hospital manager. After the completion of all seven interviews, the collected data were transcribed and analysed. As discussed in Sect. 5.2, findings from this stage suggested choosing the Department of Neurosurgery for more in-depth and focused investigation. This decision led to the interviewing of neurosurgeons, neurosurgical nurses, and TCM doctors in the main study.

- The main study: At this stage, neurosurgeons, neurosurgical nurses, and TCM doctors were approached and interviewed individually in groups of two or three. It is important to be noted that, due to the difficultis of gaining access and approaching potential interview participants as discussed in Sect. 5.1.2, the head of Neurosurgery Department and the head of TCM Department helped to pointed out who in practice was the best suitable to be interviewed next, and helped to approach potential interviewees by presenting and introducing the researchers to potential informants. Interview data were immediately transcribed and briefly analysed using open coding (as introduced in Sect. 4.2.2.4). Results from the brief analysis were used to revise the interview script and to indicate who should be interviewed next for the theory development. The data collection was stopped when the theoretical saturation was perceived as achieved. In the end, 11 neurosurgeons, six TCM doctors, and eight neurosurgical nurses were approached and interviewed. That is, in order to achieve theoretical saturation, the main study included all neurosurgeons, all TCM doctors, and half of the neurosurgical nurses. After the data collection, a much more thorough analysis was conducted, which revealed that the theoretical saturation in fact had not yet been achieved. The findings of the main study show that KS in the hospital environment was influenced by the external social environment. In this case, there was a need for a follow-up study, which not only required the interviewing of neurosurgical and TCM professionals in order to confirm and futher explain these findings from the main study, but also required the inclusion of TCM educators and healthcare politicians in order to obtain deeper understandings about the healthcare HE and about the existing national healthcare policies.

In addition, it was deemed necessary to include patients or patient relatives (carers) for the purpose of gaining opinions from people who are not from the medical background but know the needs of patients from a very close perspective. This is fundamental due to the type of knowledge sharing being studied by this book. However, the researchers were advised by healthcare professionals that almost all neurosurgical patients after surgery were not capable of talking, certainly were not capable of being interviewed or having lengthy discussion. Therefore, it was carefully decided to focus solely on patient relatives, who, after patients' surgeries, actually are the ones making decisions for patients based on negotiation with TCM and WM professionals.

- The follow-up study: In order to achieve the aim of the follow-up study, this study included neurosurgical and TCM healthcare professionals, TCM educators, healthcare politicians, and patient relatives. Similar to the main study, both heads of department (Neurosurgery and TCM) helped to approach these informants. In accordance with the interview strategy adopted in the main study, the interview participants were approached and interviewed individually in groups of two or three. However, the follow-up study differs from the main study in that interview data were immediately transcribed and thoroughly analysed. Finally, the theoretical saturation was achieved after 17 interviews, which included two neurosurgeons, two TCM doctors, three neurosurgical nurses, one TCM educator, one public administrator in the local healthcare department, and eight patient carers.

5.3.3 Supporting Tools for Data Collection

The theoretical sampling and the conduct of interviews could not be successfully finished without the assistance of two interview tools, namely: an interview question script and a digital recorder.

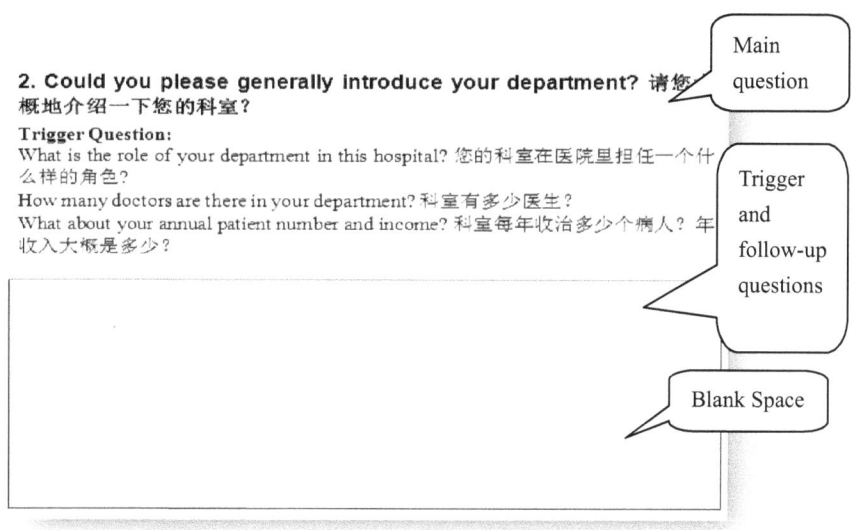

Fig. 5.4 An example of interview question script design

5.3.3.1 Interview Question Script

The interview question script was a very useful tool when conducting interviews. The script consisted of a series of open-ended questions, which guided the researchers to gather meaningful information for the needs of theory development.

Additionally, for each open-ended question, several trigger and follow-up questions were designed, for the purpose of increasing the richness and the depth of the responses, as well as informing the interviewee what level of response was desired. All questions on the script were in both English and Chinese. The English questions were used to inform the researcher for what purpose each question needed to be asked. The Chinese translations were exactly what the researchers were going to ask. Furthermore, for each main question, a blank space was designed and used for quickly jotting down emerging new issues, sparks of thoughts and ideas, potential probing or follow-up questions, etc.

A complete interview script used at the beginning of the main study is attached in Appendix 1. Furthermore, an example of the interview script design is shown in Fig. 5.4.

There were different versions of the interview script, one for each group of interviewees: TCM doctors, neurosurgeons, neurosurgical nurses, hospital manager, ICT manager, healthcare politician, TCM educator, and patient carers.

Finally, it is important to mention that interview questions in these scripts were constantly evolving with the processes of data collection and analysis. The initial version, together with all documentation offered to the informant, was subjected to ethical review and approved by the Information School in the University of Sheffield, as discussed in Sect. 5.4.

5.3.3.2 Digital Recorder

It is important to record the interview conversation accurately. As Patton (2002, pp. 380–381) stresses that, the recording needs to be done "as fully and fairly as possible" for two reasons: firstly, it protects the fluency of the interview conversation, as the interviewer can be more focused on the interviewee and be more engaged in the conversation; secondly, the accurate and intact interview recording is the foundation for detailed data analysis. Therefore, the researchers of this project used a digital recorder to document all interviews.

However, there is a problem in using the recording device, which is that the interviewee could be disconcerted and be alarmed to have his or her words preserved (Bryman 2008). In this study, two strategies were used to minimise this problem. Firstly, at the very beginning of every interview, the interviewer consulted the participant by stating:

> Your participation is potentially meaningful and greatly contributing to this study. Therefore, would you mind if I record our conversation? The recording will be kept strictly confidential and will only be used by me for the research purpose only. You can stop the recorder, for any reasons, whenever or whatever you feel uncomfortable.
>
> 您的参与很有可能为此项研究提供一些重要的信息。请问您是否介意我使用录音机记录下我们本次谈话的内容？录音记录将会严格保密，只会被我本人仅使用于本次研究。并且无论在任何时间，任何条件下，您有权利无条件的关闭录音。

The result was that all the interviewees agreed to use the digital recorder. It needs to be mentioned that one TCM doctor asked to stop the recording, because he was about to complain about some particular policies implemented by the chief hospital manager.

Secondly, the interviews were started by making some irrelevant and light conversation, such as:

> I have noticed a significant improvement in the interior decoration of your department. When was it redecorated?

or

> What is your role in the hospital?

This strategy helped the interview participants to get used to the interviewing atmosphere and to ease the discomfort caused by the digital recorder. Thus, the participants could be more at ease and provide truthful and meaningful information.

5.3.4 Data Analysis

Gathering rich and reliable data is the foundation for the data analysis and for the development of theory. This section discusses the data analysis of this research project in two main sub-sections: coding and theoretical saturation, and supporting tools for data analysis.

5.3 Data Collection

5.3.4.1 Coding and Theoretical Saturation

Coding is one of the most important analytical tools for the GT data analysis and the basis for the theoretical sampling and the comparative analysis. As introduced in Sect. 4.2.2, there are three types of coding employed by the GT data analysis, namely: open coding, axial coding and selective coding. This research project used all three types of coding for the data analysis.

Nonetheless, coding was implemented very differently in the pilot study, the main study, and the follow-up study:

- The pilot study mostly used open coding to identify concepts emerging from the data. Axial coding was also employed at this stage to link the concepts axially and to let the main categories emerge.
- The main study: In order to identify individual KS barriers and fully develop each emerging category, the main study used both open and axial coding. Moreover, selective coding was applied at the final part of this stage, due to the core category started to emerge. Furthermore, the practice of selective coding also demonstrated that a few concepts were not fully developed and needed to be investigated further in the follow-up study.
- The follow-up study applied all three types of coding. The new concepts were identified by open coding, and then linked to the emerging categories by using axial coding. Finally, the selective coding was conducted to validate the emerging theory by comparing it with the raw data.

It needs to be noted that the data analysis was stopped when the theoretical saturation was achieved; that is, when no new open codes emerged from the data analysis, categories were well developed, and relationships among categories were validated. The emergence of new open codes and the theoretical saturation can be demonstrated in Fig. 5.5.

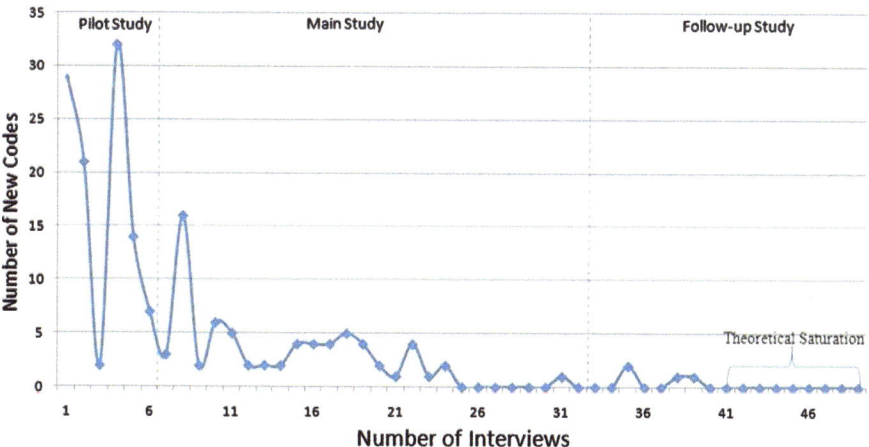

Fig. 5.5 Coding and theoretical saturation

As shown in Fig. 5.5, the burgeoning emergence of new open codes in the pilot study suggested a more focused data collection in the main study. It is worthwhile to mention that only two new open codes emerged from the third interview. This was because the ICT manager being interviewed knew very little about KS between healthcare professionals, which reflected the fact that ICT professionals in this hospital were irrelevant to this study, and hence they were not included in the main study.

In the main study, new codes were continuously emerging until the 25th interview. Although no new open codes emerged in the 26th–30th interviews, the new code identified in the 31st interview indicated a new area which had not been explored, and therefore the theoretical saturation had not yet been achieved. Thus there was a need to explore the new area in the follow-up study.

In the follow-up study, the theoretical saturation was considered as achieved after the 41st interview, but the process was continued until the 49th interview in order to obtain a better degree of certainty.

5.3.4.2 Supporting Tools for Data Analysis

In order to support the practice of coding and comparative analysis, four analytic tools were used interactively throughout all data analysis processes. These tools are computer-assisted qualitative data analysis software (CAQDAS) ATLAS.ti (version 5.0), code definition list, quotation list, and concept map.

CAQDAS ATLAS.ti

CAQDAS is one of the most significant developments in qualitative research, since this tool to a certain extent removes some of the tedious clerical tasks which come with the manual coding and retrieving of data (Bryman 2008). Additionally, ATLAS.ti is very compatible with GT and provides a number of powerful functions to support the practice of coding and to produce mind maps and memos (Fernández 2004).

Therefore, this project used the above software as the platform for the data analysis. To be more specific, once the interview data had been transcribed, the transcript was assigned into ATLAS.ti. In this way, the software became the platform for the researchers to read, retrieve, and manage the interview transcripts. Moreover, the researchers also applied open codes to the interview transcripts by using this software. A screen shot as an example of using this computer software is shown in Fig. 5.6.

However, Bryman (2008) argues that CAQDAS reinforces and exaggerates the tendency for the code-and-retrieve process. In addition, Fernández (2004) claims that ATLAS.ti creates unnecessary restrictions, inhibits the researchers' development of skills, and imposes time-consuming learning curves. In this study, two strategies were adopted to minimise these problems. Firstly, ATLAS.ti was only used to examine data closely and to tag specific pieces of data with open codes. Secondly,

5.3 Data Collection

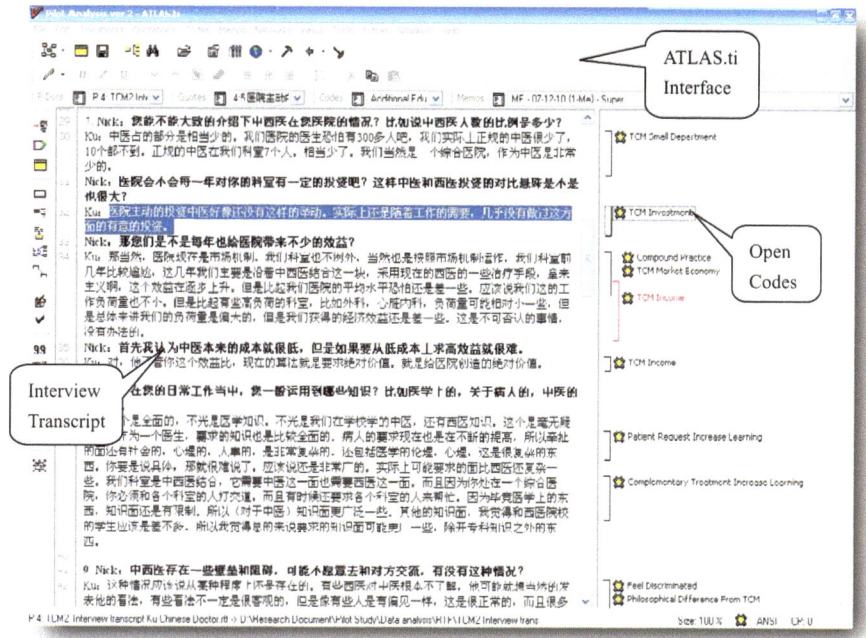

Fig. 5.6 An example of using ATLAS.ti

ATLAS.ti was used interactively with the coding definition list, the quotation list, and the concept maps.

Code Definition List

The code definition list not only presents open codes in relation to their categories and sub-categories, but also provides a definition for each open code. An example of the code definition list is shown in Table 5.2.

As shown in Table 5.2 and also in a sample in Appendix 2, the coding definition list was adopted as a fundamental tool for the comparative analysis at a generic level. By using this list, an open code can be clearly represented, in terms of both the meaning of this code and where it should be positioned. Therefore, when a new open code emerges from the data, this code is compared with the existing codes on the list for similarity and differences. Based on the comparison, the researchers can decide whether to merge this code with a similar one on the list, or to add it to the list as a new code.

According to the experience of this research project, this tool was particularly useful for the practice of open and axial coding. Moreover, this tool needs to be used in co-ordination with ATLAS.ti, the quotation list and the concept map.

Table 5.2 An example of the code definition list

Category of Philosophical Issues

Sub-Categories	3rd Level Categories	Concepts	Codes	Definition
Philosophical Conflicts	Different Conceptual Systems	Holistic VS Localised Approach to Practice	[TCM took holistic view, whereas WM took micro view of patients' problem]	TCM doctors take a holistic view to see patient, where WM doctors use a micro view.
		Different Diagnostic Methods	[TCM and WM have very different diagnosis methods]	TCM and WM professionals use very different diagnostic methods.
		Different Treatment Methods	[TCM and WM have different treatments]	TCM and WM professionals use very different treatment methods to resolve patient problems.
		Divergent Theoretical Grounds	[Non-Quantify of TCM WM]	From WM professionals' perspective, WM is based on accurate quantification, whereas TCM is not quantifiable.
			[None-Quantify of TCM	From TCM professionals' perspective,

Table 5.3 An example of the quotation list

Barrier of Chinese Healthcare Education

Sub-Categories	Codes	Quotations
TCM	[Education and Philosophy Relationship TCM]	P 6: WMD2 Interview Transcript Wang Bone Doctor.rtf - 6:61 两个不同的体系是很难沟通的，因为西医是不学中医的。 P18: TCM-D-5.rtf - 18:11 学西医的不可能接受中医，他也学中医的课程，但是学的非常少，而且他们西医的思想已经根深蒂固了，他没有办法接受中医，他会觉得中医是谬论，是不科学的。但他实际上并没有真正的了解中药配伍起来对病人有没有效果，他只是觉得你这个不科学，肯定是没效的，但实际上不是这样的。 Translation: "WM practitioners will never accept TCM. They had some TCM courses, but rarely. Their WM ideology is deep in their mind. They cannot accept TCM because they think TCM is a pseudoscience. Actually, they don't really know TCM is very effective. They just consider TCM is unscientific, must be useless. It is so not true." Interview TCM 18.11

Quotation List

The quotation list worked hand-in-hand with the code definition list and records all quotations related to an open code. An example of the quotation list is illustrated in Table 5.3.

As shown in Table 5.3 and also in a sample in Appendix 3, the quotation list was an essential tool for comparing quotations. When a new quotation is identified by using a particular open code, this quotation is then compared with the existing quotations on the list. If these quotations show different meanings, it indicates that a new open code should be applied for this new quotation.

Moreover, this list also provides a unique indicator to each quotation. For instance, the second quotation is identified as "P18: TCM-D-5.rtf—18:11", which shows that the quotation was adopted from the primary document P18 as indexed by the ATLAS.ti primary doc family. This document is named "TCM-D-5.rtf", since it was provided by the fifth TCM interviewee. Finally, the "18.11" indicates that this quotation can be found in paragraph 11 in this document.

5.3 Data Collection 67

This list also provides evidence for the translation from Chinese to English. Thus, the quotation list is essential when producing the theoretical narrative, in which the most appropriate quotations on the list were selected to present the final theory.

Concept Map

In addition to the analytical tools introduced above, Strauss and Corbin (1998) encourage the use of either memos or diagrams to assist the data analysis and to manifest the evolution of theory. The use of diagrams has a clear advantage compared to memos, as "diagrams are visual rather than written memos" (Strauss and Corbin 1998, p. 217). This study used the concept map to support the data analysis and to visualise research findings. An example of concept maps is shown in Fig. 5.7.

The concept map was a useful tool for the data analysis, particularly when practising axial coding, since it visually and explicitly demonstrates relationships between categories, sub-categories and concepts. It also facilitates the comparative analysis between sub-categories and categories. The findings chapters will show all the concept maps produced and illustrate their use in the production of the theory.

5.3.5 Research Stages

As explained in Sect. 5.2, this research project followed a four-stage design for the development of theory, consisting of a literature review, a pilot study, a main study and a follow-up study. Details of these research stages are illustrated in Fig. 5.8.

As shown in Fig. 5.8, every stage had specific aims and contributed to the development of theory. This section aims at introducing the individual stages in detail and illustrating the process of theory development.

5.3.5.1 Literature Review

As stated in Sect. 5.2, this project started by reviewing relevant literature. Although the literature review did not directly contribute to theory development, it was an important stage to this project.

Aims

There were four aims for the literature review:

- to gain general understanding about the research context and to develop contextual sensitivity. This is presented in Chap. 2.
- to enhance the theoretical sensitivity. This is discussed in Chap. 3.
- to locate appropriate theoretical frameworks to guide the remainder research stages. This is illustrated in Chap. 3.
- to draw implications for the research design and the selection of research methodology. This is clearly discussed in the conclusions of Chaps. 2 and 3.

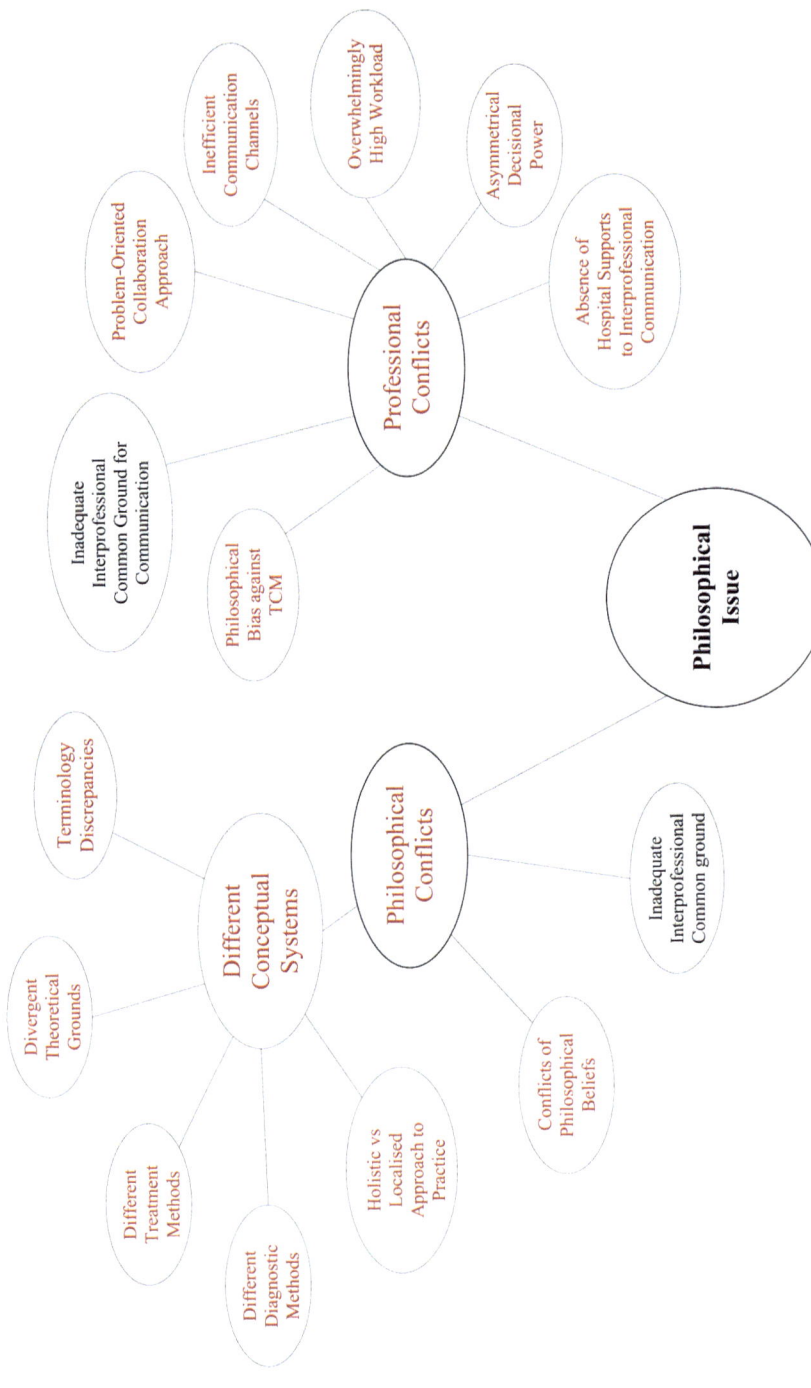

Fig. 5.7 An example of a concept map

5.3 Data Collection

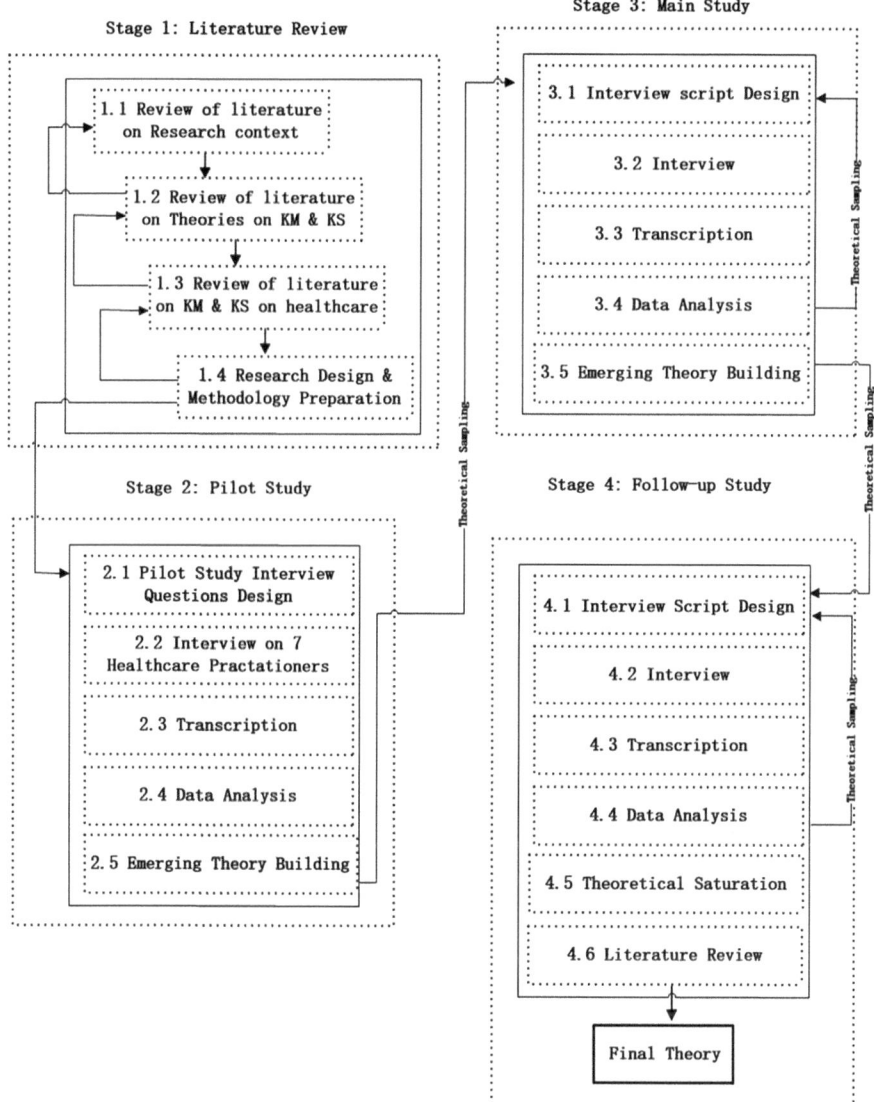

Fig. 5.8 Four-stage design of theory development

Literature Review Areas and Strategies

In order to achieve these aims, the literature review focused on the following three areas:

1. Research context included the basic philosophies of TCM and WM, the implementation of patient-centred healthcare approach in Chinese healthcare organisations, and the collaboration of TCM and WM healthcare professionals.
2. KM and KS included basic definitions and theories of KM and KS, e.g. definitions and current models of KM and KS.
3. KM and KS in healthcare organisations included definitions, theories, models, and strategies of KM and KS developed specifically for healthcare organisations.

After reviewing the three areas for the purposes of enhancing theoretical and contextual sensitivities, the researchers decided to perform a more systematised search of literature aimed at identifying theoretical frameworks to guide the collection and analysis of data. Specifically, this search aimed at identifying existing models of KM and KS between TCM and WM healthcare professionals in the context of Chinese healthcare environment.

After careful consideration, five databases were selected:

1. Emerald: Emerald Management Review
2. LLIS: Library Literature & Information Science
3. MEDLINE
4. ASSIA: Applied Social Sciences Index and Abstracts
5. Web of Science

Access to these databases was provided by the University of Sheffield, and these databases were recommended by the Information School in this university as very useful to be used in information and management research studies. Also, apart from searching articles in English language, it was considered as very important to search Chinese literature. Therefore, a Chinese academic database was included, namely, CQVIP.

Moreover, the literature search was guided by a selecting criteria: (1) relevance to the aim of this project, that is, selected literature should be related to KS between TCM and WM healthcare professionals in Chinese healthcare environment; (2) complete report and well justified research methodology and design; (3) a clear presentation of valid and reliable research findings.

Specifically, the search was performed between 2007 and 2008, and used the following search terms:

1. "Traditional Chinese Medicine"
2. "Western Medicine"
3. 1 AND 2
4. hospital*
5. health*
6. 4 OR 5

5.3 Data Collection

7. "knowledge management"
8. "knowledge sharing"
9. 7 OR 8
10. China
11. 3 AND 6 AND 9 AND 10

As the result, the search of literature identified a significant lack of literature reporting KS between TCM and WM healthcare professionals in Chinese hospitals. The search result indicated that the KS problem probably had not been studied before. In addition, it implied that this project needed to adopt an inductive approach.

Moreover, the search result led to another and more general search of literature, which aimed at identifying existing frameworks of KM or KS barriers between interprofessional medical teams in a healthcare environment. Consistent with the previous search, this search of literature included the six databases, but used different search terms:

1. "knowledge management"
2. "knowledge sharing"
3. 1 OR 2
4. Barrier*
5. Hospital*
6. Health*
7. 5 OR 6
8. Multidisciplin*
9. Interdisciplin*
10. Interprofession*
11. 8 OR 9 OR 10
12. 3 AND 4 AND 7 AND 11

This search retreived 56 articles from Emerald Management Review, one article from ASSIA, two articles from MEDLINE, and six Chinese articles from CQVIP. However, no article can be found from Web of Science and LLIS.

Nevertheless, after careful hand search and close examination of each article identified, none of the articles retrieved could be considered as sufficient to be employed as theoretical foundation for this research project. Consequently, this project essentially aimed at generating a theory, which should be grounded in and emerged from the data collected in the research context. Furthermore, the literature review provided specific implications for the selection of research methodology and the research design, as specified in Section "Implications".

Implications

As the result, the existing literature was evaluated as unable to provide a sufficient theoretical foundation. In fact, this project could be the first study to investigate the problem of KS between TCM and WM healthcare professionals in Chinese healthcare organisations. Consequently, this research project is purely inductive, and aims at establishing a theory.

Moreover, the literature review could not identify any frameworks which could be assessed as sufficient to be adopted as *a priori* framework to guide the data collection and analysis. The final theory was more likely to emerge from and be grounded in data. This also implied that GT should be adopted as the overarching research methodology to guide the data collection and analysis in a single case-study design.

The literature review also showed that there was a need to conduct a pilot study to confirm whether the KS problem anticipated did present itself in reality in the practice of a Chinese hospital, to test the selected research methodology and tools, and to identify early results and insights to guide the remaining research stages. According to the literature review, the pilot study needed to interview TCM and WM doctors, nurses, hospital managers, and ICT professionals.

Furthermore, as an end product of the literature review, a tentative framework was developed according to the perceived constructs to this KS problem. This tentative framework is introduced and discussed in the next section "Tentative Framework".

Tentative Framework

As discussed in Sect. 5.2, the literature review was performed aiming at enhancing the theoretical and contextual sensitivities. However, as explained in Sect. 5.3.5.1, the literature review process was unable to identify a robust theory to explain the phenomenon under study in this book. Nonetheless, a number of theoretical constructs emerged through the processes of theoretical and contextual sensitisation. According to Strauss and Corbin (1998), these constructs are to be used for the development of interview questions when gathering the first bit of data.

At the end of the literature review, the theorectial constructs identified were linked and categorised in order to form a tentative framework. The tentative framework was then employed as the basis for the formulation of the first version of the interview scripts. This version was only used for initial interviews in the pilot study and acted as a starting point for the collection of data, as suggested by Strauss and Corbin (1998).

It is very important to highlight that this tentative framework is very different from a priori frameworks, which are used as the foundation for the theory development. This tentative framework was only employed for the design of the interview script used in the pilot study. In addition, this tentative framework had very little influence on the data analysis and theory development, since "after first interview(s) or observation(s), the researcher will turn to questions and concepts that emerge from analysis of the data" (Strauss and Corbin 1998, p. 51).

The tentative framework consists of five main issues, namely: professional culture, ideologies and terminologies, historical issues, professional standing and power, and communication issues.

Professional Culture

The process of facilitating the interaction between TCM and WM healthcare professionals with distinct professional cultures through a single social world is undeniably a problematic proposition prone to cultural collision and conflicts. Misunderstandings, misinterpretations and a disregard for the validity of each other's discourses are significant barriers to the sharing of knowledge across these cultural boundaries. In this case, cultural collisions may be caused by even deeper cultural differences between the East and the West. To a larger extent, the problem results from the deep difference between the underlying beliefs about healing in TCM and WM. TCM theories take a holistic view of the human body, where every element is closely interrelated and interacts within one independent entity (Fruehauf 1999). In contrast, WM doctors are more interested in localised diseases or illnesses and the corresponding part of the human body. WM practitioners aim at healing that specific part of the human body rather the more general problems of the patient (Dally 2003). This may create difficulties in understanding each other's diagnosis, clashes in indications for treatment, difficulties in interpreting requirements for complementarity of treatments, and difficulties in understanding interpretations of healthcare problems. Furthermore, there are fundamental differences in the validation and acceptance of healthcare practices. TCM is based on 2300 years of evolution and accumulation of experience. On the other side, WM is based on scientific paradigms and evidence-based research. This clearly distinguishes the basic beliefs of the two communities, often producing disagreements and a disregard of the other group. This may not only result in discourses that are not compatible, but also lead to reluctance to accept each other's opinions, diagnosis and interpretations.

Ideologies and Terminologies

As discussed above, the differences in philosophical foundations result in very different professional practices, discourses and terminology. These different practices, from diagnosis to treatment, increase the separation between the two actors. TCM relies on the five element theory and yin-yang in order to explain the nature, materialism and dialectics (Cheng 2000). Diagnosis in TCM is conducted in four classic diagnostic methods: "inspection", "listening and smelling", "inquiry" and "palpation". In contrast, scientific evidence is the basis of treatment in WM. Nevertheless, as in TCM, diagnosis in Western medicine is also largely dependent on the doctor's experience. However, WM always involves modern high-technical tools to collect diagnostic evidence. Each of these different fundamental theories and practices results in an associated discourse and corresponding terminology. These are obviously different in nature and not always compatible with the counter-part group's beliefs and discourse. Thus, if each of these two actors uses a rather different set of professional beliefs, discourse and language, the communication between the two actors is very difficult, making knowledge sharing across the two communities extremely problematic.

Historical Issues

The disharmony and difficulties in coexistence between TCM and WM date back to as early as the beginning of the twentieth century. Unschuld (1985) notes that the priority in healthcare policies given to WM created resentment and conflict with the TCM community as early as 1914. In later years, the Great Cultural Revolution (1966–1976) was a disaster for research and studies in TCM. The number of Chinese Medicine colleges was dramatically decreased from 21 to 11. Furthermore, no teaching or research activities were allowed to be conducted in the area of TCM by any HE institute from 1966 to 1971 (Fruehauf 1999; Chen et al. 1999). These historical issues significantly affect the relationship between the two professional groups today, by resulting in lack of trust, professional rivalries and resentments arising from this historical background. These can therefore severely hinder knowledge sharing, due in particular to continuing professional standing and power issues within the healthcare institutions.

Professional Standing and Power
As discussed above, there is a history of rivalry and competition for professional standing and power between the TCM and WM communities. This ongoing rivalry is summarised by Tian (2003) as an ongoing inter-professional debate for supremacy. This may in turn become a strong barrier to the creation of relationships of trust, collaboration and cooperation between the two groups. This is particularly problematic due to the current imbalance in both professional standing and power within healthcare institutions. In fact, despite all the official rhetoric, in the Chinese healthcare system, WM doctors are clearly empowered and occupy most of the advantageous and powerful positions. There are three reasons behind this disproportionate power distribution. Firstly, WM is the de facto main primary healthcare service within the overall Chinese healthcare system. Secondly, according to the last statistics report provided by National Bureau of Statistics of China (2013), among approximately 9.1 million healthcare professionals in China, there are only about 117,000 TCM practitioners, an extremely small community in the Chinese healthcare system. Finally, and most importantly, WM is more profitable than TCM for the Chinese healthcare services in terms of revenue. This issue has always been blamed as the main cause of the imbalance development position in the healthcare system of these two actors. This statement is supported by Hsiao and Yip (2009), who indicates that, in the 1970s, Chinese macro-health policy shifted its healthcare financing and delivery toward a free market system by encouraging all levels of health facilities to rely on user fees to support their operation. As, by its nature, TCM is not as profitable as its WM counterpart, the development of TCM has always been limited by the implicated actor "money".

Communication Issues
Apart from all other considerations, effective knowledge sharing between TCM and WM demands efficient communication channels. These channels are usually discussed at two different levels: organisational and technological. In technological terms, communication channels usually assume form of integrated IS, supported by adequate ICT infrastructures. Knowledge emerging from both types of practitioners should be effectively acquired, stored, retrieved, disseminated and utilised. These very complex activities should be supported by appropriate IS, databases and computer-mediated communication tools integrated by effective healthcare KM

strategies. These systems should reflect the plurality and complexity resulting from the integration of TCM and WM practitioners and should serve both communities equally. However, the majority of ERP systems for healthcare clearly focus on WM philosophies, discourses and terminologies. This of course acts as a clear deterrent to communication between the two groups and results in very low acceptance by TCM practitioners. On the other hand, organisational communication issues are usually centred on formal and informal communication. Formal communication uses formal channels of communication available within the organisation, following prescribed hierarchical and functional dependencies, boundaries and systems. Conversely, informal communication is usually due to fortuitous circumstances outside formal communication channels, such as telephone conversations, informal gatherings and unplanned visits (Peng and Litteljohn 2001). According to the argument above, formal communication between the two communities is much more complicated than informal communication between individuals. Therefore, the development of knowledge sharing practices should identify and maximise instances of informal communication, study these and use the existing relationships and established trust to build more stable and durable communication.

Finally, it is worthwhile to reiterate what has been discussed at the beginning of this section, that the tentative framework had very little influence on the data analysis in this project, since the analysis was implemented entirely on the basis of the collected data. This tentative framework was only used for the design of the very first version of the interview question script used in the pilot study. Therefore, the framework was used strictly in accordance with what is prescribed by GT. The processes of data collection and analysis in the pilot study are introduced and discussed in Sect. 5.3.5.2.

5.3.5.2 Pilot Study

Aim

The purpose of the pilot study was to obtain a better understanding of the current situation in Chinese healthcare organisations with regard to KS between TCM and WM practitioners. The pilot study also aimed at confirming and exploring the KS problem identified in the literature review. More specifically the study aims at:

- confirming and further narrowing down the research gap identified in the literature review.
- testing and evaluating the inductive research methodology selected, namely, the integrated methodology of case-study and GT, the semi-structured interview as the data collection technique, and the GT data analysis methodology.
- providing initial findings to guide the remainder of the study, namely, in the choice of an adequate arena (a department in the hospital) as the case-study site for the remainder stages, and in providing an emergent theory to guide the data collection and data analysis in the main study.

Data Collection and Analysis

Data collection employed semi-structured interviews as the data collection tool. The interview script was designed according to the tentative framework produced by the literature review. Overall, seven interviewees were purposively sampled and selected from the case-study site. These participants were two WM doctors (a neurosurgeon and an orthopaedic doctor), a neurosurgical nurse, two TCM doctors, an ICT manager, and the chief hospital administrator (who was also a cardiac surgeon).

Interviews were conducted in Mandarin Chinese and generally ranged from 50 to 70 min in length. All interviews were recorded by a digital recorder. Digital recordings were transcribed all together into Word files after the completion of all interviews. Interview transcripts were then organised and assigned into ATLAS.ti for data analysis.

The data analysis followed the GT analysis methodology employing open and axial coding, as well as comparative analysis with assistance from ALTAS.ti, coding definition list, quotation list, and concept map.

As a result of the data analysis, four main categories emerged: communication issues, philosophical issues, educational issues, and professional standing and power issues. Details of the emerging results are discussed and presented in Sect. 6.1.4.1 and in Table 6.2. Futhermore, the emerging results provided specific implications for the main study.

Implications for the Main Study

The pilot study provided several important implications for the main study:

1. The pilot study confirmed and validated the usefulness and gap behind the research question identified in the literature review.
2. As discussed in Sect. 5.2, the research findings suggested choosing the Department of Neurosurgery for deeper and more focused investigation. In this case, the main study needed to interview neurosurgeons, neurosurgical nurses, and TCM doctors.
3. GT as the overarching research methodology was evaluated as appropriate for this research project, not only because using the theoretical sampling strategy could possibly gather very detailed information, but also because it is very likely that a dense and valid theory can be developed using GT data analysis methods.
4. The semi-structured interview as the data collection method had proven very useful for gathering rich and valid data. Therefore, it was decided to employ this method in the remaining stages.
5. The four tools for data analysis (the ATLAS.ti, the code definition list, the quotation list, and the concept map) were assessed as very helpful and it was decided to use them in later stages.

6. The four main categories that emerged in the pilot study were adopted in designing interview scripts for the data collection in the main study. These emerging main categories were also used as the starting point for the data analysis.

These implications which emerged from the pilot study were taken fully into consideration when designing and conducting the main study.

5.3.5.3 Main Study

Aim

The aim of the main study was to develop the theory fully. To be more specific, the main study had the following aims:

- to continue exploration of KS barriers on the basis of the findings which emerge from the pilot study.
- to develop the individual categories fully.
- to choose a main category to link other categories in order to form the final theory.
- to achieve theoretical saturation.

Data Collection and Analysis

The interview scripts were designed according to the findings which emerged from the pilot study. Before entering the field, the researchers designed three different versions of the interview script for the three types of informants chosen to be interviewed, namely, neurosurgeons, neurosurgical nurses, and TCM doctors. These interview scripts were then continuously revised throughout the main study.

When in the field, the data collection was conducted almost in parallel with the data analysis. Participants were approached individually in groups of two or three, according to the need for theory development reflected by the data analysis. After each set of interviews, the interview data were immediately transcribed and briefly analysed using open coding on the basis of the emerging theory developed in the pilot study. Results from the immediate analysis were used to revise the interview script and to indicate who should be interviewed next. The data collection was stopped when the theoretical saturation was perceived as achieved (when no new open codes emerged from the brief analysis). In the end, eleven neurosurgeons, eight neurosurgical nurses, and six TCM doctors were interviewed.

However, the data analysis conducted in the research field was not very in-depth. This led to another round of data analysis after the completion of the field study. In contrast to the data analysis in the field, which aimed at driving the theoretical sampling, this stage of data analysis aimed at the development of theory. The analysis mostly applied open and axial coding to the data. Moreover, and at the ending part of the main study, selective coding was applied, due to the core category started to emerge. Nonetheless, the practice of selective coding demonstrated that the theoretical saturation had not been achieved and a few categories and concepts were not yet fully developed, which needed to be investigated further in the follow-up study.

Four main categories emerged from the data analysis: philosophical issues, healthcare education issues, professional training issues, and political issues. These categories as well as emerging KS barriers identified are presented in Sect. 6.1.4.2 and in Table 6.3.

Also, it is important to be noted that, by the end of the data analysis, it was considered that the categories of philosophical issues, healthcare education issues and professional training issues were saturated, since no new open codes emerged. One of the main categories, the philosophical issues, started to emerge as the core category, which started to interconnect with other categories.

Nevertheless, at this stage, the theory development was not completed. As reflected in the emerging results, it was necessary to investigate the external environmental influences on KS in the follow-up study. Also, the emerging results provided specific implications for the follow-up study.

Implications for Follow-up Study

The main study indicated that the follow-up study needed to complete the theory development and to validate the emerging research findings. To be more specific, the main study provided the following implications for the follow-up study:

1. The follow-up study needed to explore the external influences on KS in the hospital environment.
2. The exploration in the follow-up study must start from the basis of the emerging theory developed in the main study. That is, the interview scripts needed to be established according to the emerging theory, which should also be the starting point for the data analysis.
3. As implied by the emerging theory, the follow-up study not only needed to interview neurosurgical and TCM healthcare professionals, but also needed to include TCM educators in HE organisations, healthcare politicians in the local government, and patient relatives and carers, who come from outside the hospital.

These implications provided by the main study impacted on the design of the follow-up study and contributed to the theoretical saturation.

5.3.5.4 Follow-up Study

Aim

Generally, the follow-up study aimed at achieving the theoretical saturation and completing the theory development. To be more specific, the follow-up study had the following aims:

5.3 Data Collection

- to develop the category of political issues fully by exploring the external influences on KS between the TCM and WM healthcare professionals.
- to identify and confirm the core category.
- to establish and confirm relationships between categories.

Data Collection and Analysis

In order to achieve these aims, a total of seventeen informants were approached at this stage. The data collection included two neurosurgeons, two TCM doctors, three neurosurgical nurses, a TCM educator (who was a TCM module coordinator in the Department of Medicine in Xiangyang Vocational and Technical College, a local HE organisation), a healthcare politician (who was in charge of supervising and controlling TCM practices and services in local healthcare organisations), and eight patient relatives, who represented the non-healthcare professionals.

Generally, the data collection strategy employed in this stage was similar to the one used in the main study. The interview scripts were designed according to the emerging theory and were then continuously revised throughout the follow-up study. Potential interview participants were approached and interviewed individually in groups of two or three. However, unlike the brief analysis of data when in the field during the main study, the follow-up study conducted a thorough analysis of data immediately after each interview bundle. Results of the analysis were then used to revise the interview scripts and to identify the participants that needed to be interviewed next.

By the end of this stage, the data analysis showed all three indicators for the theoretical saturation:

- No new open codes emerged from data.
- All emerging categories were well established.
- The relationships among categories were well established and validated.

In the light of the three indicators, the theoretical saturation was considered as achieved. It needs to be mentioned that, in fact, the theoretical saturation was considered as achieved after the 41st interview (as shown in Fig. 5.5), but the processes of data collection and analysis were continued until the 49th interview in order to obtain a better degree of certainty.

The final theory saturated on five main categories, namely: contextual influences, philosophical issues, Chinese healthcare education, interprofessional training, and hospital management. These categories and related KS barriers are discussed in Sect. 6.1.4.3 and presented in Table 6.4. In fact, the entire Chap. 6 is dedicated to discuss the five main categories and to evaluate and criticise individual KS barriers.

5.4 Research Ethics

All social research studies involve ethical issues, since they collect data from people and about people (Punch 2005). The ethical issues are even more important in a qualitative research project. This is because, as proposed by Punch (2005), while all social research studies to some extent intrude into people's lives, qualitative research studies very often intrude even more. This author adds that qualitative studies usually deal with some very sensitive, intimate, and personal matters in people's lives.

Therefore, in order to ensure research projects are ethically conducted, many professional bodies provide codes of ethical and professional conduct for research. Punch (2005) identifies four widely used ethical codes: the American Psychological Association (1992), the American Sociological Association (1989), the American Educational Research Association (1992), and the handbook for the American Anthropological Association (Cassell and Jacobs 1987).

This project follows the University of Sheffield (2012) "Ethical Policy for Research Involving Human Participants, Data and Tissue". This ethics policy was developed by consulting senior University academics and administrators, and with reference to EU and UK legislation (for instance: EU Directive on Good Clinical Practice in Clinical Trials, the Data Protection Act 1998); professional guidelines (e.g. the British Psychological Society); and higher education documents (e.g. research fund publications, other university research-related policies).

Following this ethics regulation, this project employed three main strategies to guarantee that all research processes were conducted ethically:

1. Informed Consent: All potential interview participants were approached individually by the researchers before formal interviews (usually 1–2 days). This preliminary meeting was designed to meet the interview participant in person, to provide sufficient information about the research project, and to give enough time to the participants to decide whether to take part. Moreover, during the meeting, an information sheet was provided to every potential interview participant stating necessary details about the research project, including aim and objectives, research methodology, who is undertaking and who is responsible for this project, the potential risks and inconveniences that may arise, the potential benefits, why the participant is included in this research, his/her involvement in the interview process, and confidentiality of personal information and data. This information sheet also provided contact information for the supervision authorities if anything should go wrong or if interview participants intended to make complaints. Once an interview participant agreed to be interviewed, he/she was requested to sign two copies of the Participant Consent Form, one copy for the participant and one copy for the researchers.
2. Interview Question Design: All interview questions were carefully designed, not only for the purpose of theory development, but also with the aim of protecting the privacy of individual participants. The interview questions were formulated on the basis of presumptions of the cultural, political, religious, and professional

backgrounds that were possibly possessed by the interview participants. In this way, it is perceived that the researchers could minimise the intrusiveness of the research, and avoid interview questions that could be offensive. Furthermore, because this research project is not concerned with any patient information, the interview questions were carefully designed to avoid any patient related questions. Moreover, before each interview, the researchers kindly reminded the interviewee that no specific patient names or other personal information should be mentioned.
3. Confidentiality and Security of Participants' Personal Information and Contribution: After each interview, the interview recording was immediately transcribed. During the transcription process, a very important procedure was to anonymise the manuscript and to make sure no information could be traced back to particular participants or patient cases. Both the interview recording and the transcript were kept strictly confidential and were used in this research only.

Before the researchers entered the field, the ethical strategies used in this research project were approved by the Information School Ethics Review Panel via strict and rigorous review procedures. The implementation of these strategies was supervised and monitored by the same school in the University of Sheffield.

5.5 Conclusion

This chapter describes and discusses how this research was conducted. Specifically, this chapter discusses the case-study selected for this study, explains the data collection and analysis process, tools and techniques in great detail. Moreover, this chapter presents the four-stage research design adopted in this study, consists of literature review, pilot study, main study, and follow-up study.

In sum, this chapter explains how the research was done; the next two chapters discuss the final findings and corresponding categories (Chap. 5) and present an integrative discussion on the merging of these categories into a global theory (Chap. 6).

Chapter 6
Research Findings

This chapter aims at presenting the research findings and discussing and criticising individual KS barriers. As shown in Table 6.1, the emerging theory saturated on five main categories, which consist of 13 sub-categories and 47 KS barriers, which prevent the exchange of patient knowledge between WM and TCM healthcare professionals.

As shown in Table 6.1, this chapter uses five Sects. (6.2, 6.3, 6.4, 6.5, and 6.6) to discuss the five main categories that emerged from the data analysis, one section for each category. Nevertheless, before the in-depth discussion of individual KS barriers, this chapter starts from Sect. 6.1, which lays a necessary foundation for the understanding of the theory and discusses issues relating to the research context.

6.1 Introduction to the Research Findings

This section is a contextual discussion to the presentation of research findings and aims at providing a social context, which is emerged from the data analysis. This section is considered as essential in order to rationalise and contextualise the discussion of barriers in the following sections. Moreover, it is important to highlight that, although these issues have emerged from the data collected, these contextual issues are not KS barriers. Instead, they are explanatory contextual issues that will help understand the theory produced.

To be more specific, this section addresses three main contextual issues: collaboration and complementarity of neurosurgical and TCM practitioners, the position of the patient, and KS processes in the interprofessional collaboration. In addition, at the end of this section, an evolvement of theory is presented by showing the results emerged from the pilot study, the main study and the follow-up study.

Section	Main category
6.2.	Contextual influences
6.3.	Philosophical issues
6.4.	Chinese healthcare education
6.5.	Interprofessional training
6.6.	Hospital management

Table 6.1 Arrangement for the presentation of the final theory

6.1.1 Collaboration and Complementarity of Neurosurgical and TCM Medical Teams

It was identified in the data gathered that the neurosurgical and TCM medical teams share a strong interprofessional collaborative relationship.

> WM and TCM are connected by a complementary relationship, in which WM takes the unchallengeable primary position and is complemented by TCM. Interview WMD 2.13

> In neurosurgery, the primary method is the craniotomy, which is assisted by a series of procedures and bio-chemical drugs. After the surgery, at the rehabilitation stage, we need to include TCM treatment, such as acupuncture, massage, and sometimes we use traditional herbal medicine. Interview TCM 17.19

Thus, it could be perceived that when dealing with neurosurgical patients, WM is considered as the main approach and is applied first to patients. However, the application of WM is often complemented by TCM methods.

> At acute stages, WM methods are better and more effective. But these WM methods show lack of efficacy at the rehabilitation and post-surgical stages. Interview WMD 20.11

TCM methods are mostly used at the post-surgery and rehabilitation stages, where WM doctors "do not have good methods" (Interview TCM 4.71) and "are less effective" (Interview WMD 20.12).

> Patient usually has some problems after the brain surgeries. These problems may lead to some serious sequelae. For these problems, patients can use TCM herbal medicine and acupuncture to assist rehabilitation after surgeries. TCM is not usually used before surgeries. Interview WMD 20.15

> [The interprofessional collaboration] is actually very useful. We [TCM doctors] usually mention to neurosurgeons that it is our work that woke up those deep coma patients. Interview TCM 16.25

Therefore, as asserted by a number of interviewed practitioners, TCM and neurosurgical healthcare professionals have formed a strong complementary relationship. This relationship is deemed to be very useful and thus is widely used on neurosurgical patients, since "half of our [neurosurgical] patients are using TCM treatments" (Interview WMD 2.72). Therefore, TCM healthcare professionals are frequently invited by neurosurgical practitioners for intervention in patient rehabilitation.

6.1.2 The Position of the Patient

A number of interviewed healthcare professionals claimed that the collaboration of neurosurgical and TCM healthcare professionals is "purely for the benefits of patients" (Interview WMD 10.30).

> As a healthcare professional, the basic aim is to help the patient to achieve a better health condition. Interview WMN 29.13

As reflected in the above quotation, the collaboration essentially aims at helping the patient and resolving patient health problems. In this case, the patient probably stands at the centre of interprofessional collaboration and could be seen as an essential link connecting the two medical teams.

Nevertheless, these idealistic statements provided by healthcare professionals might not be entirely true in day-to-day practice. Some interviewed patient relatives stated that patients' needs and requirements are in fact not very well protected. For instance, two patient relatives stated:

> My husband is suffering from a severe high fever after surgery. Neurosurgeons suggest using antibiotic injections. But this method cannot be used more than 18 days. At the 18th day, the injections must be stopped. Once it's stopped, the fever is back. It has been on and off like this for a few months. Therefore, I was thinking of contacting TCM doctors to use some herbal medicines to solve the problem. I have been complaining and requested this several times. But the neurosurgeon in charge said that there is no need for that. I reckon they are [solely] relying on those antibiotics. Personally, I think TCM could be more effective. Interview PC 36.19

> We do not choose [between TCM and WM methods], they [neurosurgeons] decide for us. In other words, what we say does not count. They have operated [on my son] for three times. They did not leave any space for us to make a decision. Interview PC 43.13

Thus, as reflected by both quotations, patient requests are probably not treated very seriously. It is perceived that patients' voices and rights are not clearly represented and well protected by healthcare professionals. Additionally, patients probably do not have the power to make decisions for themselves, since "what we say does not count" (Interview PC 43.13).

> Neurosurgeons usually suggest to us what to do. We are using acupuncture because they introduced it could be very effective, especially after a brain surgery. Interview PC 35.21

Therefore, and as shown in the quotation above, it is perceived that due to a lack of power, patients and their relatives probably have to passively accept the decisions made by healthcare professionals. Thus, it is probable that patients, as a less empowered and almost silent party involved in the interprofessional collaboration, are unable to protect their rights, requirements and needs. In fact, according to the discussion in this section, the WM doctors seem to be a dominant force in the process, not always open to discussion with either patients or TCM doctors.

6.1.3 KS Processes in Interprofessional Collaboration

As emerged from statements provided by informants, interaction and collaboration between TCM and WM professionals usually occur in consultation sessions, which are also the main vehicle for the sharing of patient knowledge.

> Ordinarily we have consultations. In cases where are some problems we cannot treat from the WM perspective, we would invite TCM doctors to help and find out whether they have better solutions. The consultation is a very common method and is frequently used. At late stages [post-surgery and rehabilitation stage], we [the neurosurgical professionals] almost entirely depend on TCM doctors. Interview WMN 7.109

> If patients in our Neurosurgery Department need TCM doctors to prescribe herbal medicines and to apply acupuncture, I will let the nurse in charge telephone those TCM doctors. In this case, we can arrange time for their consultation. We also need to initiate a consultation note to them as a formal invitation. After they receive the consultation note, they can come over and collaborate with us. Interview WMD 21.15

As shown in the quotation above, a consultation is usually requested by a neurosurgeon, when a patient's condition is perceived to be better treated by TCM doctors. The nurse in charge usually initiates the process at the request of the neurosurgeon and contacts the TCM doctors directly to make an informal enquiry. If the TCM doctor agrees his/her commitment, the neurosurgeon initiates a consultation note as a formal invitation for collaboration. After this consultation session, WM and TCM professionals never meet again to discuss that particular patient, except in the case of emergencies.

It is worthwhile to mention that the consultation note is a formal document used to record all information related to the consultation. One of the interviewed neurosurgeons provided an unused consultation note to the researchers as an example. A consultation note consists of two sections. The first section needs to be filled in before the consultation. This section includes basic patient information (patient name, patient number, gender, age, etc.), a brief introduction to the patient problem, the purpose and aim of the consultation, and when and where to meet. The second section focuses on the outcomes of consultation. Finally, the consultation note must be signed by doctors from both sides and documented in the patient records.

Both sides perceive these consultation sessions as "a relatively good communication channel for KS" (Interview WMD 11.09). However, as a communication channel, these meetings can only play a very limited role in real KS between the two professional groups. In reality, as expressed by a number of informants, the meetings last usually "no more than 10 or 20 min" (Interview WMN 7.119), in which "the diagnosis of the patient is presented by a WM doctor and then usually we [the visiting TCM doctor and the neurosurgeon in charge] need to have a brief discussion" (Interview TCM 4.92). This is of course not conducive to in-depth in-terprofessional discussions.

Moreover, all the participants in the consultation are extremely pressed for time. This was evident from the statements of a number of informants.

6.1 Introduction to the Research Findings

> [In the consultation] usually they do not ask many questions, and we do not talk that much. We all are very busy. As long as we can treat the patient, that is all right. We all are too busy to actually sit down and have a deep conversation. Interview TCM 37.63

> [In consultation] sometimes neurosurgeons can introduce patient conditions. But normally they [neurosurgical professionals] are very busy. Therefore, we mainly rely on the patient records. Interview TCM 15.23

Thus, the consultation meeting becomes a formal handover of patients and not a vehicle for the exchange of knowledge and interprofessional communication.

Furthermore, the patient records are the main vehicle for the exchange of patient knowledge. The researchers also obtained an unused copy of a patient records form (in this hospital, patient records had not yet been digitised). According to this form, the patient records are indeed very useful for transferring explicit technical knowledge. Nevertheless, it does not include any of the ethical and emotional knowledge or the social and behavioural knowledge about individual patients that are studied in this research. Therefore, these two types of patient knowledge are lost in the 20-min process of patient handover.

Also, the knowledge on which this research is focused is inherently tacit and centred around patient needs, requirements and expectations. Crucially, the healthcare professionals that usually possess more of this knowledge, the nurses, are mere spectators in these consultation meetings.

Nurses, as the healthcare practitioners closest to the patient, are the ones that have a better understanding of the ethical and emotional knowledge about a particular patient, as well as the social and behavioural knowledge pertaining to their family, social and even religious background. However, due to a combination of Chinese and hospital culture, their role in the consultation meetings is secondary at best. Nurses, although present in the meetings, very rarely intervene and never have direct contact with their counterparts on the other side.

> I rarely get into deep conversation with TCM doctors. We [neurosurgical nurses] never talk in such detail [for the purpose of sharing patient knowledge]. Interview WMN 33.15

> We after all are just nurses. If a patient needs help from TCM doctors, it is entirely the neurosurgeon's responsibility. They need to make decisions. Then, we just work on those decisions. Interview WMN 31.13

Thus, all the knowledge accumulated by direct care and interaction with a particular patient is lost and never transmitted to the TCM professionals.

6.1.4 The Evolution of Research Findings

Before the presentation and discussion of KS barriers identified, it is important to present results emerged from each research stages (the pilot study, the main study, and the follow-up study), in order to show the progression of the theory and to provide evidence for the identification of individual KS barriers.

Table 6.2 Presentation of findings of the pilot study

Main category	Sub-category	KS barriers
Communication issues	Formal communication	Different professional terminologies
		Consultation as an ineffective communication channel
	Informal communication	Lack of communication motivation
		Absence of hospital communication strategy
Philosophical issues		Philosophical difference between TCM and WM
		Lack of mutual knowledge
Educational issues	Education structure	Lack of mutual education
		Lack of WM education in TCM universities
		Lack of TCM education in WM universities
	Professional learning	High workload for active learning
Professional standing and power issues	TCM economy	The implementation of market economy
		The decrease of TCM market
	Biases against TCM	Unequal political support to TCM and WM
		Management bias against TCM
		Career progression difficulty for TCM doctors

6.1.4.1 Brief Description of Emerging Results from the Pilot Study

As discussed in Sect. 5.3.5.2, the pilot study identified four main categories: communication issues, philosophical issues, educational issues, and professional standing and power issues. These emerging main categories, sub-categories and KS barriers are shown in Table 6.2.

The pilot study provided initial insights into the KS problem between TCM and WM healthcare professionals in Chinese hospitals. The research findings also indicated that it was necessary to carry out a more thorough and focused investigation in the main study.

6.1.4.2 Brief Description of Emerging Results from the Main Study

As discussed in Sect. 5.3.5.3, four main categories emerged from the main study, namely, philosophical issues, healthcare education issues, professional training issues, and political issues. These categories are shown in Table 6.3. Moreover, in

6.1 Introduction to the Research Findings

Table 6.3 Presentation of findings of the main study

Main category	Sub-category	KS barriers
Philosophical issues	Philosophical conflicts	Different conceptual systems
		Conflicts of philosophical beliefs[a]
		Inadequate interprofessional common ground
	Professional conflicts	Inefficient communication channels
		Problem-oriented collaboration approach[a]
		Overwhelmingly high workload[a]
		Asymmetrical decisional power[a]
		Inadequate interprofessional common ground as motivation for interaction
		Absence of hospital supports to interprofessional communication
		Philosophical discrimination against TCM[a]
Healthcare education issues	Lack of interprofessional education in WM HE	Structure of WM HE
		Perceived value of TCM education in WM HE[a]
		Lack of systematic TCM education in WM HE
		Decrease of TCM teaching in WM HE[a]
		Progressive erosion of TCM knowledge[a]
	Lack of deep interprofessional education in TCM HE	Structure of TCM HE
		Perceived value of WM education in TCM HE[a]
		Increase of WM teaching in TCM HE[a]
		Insufficient WM understanding for TCM doctors
		Political bias against TCM education[a]
Professional training issues	Existing interprofessional training structure	Absence of hospital attention to interprofessional training[a]
	Absence of interprofessional training in the neurosurgery department	Political influences to interprofessional training[a]
		High workload against interprofessional training
		Lack of personal interests in interprofessional training[a]
		Philosophical discrimination against interprofessional training[a]
	Absence of interprofessional training in the TCM department	Career progression difficulty for TCM professionals[a]
		Political bias against interprofessional training for TCM doctors[a]

Table 6.3 (continued)

Main category	Sub-category	KS barriers
Political issues	External political environment	Invalidity of current healthcare policy
		The implementation of market economy policy[a]
		Economical influence to hospital management[a]
		Political influence on hospital management[a]
	Hospital management	Management bias against TCM
		Career progression inequality
		Recruitment inequality[a]
		Investment inequality[a]
		Decrease of the TCM department[a]

order to differentiate from KS barriers emerged from the pilot study, barriers identified in the main study are labeled with 'a'.

The main study brought significant findings to the development of theory. It is worthwhile to mention that, by the end of the data analysis, it was considered that the categories of philosophical issues, healthcare education issues and professional training issues were saturated, since no new open codes emerged. Moreover, one of the main categories, the philosophical issues, started to emerge as the core category, which started to interconnect with other categories.

Nevertheless, at this stage, the theory development was not completed. To be more specific, as reflected in the emerging results, it was important to investigate the external environmental influences on KS in the follow-up study.

6.1.4.3 Brief Description of Emerging Results from the Follow-up Study

The theoretical satuation was achieved in the follow-up study. Specifically, the final theory saturated on five main categories, namely: contextual influences, philosophical issues, Chinese healthcare education, interprofessional training, and hospital management. These categories and related KS barriers are shown in Table 6.4. Additionally, in order to differentiate from barriers identified in the main-study as presented in Table 6.3, KS barriers emerged from the follow-up study are labeled with 'a'.

Categories and KS barriers shown in this table will be discussed in depth in Sects. 6.2, 6.3, 6.4, 6.5, 6.6. One issue that must be highlighted is that the category of philosophical issues emerged as the core category, on the basis of which the final theory was fully established.

6.1 Introduction to the Research Findings

Table 6.4 Presentation of findings of the follow-up study

Main category	Sub-category	KS barriers
Contextual influences	Political influences	Inefficiency of current healthcare policy
		Ineffectiveness of patient-centred policy[a]
		Negative effects of market economy policy
	Economical influences	Negative effects of social materialism[a]
		Negative economical influences to medical belief[a]
	Social influences	Social preference for WM[a]
		Social bias against TCM[a]
		Decrease of TCM market
Philosophical issues	Philosophical conflicts	Different conceptual systems
		Conflicts of philosophical beliefs
		Inadequate interprofessional common ground
	Professional conflicts	Inefficient communication channels
		Problem-oriented collaboration approach
		Overwhelmingly high workload
		Asymmetrical decisional power
		Inadequate interprofessional common ground for communication
		Absence of hospital requirement for interprofessional communication
		Philosophical bias against TCM
Chinese healthcare education	Lack of interprofessional education in WM HE	Lack of convergence in WM HE structure
		Perceived value of TCM education
		Lack of systematic TCM education in WM HE
		Decrease of TCM education in WM HE
		Progressive erosion of TCM knowledge
	Lack of deep interprofessional education in TCM HE	Lack of convergence in TCM HE structure
		Perceived value of WM education in TCM HE
		Increase of WM education in TCM HE
		Insufficient WM understanding for TCM doctors
	External influences on healthcare HE	Imbalanced political supports to WM and TCM education
		Negative Economical Influences on Healthcare Education[a]
		Overly Strong Social Preference for WM Education[a]

Table 6.4 (continued)

Main category	Sub-category	KS barriers
Interprofessional training	Existing professional training structure	Lack of convergence in professional training structure in neurosurgery department
		Lack of convergence in professional training structure in TCM department
		Lack of political emphasis on interprofessional training
	Absence of interprofessional training in the neurosurgery department	High workload against interprofessional training
		Lack of personal interest in interprofessional training
		Philosophical bias against interprofessional training
		Lack of hospital attention on interprofessional training
	Absence of interprofessional training in the TCM department	Management bias prevents interprofessional training
		Career progression difficulty prevents professional training
Hospital management	External influences on hospital management	Overly strong social preference on WM services[a]
		Negative Economical Influences on Hospital Management
	Management bias against TCM	Management philosophical bias against TCM
		Financial bias against TCM[a]
		Career progression inequality
		Recruitment inequality
		Investment inequality
		Decrease of the TCM department

6.1.5 Section Summary

This section discusses three issues about the research context: firstly, the complementary collaboration of the two types of healthcare professionals; secondly, the role of patient in the interprofessional collaboration; finally, KS processes that occur during the interprofessional collaboration. In addition, this section shows the evolution of the theory by presenting and comparing emerging results from the pilot study, the main study, and the follow-up study.

On the basis of the discussion in this section, Sects. 6.2, 6.3, 6.4, 6.5, and 6.6 present research findings, discuss the five main categories that emerged from the data analysis, evaluate and criticise individual barriers to sharing patient knowledge between TCM and WM healthcare professionals in their patient-centred interprofessional collaboration.

6.2 Contextual Influences

This section discusses external contextual barriers, which is the first category introduced in this book. According to a number of interviewees participated in this study, there are some negative influences from the hospital's external environment, which can be identified as KS barriers and which hinder activities and processes of KS between the neurosurgical and TCM healthcare professionals within the hospital environment. To be more specific, this section discusses three sub-categories, namely, political influences, economical influences and social influences. The final theoretical construct for this category is shown in Fig. 6.1.

6.2.1 Political Influences

This section focuses on the sub-category of political influences. This sub-category is formed by three barriers, as shown in Fig. 6.2.

This section discusses three KS barriers: inefficiency of current healthcare policy, ineffectiveness of patient-centred policy, and negative effect of Market Economy Policy (MEP).

6.2.1.1 Inefficiency of Chinese Healthcare Policy

The practice of coding on the data collected revealed that, at a high political level, the Chinese central government intends to support TCM and WM equally. For instance, the interviewed healthcare politician stated:

> Currently, the central government provides relatively strong political supports to TCM. Firstly, in the national healthcare policy, there is a fundamental point of "equal support for TCM and WM" and "WM is the primary and complemented by TCM". It is a rather fundamental point. Secondly, the healthcare system reformation, which is going to happen in the near future, clearly points out the importance of TCM participation. It is a very high-level policy. Thirdly, the central government requires our local healthcare administrators to provide support to TCM philosophy, TCM education, TCM institutions, and TCM practitioners. [...] Fourthly, for the local healthcare administration, a basic guidance for us is that TCM needs political support. The national policy has such a requirement. Therefore, we need to think about what exactly should we do and what actual strategies we should implement. Interview TCM Politician 34.7

To summarise the above statement, the Chinese central government have established two high-level policies, namely, "TCM and WM should be equally treated and supported" (Interview TCM 4.24) and "WM is the primary and complemented by TCM" (Interview WMN 7.59). As discussed by this healthcare politician, top politicians in the Chinese central government probably consider that it is important to maintain the coexistence and the balance of TCM and WM communities in the national healthcare system and to protect the complementary relationship between

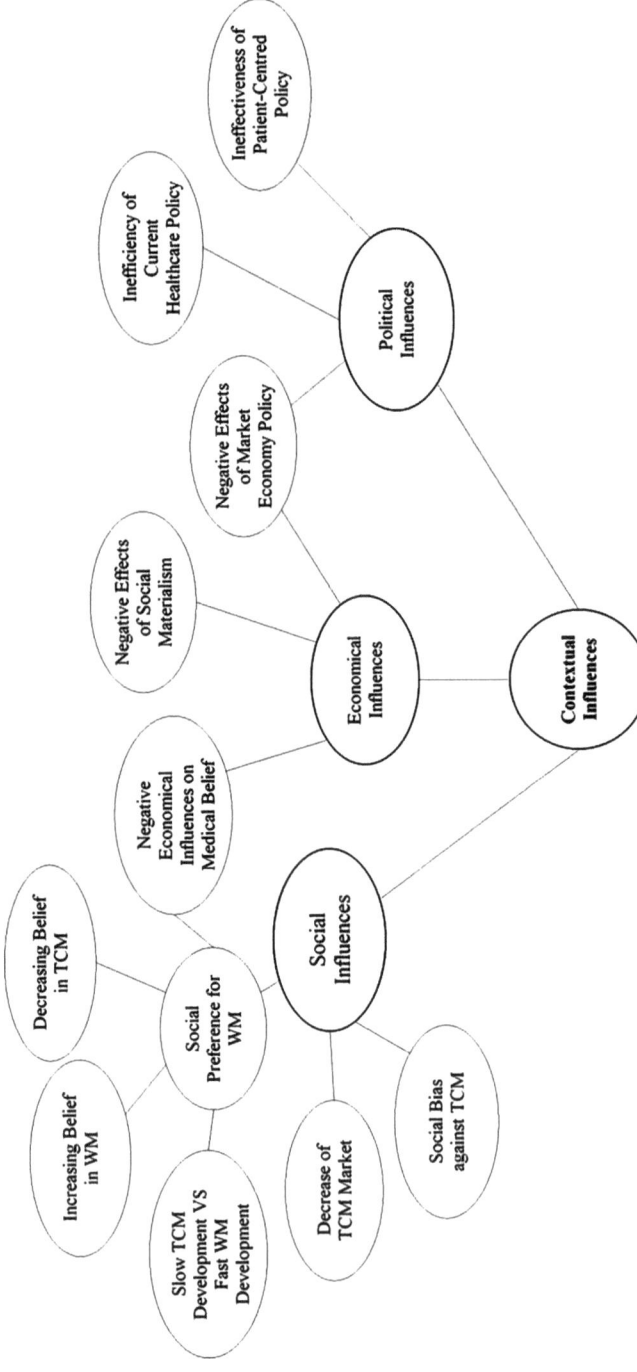

Fig. 6.1 Concept map for contextual influences

6.2 Contextual Influences

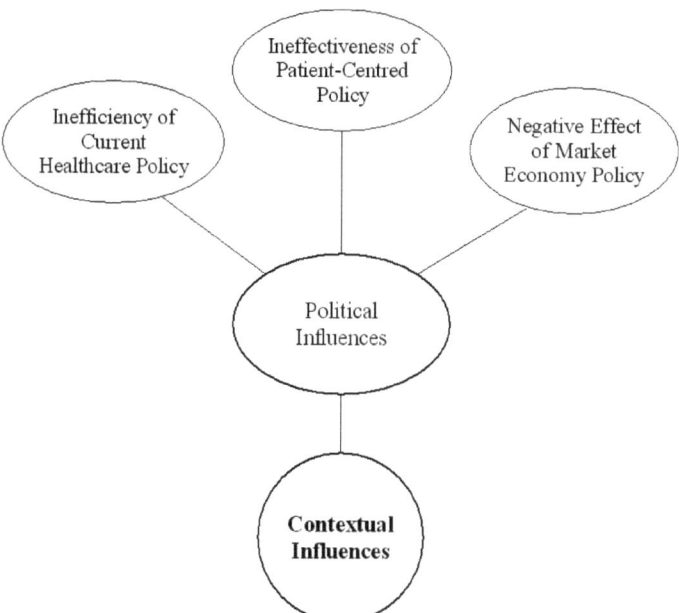

Fig. 6.2 Concept map for political influences

TCM and WM healthcare professionals. This confirms the findings of the initial literature review.

Moreover, both high-level policies discussed above are expected to be implemented by local healthcare politicians and management in each hospital. However, it was identified that the central government might not have a detailed plan to guide the implementation of these high-level policies at operational level in hospitals. Therefore, as stated by the interviewed healthcare politician, "we need to think about what exactly should we do and what actual strategies we should implement" (Interview TCM Politician 34.7). In this case, it became clear that these national healthcare policies are probably not very well implemented.

> In the national policies, top level politicians believe TCM and WM should be equally supported, but it is difficult to be executed. Interview TCM 17.31

Also, from the perspective of interviewed TCM practitioners, these policies are "just political slogans" (Interview TCM 6.52), and thus have little real impact.

> [TCM national policies] are not eminent and not very effective to our level of hospitals, because they are not compulsory policies, they are just suggestions. Interview WMD 12.8

> The central government requires the TCM and WM collaboration, but I have never heard of any actual strategies. Interview WMN 13.15

Very similarly, many interviewed neurosurgical healthcare professionals commented that these national policies are "just suggestions" (Interview WMD 12.8) and some of them claimed that "never heard of any actual strategies" (Interview WMN 13.15).

As reflected in the discussion above, both policies create imbalances of power in hospital, in which WM professionals possess considerably stronger power, almost dominating the processes of TCM and WM collaboration. These imbalances do not motivate the empowered WM professionals to communicate and share knowledge with the perceived inferior group of TCM professionals. Moreover, it is necessary to highlight the second policy, "WM is the primary and complemented by TCM", which reinforces the dominant position of WM and exaggerates imbalances between TCM and WM communities in the hospital environment. This is augmented by the traditional very high power distance culture of China, which encourages WM professionals not to be open to communication, and prevents spontaneous and voluntary interaction and KS.

6.2.1.2 Ineffectiveness of Patient-Centred Policy

As reflected in the data collected, patient-centre healthcare is a national policy clearly demanded by the central government. For instance, one of the interviewed neurosurgical nurses claimed that:

> The patient-centred approach is repeatedly emphasised by the government these years. It is a basic requirement to all doctors and nurses. In truth, our collaboration with TCM doctors is to satisfy patient needs. Interview WMN 30.20.

As discussed in Sect. 6.1.2, many interviewed professionals claimed that they are collaborating with the aim of helping patients; for example, one of the TCM doctors stated that:

> When treating individual patients, if necessary we would voluntarily communicate with WM doctors. Interview TCM 5.81

However, as also discussed in Sect. 6.1.2, patients are not really always guaranteed to be at the centre of all health services, including TCM and WM collaboration. In truth, as shown in data, the needs and requirements of patients are not very well protected by TCM and WM healthcare professionals.

Therefore, without respecting the central role of the patient and without the true implementation of the patient-centred approach, the activities of sharing ethical and emotional knowledge and social and behavioural knowledge about individual patients could be seen as not important and not necessary.

6.2.1.3 Negative Effects of Market Economy Policy

As discussed in Sect. 6.2.1.1, national policies, in particular the one stating "WM is the primary and complemented by TCM" (Interview TCM Politician 34.7), have created substantial imbalances of power between communities of TCM and WM professionals in hospital. Also, as discussed in that section, these imbalances

6.2 Contextual Influences

emerged as a severe barrier to KS. In addition, it was identified by the practice of coding that this barrier is compounded and augmented by the implementation of the Market Economy Policy (MEP).

> I think under the Market Economy, they [TCM doctors] have no way out of this. But I am sure the central government supports TCM. I think that if the Market Economy has a huge impact, it [TCM] cannot survive. Their [TCM doctors] treatments are very cheap, such as acupuncture. Interview WMD 9.36

MEP has been introduced and discussed in the initial literature review (Sect. 2.5.2). Additionally, according to the statement provided by many informants, the implementation of MEP has had a very negative impact on the existence of TCM and its professional community. For instance, as discussed in the quotation above, after the implementation of MEP, TCM cannot survive in the healthcare system, especially when competing with WM.

> Now, [because of MEP] they [hospital management] only evaluate you [individual departments] according to how much financial profits you can make. This is the only way [method of evaluation]. We cannot compete with WM departments. I think if we can make more money, the situation would be better. Interview TCM 15.65

Moreover, many interviewed TCM doctors further discussed the implementation of MEP in greater detail. For example, a very detailed statement by an interviewed TCM doctor mentioned that:

> [The TCM department's lack of management attention] is a very big topic, it is a little complicated. It is related to the national policy. The governmental financial support to all hospitals is rather fundamental. Currently, hospitals receive very little financial funds from the government. The hospital needs to survive, which is inarguable. Although they [hospital management] literally claim that the healthcare quality needs to be improved, [in fact] what they are more concerned about is finance. Therefore, here we have political and management problems. If you want to confront this with them, they would deny this. But what they are doing is just leave you [the TCM department] as what you are. If you survive, you survive. If you die, you die. Interview TCM 4.27

To summarise the quotation above, due to the implementation of MEP, the central government no longer provides financial support to healthcare organisations. Therefore, all hospitals in China are themselves responsible for all hospital operation expenses. In this case, in order to maximise financial income, the management of the hospital where this study was conducted possibly decided to provide more support to those more profitable WM departments. In other words, the TCM department receives less management support, as the department "is less profitable" (Interview TCM 17.15), and it is very difficult for the TCM department to survive.

It is also important to highlight that, as discussed in the previous quotation, the interviewed TCM doctor stated that "what they [hospital management] are more concerned about is finance". This statement implies that the hospital management is probably more concerned about hospital financial income and profitability than about promoting the quality of healthcare services and ensuring communication and sharing of patient knowledge between healthcare professionals.

Consequently, the negative effects of MEP was identified a significant barrier to KS. Firstly, as discussed above, it presses hospital management to pay less attention to communication and KS between healthcare professionals and on protecting the rights and benefits of individual patients. Moreover, it compounds with the KS barrier resulting from the inefficiency of Chinese healthcare policy (as discussed in Sect. 6.2.1.1) and reinforces imbalances of power between groups of TCM and WM professionals. In addition, MEP encourages competition between the two medical communities for pursuing higher financial incomes. This competition demotivates professionals from voluntary communication and interaction of patient knowledge. Finally, the implementation of MEP has developed an economical environment in which TCM and its practitioners are not only seen as inferior but are also perceived to have no chance of survival. Therefore, WM professionals as a superior party are clearly not motivated to communicate and voluntarily share knowledge with TCM doctors, who have considerably less power and can hardly survive.

In addition, more discussion about MEP and hospital management strategy is presented in Sect. 6.6.

6.2.2 Economical Influences

In addition to the political influences, several economical influences also emerged as barriers to KS between TCM and WM healthcare professionals. This section discusses these economical influences.

As shown in Fig. 6.3, three economical influences were identified as barriers to KS. These barriers are discussed in three sections, namely, negative effects of MEP, negative effects of social materialism, and negative economical influences on medical belief.

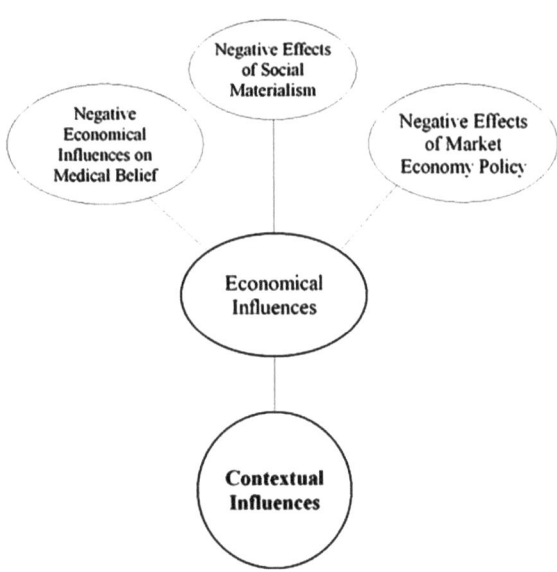

Fig. 6.3 Concept map for economical influences

It is important to note that MEP is a national economic policy, which not only results in significant changes in Chinese economy, but also negatively influences KS in hospitals, as discussed in Sect. 6.2.1.3. Therefore, the barrier "negative effects of MEP" links both sub-categories of political influences and economical influences. This barrier has been discussed in-depth in Sect. 6.2.1.3, and for this reason is not repeated in this section, which focuses on the remaining two barriers in this sub-category.

6.2.2.1 Negative Effects of Social Materialism

It is widely known that the implementation of MEP has significantly boosted the Chinese economy. However, the practice of coding on the data collected identified that MEP has developed a materialistic social environment, in which Chinese people are probably getting "more and more materialistic and money-oriented" (Interview TCM 16.21).

> I think the current society is developing very fast. Everyone is pursuing materials, pursuing money. It is fairly difficult [as a doctor] to calm down and practise medicine. TCM doctors treat patients, they use herbal medicine. They could not make much money out of it. Therefore, they cannot demonstrate their value in this society. Consequently, many TCM students and even professors have changed their professions. Therefore, fewer and fewer people want to learn TCM, fewer and fewer people practise TCM. It is all because of financial profits. Interview WMD 24.34

In the materialistic social environment described in the above quotation, the survival of the TCM community could be very difficult, because "they could not make much money out of it". Therefore, the materialism in the social environment further exaggerates imbalances of power between TCM and WM communities in hospitals, and compounds with KS barriers discussed in political influences (Sect. 6.2.1).

The negative effects of social materialism emerged as an additional barrier to KS, since it has created severe imbalances in the social standing of TCM and WM healthcare professionals. TCM doctors have much lower social standing, because, as stated in the above quotation, "they could not make much money out of it", they "cannot demonstrate their value in this society", and therefore "fewer and fewer people want to learn TCM, fewer and fewer people practise TCM".

> The problem is that TCM is very cheap. In this case, a TCM doctor cannot make enough money for living. In other words, one should live a dignified and decent life based on being honest and hard-working. Interview TCM Politician 34.23

The imbalances in social standings could result in imbalances in professional standings, reinforce imbalances of power in hospitals, and thus demotivate and discourage both types of healthcare professionals from interacting and KS with each other.

6.2.2.2 Negative Economical Influences on Medical Beliefs

In addition to the social materialism, it became clear that the rapid economic growth in China has influenced people's medical beliefs.

> TCM is slower and less efficient [than WM]. With the economic development and the development of WM, people think TCM is too slow. For some acute diseases, they would choose WM, at later stages they would use TCM treatments. Interview TCM 16.23

In China nowadays, people are more interested in WM. As explained in the above quotation, there are two reasons for this: first, "the [rapid] development of WM", which will be explained in Sect. 6.2.3.2; and second, "the economic development".

Specifically, a few interviewed neurosurgeons asserted that, with the development of the Chinese economy, people consider TCM as increasingly less important.

> The collaboration of TCM and WM, in the 1970s and 1980s, had a very very strong advantage which was that TCM herbal medicine is widely accessible, since it can made from animals and plants. And TCM treatments were very cheap. In the 1970s and 1980s, the Chinese economy was not as developed as at this moment. At that time, the economy, healthcare, and scientific development were relatively low. Therefore, at that time the TCM and WM collaboration was a big issue. However, with the fast development of WM and the Chinese economy nowadays, this kind of collaboration is less and less important. Interview WMD 39.21

Interpreting the quotation above, in the 1970s and 1980s, people could not afford for the more effective and more expensive WM. TCM offered less effective, but much cheaper and widely accessible medical services. Therefore, the collaboration of TCM and WM provided healthcare solutions, which were seen as not only relatively effective, but also affordable by people. Nevertheless, in the current economic and social environments, the value of TCM could be seen as less evident and important, since people have enough money to pay for the more effective WM. In this case, not only is the collaboration of TCM and WM considered as less important, but also communication and KS between the two types of healthcare professionals could be considered as not wholly necessary.

Furthermore, the application of coding identified that in the current economic environment of China, people prefer to use WM, because it is more effective and works faster.

> WM is much faster and more effective. Many people like me are living a big city with a very high pressure working environment. If I get ill, I think, well, I think the difference between TCM and WM is that, WM can resolve your problem rapidly. Interview PC 41.9

This statement was made by one of the interviewed patient relatives. He was an ERP project manager in a software company based in Beijing. Like some other interviewed patient relatives, he clearly pointed out his preference for WM methods, because WM "can resolve your problem rapidly" (Interview PC 41.9) and "works faster" (Interview PC44.11). Moreover, the preference for WM is related to the "high pressure working environment" (Interview PC 41.9) and hence Chinese people are "too busy to consider using TCM" (Interview PC 46.15).

According to the above discussion, rapid economic developments in China have resulted in a social preference for WM, which not only further strengthens imbalances in the social standing of WM and TCM healthcare professionals, but also reinforces the dominant power and positions of WM healthcare professionals in hospitals. Therefore, rapid economic developments have become a barrier to KS,

6.2 Contextual Influences

by forming a social environment and culture not encouraging for interprofessional communication and not conducive to the sharing of patient knowledge between TCM and WM professionals. Moreover, this barrier compounds with the social materialism discussed in Sect. 6.2.2.1 and political influences discussed in Sect. 6.2.1.

Finally, there is an additional reason for the social preference for WM. That is, WM is developing at a much faster pace than TCM, and is therefore preferred by people. This issue is discussed in the following section, Sect. 6.2.3.

6.2.3 Social Influences

In addition to those KS barriers discussed in the sections on political issues and economical issues, some social influences also emerged as barriers to KS.

As shown in Fig. 6.4, this section discusses three KS barriers, namely, social preference for WM, social bias against TCM, and decrease of the TCM market. Furthermore, the social preference for WM consists of four constructs: negative economical influences on medical belief, decreasing belief in TCM, increasing belief in WM, and slow TCM development vs fast WM development.

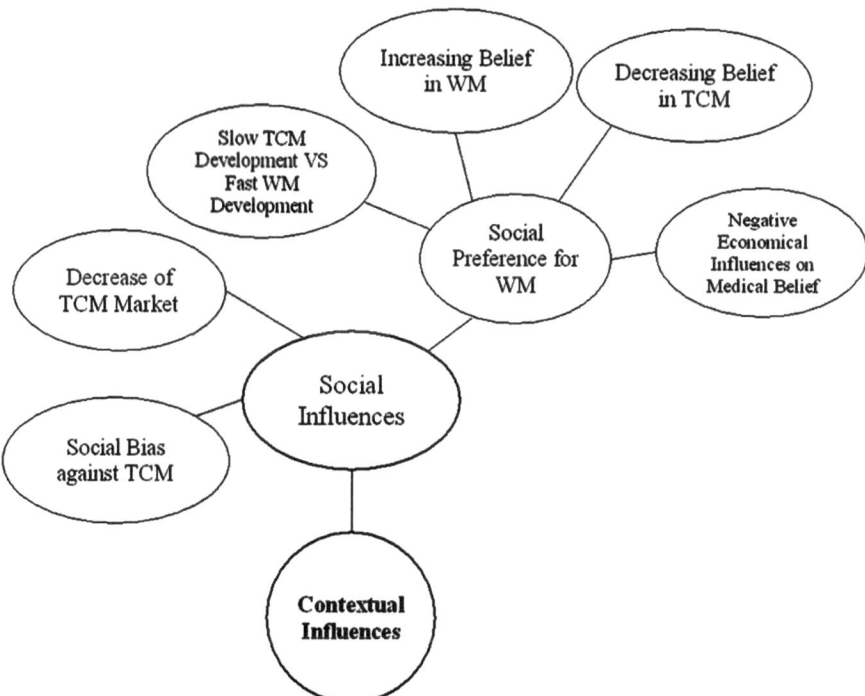

Fig. 6.4 Concept map for social influences

6.2.3.1 Social Preference for WM

This section discusses four KS barriers, namely, negative economical influences on medical belief, decreasing belief in TCM, increasing belief in WM and slow TCM development vs fast WM development.

It needs to be noted that the negative economical influences on medical belief is a barrier appears in two sub-categories, namely: economical influences, and social influences. It is because this barrier not only is related to the Chinese economic environment, but also could be considered as a social influence, due to the changes of economic environment could influence on people's understandings toward TCM and WM. Moreover, this barrier has already been discussed in Sect. 6.2.2.2; therefore, this section is not going to repeat the discussion and will focus on the last three issues.

Decreasing Belief in TCM

> In China, TCM has thousands of years of history. In this case, it does not matter if you are a doctor, or an ordinary person, we all have the concept of TCM [in mind]. Interview WMD 26.31

A number of interviewed healthcare professionals from both medical departments regarded TCM as "a classic legacy that has been evolving throughout thousands of years of Chinese history" (Interview WMN 14.11).

> Patients still think TCM cures the roots of diseases, but it is slow in treating surface symptoms. WM treatments are very effective in treating those surface symptoms, but cannot cure the roots. Based on my knowledge of TCM, treatments need a long period of time. WM is very effective and efficient in controlling the surface symptoms, but it is relatively weak in treating the root. Interview WMN 40.5

The application of coding and comparative analysis on the data gathered confirmed that nowadays TCM is well accepted by the public and is regarded as effective for curing the roots of diseases, although "TCM is slower in treating surface symptoms" (Interview PC 44.11).

> TCM is our old and traditional medical methodology in our country. WM is just relatively faster and more effective, such as surgeries. I think we need to preserve TCM, and I think TCM doctors and WM doctors should collaborate. Therefore, they can overcome one's weaknesses by acquiring the other's strong points. Interview PC 42.13

Due to the advantages and disadvantages of TCM, practitioners of TCM and WM are better when they work together and collaborate with each other in order to "complement each other" (Interview WMD 1.06).

Therefore, TCM could be considered as a very important component of the Chinese healthcare system, coexisting with and complementing WM. TCM and WM professionals should collaborate with each other and that their communication and KS can benefit patients substantially.

However, it was found that TCM and WM professionals do not really coexist harmoniously, collaborate unconditionally and communicate with each other

6.2 Contextual Influences

spontaneously and voluntarily, since WM is usually perceived as more effective, more useful and better than TCM. As emerged, the belief in the traditional healing philosophy is decreasing. This issue is explained and discussed in the following Section "Increasing Belief in WM".

Increasing Belief in WM

Even though people may still trust and sometimes use the traditional healing methodology, many interviewed healthcare professionals claimed that patients always choose WM as their first choice; for example, a TCM doctor and a neurosurgical nurse stated:

> In terms of acute diseases, patients certainly would select WM. For those patients who have chronic diseases, when WM fails, they would use TCM. I think people still believe in TCM and believe in the traditional methods, such as inspection, listening and smelling examination, inquiry, and palpation. Interview TCM 38.5

> People think TCM is slow. Only when WM methods failed, people would think about using TCM. Ordinarily, the first choice is WM, because people think TCM is relatively slower and cannot be as effective as WM. I think it is a reason. Interview WMN 7.126

Usually, patients would select WM methods as their first choice, because it "works faster" (Interview TCM Politician 24.17) and is "more effective" (Interview PC 41.9). TCM methods would only be used when WM methods failed and are thus considered as less valuable and less important.

In fact, through the process of coding, it was confirmed that people are losing belief and trust in the traditional methodology. For example, one of the interviewed patient relatives stated that:

> TCM is entirely based on experience. Therefore, it is not very accurate. It is almost impossible [to be accurate]. Otherwise, they [TCM doctors] are lying. Why in these years do people not believe in TCM? Some people even think it is a superstition or some other things. It is because there is no precision in TCM treatments. It is entirely based on doctor's experience. WM is different. WM doctors rely on equipment. They have visible evidence. In terms of diagnosis, I think WM is more reliable. Interview PC 45.29

Modern Chinese people probably have more trust and confidence in WM, because it relies on hi-tech "equipment" (Interview PC 45.29) and "scientific evidence" (Interview PC 45.29). In comparison, TCM is less accurate and is based on doctors' "experiences" (Interview TCM 4.18).

According to the discussion above, it became clear that there is a strong social preference for WM. This social preference compounds with the KS barriers which have been discussed in political influences (Sect. 6.2.1) and economical influences (Sect. 6.2.2), reinforces and further exaggerates the imbalances in the professional standing and power of the two types of healthcare professionals in hospitals, and adds extra difficulties for interprofessional communication and KS. Moreover, the social preference emerged as an additional barrier to KS, as it encourages the two types of healthcare professionals to compete not only for financial income (as discussed in Sect. 6.2.1.3), but also for people's preference and recognition. These forms of competition discourage individual professionals from voluntary collaboration and spontaneous communication and KS.

Slow TCM Development vs Fast WM Development

In addition, the social preference for WM could have been caused by the "rapid development" (Interview TCM 16.43) of WM methodology in recent years, whereas "TCM is developing at a much slower speed" (Interview WMD 1.36). In this case, because "the development of TCM is too slow" (Interview TCM 16.43), "people usually think WM is better" (Interview TCM 17.29). For instance, an interviewed TCM doctor and an interviewed neurosurgeon stated:

> With the rapid development of WM, and with the acceleration of importing and implementing newly developed WM methods from foreign countries, people think the position of WM is relatively higher than TCM. It is true, for example, that TCM is very weak in treating acute diseases. Interview WMD 20.35

> TCM is developing very slowly; as Chairman Mao said, 'Traditional Chinese Medicine is a great treasure'. At this moment, we are still trying to discover the treasure. This is a reason for the slow development. [...] Personally, I think TCM has potential spaces to be improved. However, we have not found a breakthrough point yet. All TCM doctors are talking about inheritance [from traditional methods, concepts, and methods]. I think it is not enough. It [TCM methods] also needs to be developed and advanced. I think we have not done enough for the development. TCM has developed for thousands of years. In its thousands of years of development, it has developed a form. But in recent decades or in this century, this form has not changed too much. Well, it has developed, but in a very limited way. In comparison, WM is developing at a very fast velocity. So, people usually think WM is better. Interview TCM 17.29

Therefore, in the hospital environment, WM could be considered as more important, and WM professionals thus have higher professional standing and hold more power than TCM doctors. This hospital environment does not motivate healthcare professionals from both medical communities to communicate and share patient knowledge with each other. Moreover, this environment promotes competition for methodological superiority between TCM and WM and therefore could hinder interprofessional communication and KS.

6.2.3.2 Social Bias Against TCM

As asserted by many interview participants from both medical teams, recently there have been several public debates concerning the legitimacy of TCM. Some people have even appealed for political actions aiming at excluding TCM from the national healthcare system. For instance, a neurosurgeon stated:

> I think in the recent Chinese history, the development of TCM was very much behind the development of WM. I have noticed that in these years there are many of these kinds of public discussions, [in which] some people believe TCM can be abolished. Interview WMD 11.47

6.2 Contextual Influences

Some WM interviewees claimed that the WM approach is more scientific and should be superior to TCM. In comparison, traditional medicine is sometimes referred as "unscientific" (Interview WMD 12.22) and as a "superstition" (Interview WMD 6.44). Therefore, some people claimed that TCM need to be abolished and excluded from the national healthcare system. Actually, when in the field, the researchers witnessed a hot online debate around the topic of "abolishing TCM".

Several interviewed TCM doctors expressed their personal opinions about these public debates. Some of them even expressed clear resentment, for instance:

> There was a certain time last year, [there are some people] appealed to abolish TCM. I think it is rather ridiculous. You cannot abolish thousands years of accumulation by only a few words. How can you abolish Chinese history? After all, TCM has been in existence for four or five thousands of years. You cannot say TCM is not evidence based, and then it must be destroyed. Interview TCM 6.75

> Some WM doctors, who think they are very good at what they are doing, are so arrogant. Even though they do not understand TCM at all, they consider TCM is a lie and a superstition. Interview TCM 19.39

Although TCM still exists in the national healthcare system today, these public debates have created a pessimistic attitude among TCM professionals and have developed distrustful, uncooperative, and even resentful relationships between TCM and WM professionals. Moreover, these public debates further reinforce imbalances of professional standing and power in hospitals. These public debates indicate strong social bias against TCM and its professionals, disharmonise the coexistence of TCM and WM, and create interprofessional tensions preventing both types of healthcare professionals from actively communicating and sharing knowledge with each other.

6.2.3.3 Decrease of TCM Market

> TCM philosophy is degenerating. Its market is decreasing. The reason is that the TCM philosophy needs a scientific explanation. If they only used modern scientific methods to explain it, people could believe it. TCM needs this. Interview WMD 2.101

Due to the strong social preference for WM, the market for TCM is decreasing.

> We have several thousands of outpatients annually. […] The patient number has decreased a lot. We used to have several thousand patients a month. Interview TCM 4.33

Moreover, on the basis of the analysis of data and the practice of coding, it was confirmed that the decrease in the TCM market results in problems causing barriers to KS. Firstly, TCM doctors cannot make enough financial income to meet the requirements demanded by the hospital management. Thus, they are less supported by the management. Secondly, TCM does not fit in the hospital environment dominated by WM, and thus finds it very difficult to survive, and is considered as not important. Thirdly, the decrease in the TCM market could be caused by a strong social preference for WM (discussed in Sect. 6.2.3.1) and by social bias against TCM (discussed in Sect. 6.2.3.2). Therefore, TCM doctors are less respected by patients, have lower professional standing and hold much less professional power.

All these three issues result in severe imbalances of power and professional standing, and have developed untrusting and uncooperative relationships between TCM and WM professionals. Therefore, interprofessional communication and the sharing of patient knowledge are not always voluntary, spontaneous and sufficient.

6.2.4 Section Summary

This section discusses the contextual influences, which emerged as one of the main categories. To be more specific, this section discusses KS barriers relating to three sub-categories: political influences, economical influences, and social influences.

As discussed in this section, these political, economical and social influences from the hospital's external environment result in imbalances in the power possessed by TCM and WM healthcare professionals. These imbalances of power demotivate both TCM and WM healthcare professionals from active communication and KS. Moreover, the contextual influences from the external environment have caused imbalances in the professional standing of TCM and WM professionals in hospitals. These imbalances of professional standing hinder processes of communication and KS between the two medical communities.

Also, the external political, economical and social influences have resulted in competition between TCM and WM communities, not only for power and professional standing, but also for financial income, people's preference and recognition, and methodological superiority. As discussed in this section, these forms of competition have caused uncooperative and even resentful relationships between the two medical communities, discourage both types of healthcare professionals from collaborating with each other, and prevent voluntary and spontaneous communication and KS.

Finally, the three types of contextual influences are interconnected and interact with each other. Also, the contextual influences discussed in this section are related to the other main categories: philosophical issues, Chinese healthcare education, interprofessional training, and hospital management. The next Sect. (6.3) concentrates on and discusses the philosophical issues, which emerged as the core category.

6.3 Philosophical Issues

This section discusses one of the main categories that emerged from the comparative analysis, namely, the philosophical issues. The final construct for this category is shown in the concept map as shown in Fig. 6.5.

The application of coding and comparative analysis on the data gathered indicated that healthcare professionals in neurosurgery and TCM have completely different conceptual, philosophical and methodological systems. These differences were considered as barriers to interprofessional communication and KS. These barriers will be discussed in this section. As shown in the concept map, two sub-categories are discussed: philosophical conflicts and professional conflicts.

6.3 Philosophical Issues

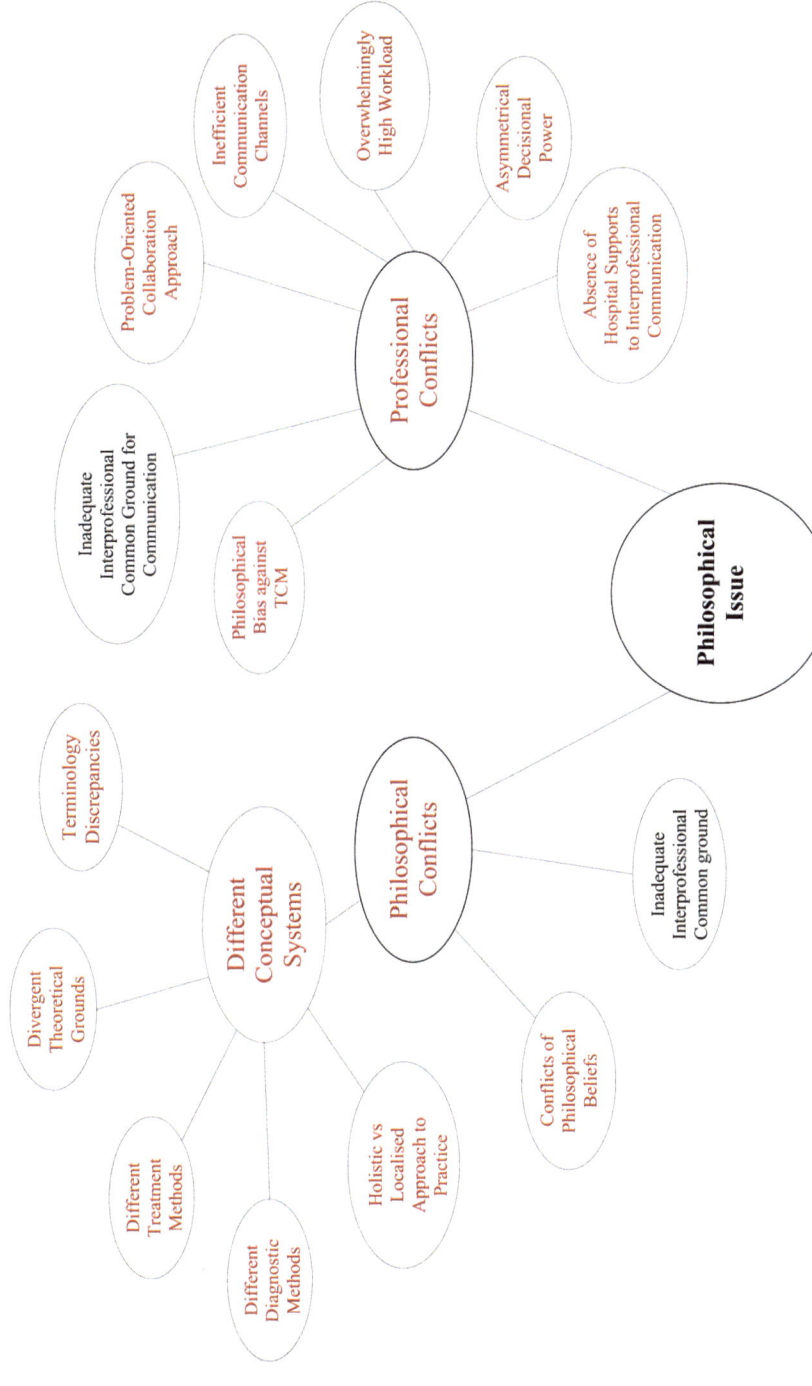

Fig. 6.5 Concept map for philosophical issues

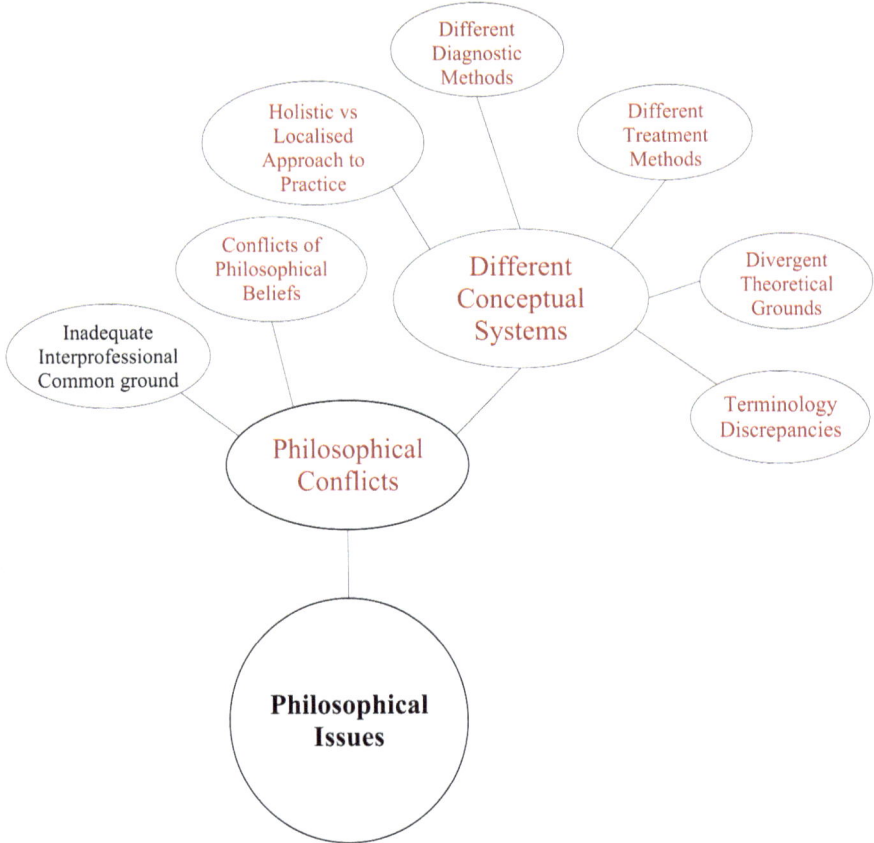

Fig. 6.6 Concept map for philosophical conflicts

6.3.1 Philosophical Conflicts

This section presents and discusses KS barriers relating to the sub-category of philosophical conflicts. Specifically, this section discusses three main barriers: different conceptual systems, conflicting philosophical beliefs and inadequate interprofessional common ground. These barriers are shown in Fig. 6.6.

6.3.1.1 Different Conceptual Systems

TCM and WM are two entirely different medical philosophies, with very distinct conceptual foundations and diagnostic and treatment methods. WM and TCM informants asserted that the substantial differences between the two systems are barriers to the exchange of patient knowledge between professionals of TCM and WM in their patient-centred collaboration.

6.3 Philosophical Issues

To be more specific, five main differences between WM and TCM emerged and were considered as barriers to KS, namely: holistic vs localised approach to practice, different theoretical grounds, different diagnostic methods, different treatment methods and terminology discrepancy.

Holistic VS Localised Approach to Practice

When discussing differences between TCM and WM, a TCM doctor claimed:

> It is almost impossible to integrate both TCM and WM methods into one medical procedure. It is because TCM takes a holistic view of the human body, which is the philosophical foundation for TCM. Interview TCM 18.7

TCM doctors employ a holistic philosophical perspective toward the human body, which is the "philosophical foundation" for the practice of TCM.

Conversely, many neurosurgical interviewees claimed that WM is entirely different from TCM. For example, a neurosurgeon stated:

> WM always localises diseases into particular parts of the human body. If you have a head problem, then treat the head. If you have problems with your feet, then treat the feet. However, TCM treats a patient as a whole. They [TCM doctors] are not just dealing with the disease itself. Therefore, WM is from a micro perspective, TCM is holistic. Interview WMD 24.9

Summarising the discussion above, TCM and WM adopt two contrasting philosophical perspectives. WM takes a 'micro' approach, in which practitioners are more interested in localising a disease in a specific part of the human body instead of the patient with the problem. Very differently, TCM adopts a holistic perspective, in which patients are diagnosed and treated as an integral entity.

The divergent philosophical approaches (holistic or localised) to practice could become barriers to the sharing of patient knowledge between the two types of healthcare professionals. Specifically, the divergent philosophical views form two very distinct professional groups of TCM and WM practitioners, which have very different understandings of patient problems and different approaches to diagnosis and treatment, and which could have conflicting interpretations of the patient's needs and requirements. Therefore, for individual professionals from both groups, communication and KS could be seen as very difficult. Even if they intended to communicate with each other, very often, knowledge shared by either medical group might have very little meaning or value to the other group. Finally, the divergent philosophical views have undeniably resulted in untrusting relationships between the two medical communities, which do not permit the sharing of patient knowledge.

Different Theoretical Grounds

In addition to the holistic and localised approaches to practice adopted by TCM and WM practitioners, a number of interviewed healthcare professionals pointed out that WM and TCM have entirely different theoretical grounds.

> TCM is not quantifiable. It can define on the nature of diseases. Therefore, it needs practitioners' experience. [For example] I can use a specific drug for a patient. You can use the same drug for this patient. I may use ten mg, but you may disagree with me and you propose to use 30 mg. There is no quantified rule to provide a unified understanding. Consequently, it needs experience. For a patient, one may think of only one symptom, others may be able to think of more problems. Interview TCM 4.18

The practice of TCM needs "individual practitioners' personal experiences" (Interview TCM 5.67). TCM theories, diagnosis, and treatments do not have standard guidelines or rules for individual TCM professionals to follow. Moreover, TCM is "very difficult to quantify" (Interview TCM 6.44). Therefore, for a particular patient condition, different TCM doctors can have different interpretations, derive different results from diagnosis, and use different treatments. Also, a particular treatment method can be used for different patient conditions.

In contrast, a number of interviewed neurosurgeons emphasised that the practice of WM depends on "quantification" (Interview WMD 1.56) and "locating medical evidences" (Interview WMD 2.137). For instance, a neurosurgeon stated:

> WM has very clear evidences. Based on these evidences, treatments are very clear; for example, I need to use this particular drug to control this particular symptom. But TCM is very different. In TCM, doctors can use the same treatment method to deal with different patient problems. It is based on doctors' experience. I think this is one of the most basic differences between TCM and WM. Interview WMD 2.96

Thus, WM has a completely different theoretical basis from TCM. Instead of largely relying on personal experience, WM professionals need to make informed medical decisions based on "obtaining accurate medical evidences" (Interview WMD 8.23). Therefore, their treatments should be precisely implemented.

Because of the significant differences in theoretical foundation, professionals from either medical group may not fully understand, entirely agree with and trust the knowledge shared by the other professional group. In this case, activities of KS could be devalued, and healthcare professionals will not necessarily be motivated for interprofessional communication and KS. Thus, this was identified as a barrier to sharing patient knowledge.

Different Diagnostic Methods

Many interviewees stated that they use entirely different methods and techniques to diagnose patients on the basis of divergent philosophical views and theoretical grounds. Two good examples were provided by a TCM doctor and a WM nurse:

> TCM is based on the Bian-zheng theory for diagnosis. WM focuses on evidences. For example, a patient has a problem with his liver. WM doctors base their diagnosis on laboratory tests, CT and MRI results. Differently, TCM doctors rely on classical methods of inspection, listening and smelling examination, inquiry, and palpation to observe the patient's symptoms. Then, we decide what problem he has. Interview TCM 6.35

> TCM diagnosis uses inspection, listening and smelling examination, inquiry, and palpation. These methods are very different from ours. Sometimes we suspect how accurate these methods are. Interview WMN 27.15

6.3 Philosophical Issues

Diagnosis in TCM uses the Bian-zheng theory and adopts classical diagnosis methods of "inspection, listening and smelling, examination, inquiry, and palpation" (Interview TCM 19.35). In contrast, diagnosis in WM is usually based on conducting accurate medical tests and locating explicit medical evidences from laboratory tests, CT and MRI results, etc.

These differences in diagnostic approaches were identified as a KS barrier. Because they have very different conceptual foundations and diagnostic methods, TCM and WM professionals could have very different diagnosis results, which could cause conflicts of understandings of patient problems and requirements, and result in conflicts in actions aimed at solving patient problems and achieving patient requirements. These conflicts could hinder processes of interprofessional communication and hinder activities of sharing patient knowledge.

Different Treatment Methods

TCM and WM healthcare professionals employ very different treatment methods to resolve patient problems. For instance, a TCM doctor stated:

> In neurosurgery, the primary method is the craniotomy, which is assisted by a series of procedures and bio-chemical drugs. After the surgery, at the rehabilitation stage, we need to include TCM treatments, such as acupuncture and massage, and sometimes we use traditional herbal medicine. Interview TCM 17.19

Similarly, the differences in TCM and WM treatment methods are also reflected in many statements provided by interviewed neurosurgical practitioners; for example, a neurosurgical nurse mentioned:

> In our Neurosurgery Department, WM methods are primarily used, particularly the craniotomy surgeries. After these WM treatments, we invite TCM doctors for patient rehabilitation, such as acupuncture. Interview WMN 7.19

According to the quotations and discussion above, it became clear that, when treating neurosurgical patients, WM practitioners mainly use "craniotomies and some bio-chemical drugs" (Interview WMD 10.20). To complement treatments applied by WM professionals, TCM doctors employ traditional methods, such as acupuncture, massage, and herbal therapies.

These differences in treatment methods are a barrier to interprofessional communication and sharing of patient knowledge. This barrier not only compounds with the issue of holistic vs localised approaches to practice, different theoretical grounds and different diagnostic methods, but also enhances the professional boundary, further distances the two medical communities and reinforces untrusting relationships between the two types of healthcare professionals.

Terminology Discrepancy

In addition, TCM and WM professionals are using entirely different professional terminologies, which are an additional barrier to interprofessional communication and KS. For instance, a TCM doctor and a neurosurgical nurse stated:

> [WM and TCM] have two terminological systems. Maybe both of them have an identical purpose, but how they express the purpose is entirely different. Interview TCM 15.35

> Most of the time, when TCM doctors are proposing their ideas, we can't understand. We ask for further explanation, but still, we can't understand. It's not like in WM, very demonstrative and clear, such as in some cases we focus on the evidences. Interview WMN 7.135

The above two quotations show that TCM and WM healthcare professionals have two completely different systems of terminology and use very different professional terms and jargon to describe and explain patient problems and requirements.

> I can understand some WM words. But I found it is difficult for me to understand when they explain their treatments and analysis. Interview TCM 18.39

> In terms of terminological systems between WM and TCM, it is usual that we can't understand each other. Interview TCM 17.35

Since these professionals cannot understand each other's terminology, KS between could be very difficult. Patient knowledge shared by one side probably cannot be correctly received and comprehended by the other side. Therefore, the discrepancy in terminology is a significant barrier to communication and KS.

Furthermore, it was identified in data that TCM doctors could probably understand some WM technical terms, whereas WM professionals usually cannot understand the TCM language at all.

> For me, I can easily communicate with WM doctors, because I nearly learnt all WM knowledge. But if WM doctors do not learn TCM, they will never accept our philosophy. Interview TCM 6.72

As discussed in this quotation, TCM doctors generally can understand some WM language, since they "learnt nearly all WM knowledge in the TCM university" (Interview TCM 6.69). Sometimes they can even speak "their [WM] language" (Interview TCM 17.73). In contrast, because WM doctors have almost never received any TCM education and training in WM HE, they usually cannot understand TCM language at all. Therefore, the discrepancy in terminology is related to Chinese healthcare education, which will be discussed in Sect. 6.4.

6.3.1.2 Conflict of Philosophical Beliefs

KS barriers presented and discussed in Sect. 6.3.1.1 illustrate how the divergent conceptual systems of TCM and WM could hinder the activities of sharing patient knowledge.

In addition, many TCM and WM interviewees claimed that the divergences in conceptual and theoretical foundations could have caused conflicting philosophical views that adopted by TCM and WM professionals; for example, an interviewed neurosurgeon stated:

> Theories of TCM and WM are very different, such as TCM requires thinking by heart, but as we know actually thinking is by brain. TCM does not have a clear definition and description about the brain. I think TCM and WM are two different systems. I can generally understand TCM, but from a professional point of view I think TCM is not good, not accurate, not rich. Interview WMD 39.13

6.3 Philosophical Issues

Neurosurgical practitioners often evaluate and criticise the philosophical beliefs, concepts and techniques of TCM from a WM perspective. In their opinion, TCM is often considered as "not scientific enough" (Interview WMD 23.22).

Moreover, many interviewed WM professionals showed strong disbelief, distrust and disagreement against TCM. In many statements provided by WM informants, TCM is repeatedly described as "unscientific" (Interview WMD 1.64) and "superstitious" (Interview WMN 14.17). Thus, it is perceived that WM professionals consider WM as superior to TCM.

On the other side, several TCM interview participants also criticised WM from a TCM professional point of view. For instance, a TCM doctor claimed:

> In many cases, we have different opinions from WM doctors. For example, when dealing with a patient with symptoms of urination difficulty, we think acupuncture would be the best solution. But WM doctors think differently, they always use methods to force the patient to urinate. It is wrong, very wrong. Interview TCM 15.25

To some TCM doctors, a few WM techniques frequently used by WM professionals may not be entirely appropriate to the patient, and some may even be harmful to the patient's health. Moreover, TCM doctors strongly disagree that TCM should be inferior to WM. For instance, one of the TCM interviewees stated:

> Some WM doctors, who think they are very good at what they are doing, are so arrogant. Even though they do not understand TCM at all, they consider TCM is a lie and a superstition. [In fact, WM is not perfect], when treating a patient, we would use the traditional herbal medicines as much as possible. We normally do not suggest to the patient to take any WM drugs, which are bad for the heart and the liver, because they are all chemicals. Interview TCM 19.39

Therefore, there are strong philosophical conflicts between the two medical groups. As shown in the discussion in this section, the divergence of TCM and WM conceptual systems may have caused substantial philosophical tensions between the two professional communities, which have conflicting professional views and opinions, and which compete for the superiority of philosophy. These philosophical tensions could not only prevent the sharing of patient knowledge, but also cause substantial professional boundaries separating and distancing the TCM and neurosurgical medical communities.

Nevertheless, the practice of coding and constant comparison identified that TCM professionals can generally accept WM beliefs. For instance, one of the TCM interviewees stated that:

> [Because we TCM doctors learnt WM] therefore we understand both TCM and WM. [...] We TCM practitioners can accept WM theories and we can treat patients by using WM methods. But WM doctors will never accept TCM methodological system. Interview TCM 18.09

This quotation indicates that, because TCM doctors have learnt WM in their HE and have a general knowledge basis of WM, they can generally accept WM beliefs and concepts. On the other side, WM doctors "will never accept TCM" (Interview TCM 18.11), because they "never learn TCM" (Interview WMN 7.30). Therefore, the philosophical conflicts and tensions could have been caused by the absence of shared basic knowledge, overlapping interests and mutual conceptual understandings. These issues also emerged as KS barriers and are discussed in Sect. 6.3.1.3.

6.3.1.3 Inadequate Interprofessional Common Ground

> [Because we TCM doctors learnt WM] we therefore understand both TCM and WM. [...] We TCM practitioners can accept WM theories and we can treat patients by using WM methods. But WM doctors will never accept the TCM methodological system. Interview TCM 18.09

As discussed by interviewed professionals from both groups, and as shown in the quotation above, there is a lack of interprofessional common ground, which can be conceptualised as a knowledge base of overlapping interests and shared conceptual understandings.

Many interview participants asserted that the interprofessional common ground is very important to interprofessional communication and KS. For example, a TCM interviewee stated:

> WM practitioners will never accept TCM. They had some TCM courses, but rarely. Their WM ideology is deep in their mind. They cannot accept TCM because they think TCM is a pseudoscience. Actually, they don't really know TCM is very effective. They just consider TCM is unscientific, must be useless. It is so not true. Interview TCM 18.11

The lack of interprofessional common ground could result in philosophical conflicts and disagreements with each other's views and opinions, enhance untrusting relationships between the two medical communities, and reinforce the professional boundaries. Furthermore, a lack of interprofessional common ground could strengthen the philosophical tensions between TCM and WM professional teams and prevent both types of healthcare professionals from actively and spontaneously sharing patient knowledge.

> I do not have a deep understanding of the TCM system. I am taking a suspicious attitude toward TCM. I think there is something that cannot be explained in TCM. I do not have a deep understanding about TCM, because I do not believe in TCM. In this case, I am not particularly interested in it. Once you entered the door of WM, you would exclude TCM. Interview WMD 24.29

Through the analysis of data and the practice of coding, it was identified that the lack of interprofessional common ground is caused by insufficient interprofessional education in the Chinese healthcare education system (which will be discussed in Sect. 6.4) and by inadequate interprofessional training in hospital environment (which will be discussed in Sect. 6.5). Finally, it was also identified that the key to resolving these philosophical tensions is to increase the interprofessional common ground.

6.3.2 *Professional Conflicts*

This section focuses on professional conflicts, which emerged from the comparative analysis as one of the sub-categories. This sub-category is formed by seven barriers, as shown in Fig. 6.7:

6.3 Philosophical Issues 115

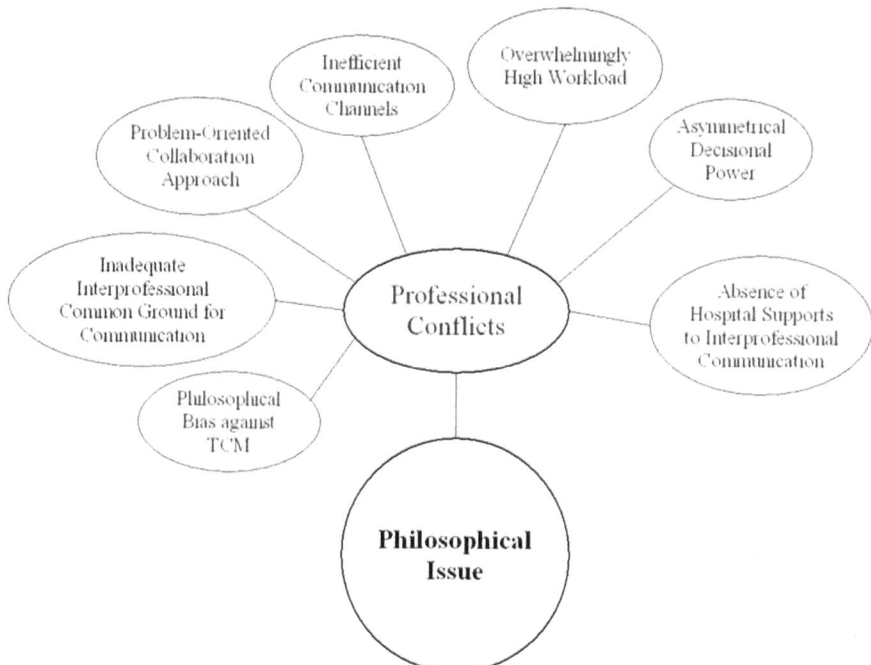

Fig. 6.7 Concept map for professional conflicts

This section discusses seven KS barriers in-depth: philosophical bias against TCM, inadequate interprofessional common ground for interaction, problem-oriented collaboration approach, inefficient communication channels, overwhelmingly high workload, asymmetrical decision-making power and the absence of a hospital requirement of interprofessional communication.

6.3.2.1 Philosophical Bias Against TCM

Discussion in Sect. 6.3.1 clearly points out that there are philosophical tensions preventing necessary communication and the exchange of patient knowledge between neurosurgical and TCM professionals. In addition, as reflected in statements by a number of interviewees, the philosophical tensions could have resulted in clashes of professional opinions, behaviours and attitudes that could hinder the sharing of knowledge. Therefore, it was considered as a professional problem that stems from a philosophical dissonance.

> TCM relies on experience [of TCM doctors], I think TCM is unreliable. It is just complementary to WM. Its theories are very vague and visionary. I do not like TCM. Interview WMD 24.07

Many interviewed WM professionals showed a sense of superiority over TCM doctors. In their statements, TCM is often dismissed as "unscientific" (Interview WMD 1.64) and "superstitious" (Interview WMN 14.17), even though they frequently invite TCM doctors for interventions for patient rehabilitation.

Moreover, many interviewed TCM doctors took the criticisms of WM professionals very personally, rather than as an active debate of philosophies and medical beliefs.

> I know that TCM is very effective against various diseases, but TCM is considered as unscientific when evaluated in WM methodology. In fact, TCM and WM have rather distinct systems; there is no similarity. You cannot define TCM by using WM theories [...] because WM is microcosmic, whereas TCM takes a holistic and integral view. Interview TCM 17.7

> The current problem is that a large number of WM practitioners, in fact a very large number of WM practitioners, do not believe TCM is scientific. For example, there are some professors in the Chinese Academy of Science who appealed to exclude TCM out of the Chinese healthcare system. I think they are wasting their time. If you (those professors) are really free, please do your own research. Do not criticise TCM. Why would they do that? The existence of TCM means there is a need for it. It means TCM is effective. You cannot just simply ignore the value of TCM. Interview TCM 4.12

As shown in both quotations above, the philosophical bias against TCM enhances the philosophical conflicts and tensions discussed in Sect. 6.3.1. Moreover, it formulates professional tensions, which encourage interprofessional competition, reinforce professional boundaries and further increase the distance between the two communities. Therefore, the philosophical bias could prevent interprofessional communication and hinder the processes of sharing patient knowledge, and thus was identified as a barrier to KS.

6.3.2.2 Inadequate Interprofessional Common Ground for Communication

Due to a lack of interprofessional common ground, as discussed in Sect. 6.3.1.3, both TCM and WM healthcare professionals are insufficiently motivated to participate in interprofessional communication and KS.

> WM students learn TCM, but in a very limited way. These students do not have enough TCM knowledge. In this case, WM doctors usually do not have a natural motivation to voluntarily collaborate with TCM colleagues. Interview WMD 1.36

> [Communication and collaboration] require WM practitioners to accept TCM. For instance, doctor A accepts acupuncture, therefore he invites us for collaboration. He introduces patients to us. If a WM doctor has no basic TCM knowledge, he would not trust TCM, therefore no [collaborations]. Interview TCM 16.18

As shown in both quotations above, interprofessional common ground could be an important element in enabling, encouraging and motivating interprofessional communication, KS and collaboration. However, due to the lack of an adequate interprofessional common ground, healthcare professionals are usually not sufficiently motivated.

6.3 Philosophical Issues

> [Communication and collaboration] depend on how much a WM doctor knows TCM. If you know less, you are less motivated. If you know more, you are more motivated. According to our current situation, WM practitioners do not know TCM very well. Interview WMD 9.21

Furthermore, when compared with TCM doctors, WM professionals usually are less motivated in communicating and collaborating with TCM doctors, because they "do not learn TCM" (Interview TCM 6.72), as some TCM interviewees complained. In comparison, TCM doctors are usually more motivated, since they "learnt nearly all WM knowledge in the TCM university" (Interview TCM 6.69). Therefore, it is perceived that KS could be much improved and individual healthcare professionals could be much more motivated if an appropriate interprofessional common ground could be developed. This issue is related to Chinese healthcare HE and interprofessional training in the hospital environment, which emerged as two main categories and will be discussed in depth in Sects. 6.4 and 6.5.

6.3.2.3 Problem-Oriented Collaboration Approach

In addition, the practice of coding and comparative analysis further identified that the process of sharing patient knowledge is limited and hindered by the adoption of a rigid problem-oriented approach to collaboration.

As discussed in Sect. 6.2.1.2, neurosurgical and TCM healthcare professionals asserted that they are collaborating purely for the benefit of the patient. It is also discussed in that section that this kind of interprofessional collaboration should be supported and facilitated by effective, timely and sufficient communication of knowledge about individual patients. However, the data collected revealed that in reality the interprofessional collaboration only aims at solving patient problems, and is not necessarily combined with adequate and effective communication and KS. For instance, a neurosurgeon stated:

> (In WM and TCM collaboration) we do not need to know TCM theory and method. We just want them (TCM doctors) to help us to solve patients' problems. Interview WMD 48.12

Similarly, one of the interviewed TCM doctors stated:

> The reason why neurosurgeons invite us to join a consultation is that they want us to solve their problems. I don't think they are trying to understand TCM or how we think of the patient. Interview TCM 4.81

Both quotations above point out that, when adopting the problem-oriented approach to collaboration, individual professionals only aim at dealing with the immediate problems of the patient. Therefore, as long as those patient problems can be resolved, interprofessional communication and KS could be considered as not really important and as something that can probably be largely ignored. Thus, the problem-oriented collaboration approach is a KS barrier.

6.3.2.4 Inefficient Communication Channels

Before discussing this KS barrier, it is necessary to recall that, as discussed in Sect. 6.1.3, the processes of sharing patient knowledge occur during consultation sessions. It is also mentioned in that section that these consultation meetings are an important vehicle for exchanging patient knowledge.

However, these consultation sessions, as a communication channel, are not conducive to communication or the sharing of patient knowledge.

> Consultation is very clearly oriented by patient problems. When WM doctors invite us for consultation, they expect us to solve their current problems. In terms of sharing knowledge, well, I do not think so. Our interactions are very superficial. Interview TCM 5.81

Some interviewed neurosurgical practitioners provided very similar statements, for instance:

> Very often we invite TCM doctors for consultations. This consultation usually starts when we find some problem. TCM doctors provide their treatments based on their understandings, theories, and diagnosis. This consultation is purely an invitation for them to help us to solve problems. It is a pure supply-demand relationship. Very rarely, we share our professional understandings and knowledge. We have not achieved that level. Interview WMD 15.39

Consequently, consultation cannot be considered as an efficient communication channel, and was identified as a barrier to the sharing of patient knowledge, because the main (and perhaps the only) purpose for these consultation meetings is to solve the patient's problems.

Besides, it must be mentioned that, as shown in the above quotation, the interviewed neurosurgeon described the relationship between neurosurgical and TCM healthcare professionals as "a pure supply-demand relationship" (Interview WMD 15.19). It implies that patients are probably handed over between healthcare professionals like a product, instead of being the centre of all healthcare services. Therefore, their feelings, needs, rights and requirements could be considered as not important and may not be carefully protected in TCM and WM collaboration. In this case, the processes of sharing patient knowledge could be largely overlooked and neglected by both types of healthcare professionals during consultation meetings.

6.3.2.5 Overwhelmingly High Workload

When collecting data in the case-study site, the researchers had chances to have glimpses of both medical departments. It was noticed that practitioners from both departments were extremely busy and had very high workloads. For instance, an interviewed neurosurgeon and an interviewed neurosurgical nurse stated:

> We are suffering from having too many patients. You can have a look of our corridor. It is full of patients. We have 44 patient beds in 18 wards. They are all full, so we have to put

6.3 Philosophical Issues   119

> new patients in the corridor. We [neurosurgical practitioners] are working at almost 120% efficiency. Annually, we need to conduct more than 400 craniotomy surgeries. Interview WMD 9.05

> We are very busy, no less than those surgical departments. We are short of staff [nurses]. For ICU [Intensive Care Unit], we used to have only two nurses. But now, there are four of us working in the ICU during the night shift. This means we have fewer nurses working outside the ICU [on normal wards]. Therefore, we are short of staff. I need to mention that our department has very high standards for staff. We are under a lot of stress and working overload. Interview WMN 10.08

Similarly, in the TCM department, many interviewed TCM professionals also claimed that they have very high workloads. For instance:

> We not only need to take care of our own patients, but also very often need to solve problems in other departments. Moreover, patients in the TCM department need to be treated repeatedly. For example, acupuncture patients usually need to be treated every day for two weeks. Interview TCM 15.45

As asserted by a number of interviewed healthcare professionals, the overwhelmingly high workloads are a barrier to sharing patient knowledge and could prevent necessary interaction and KS in the processes of collaboration. For instance, a TCM doctor and a neurosurgical nurse stated:

> [In the consultation] usually they do not ask many questions, and we do not talk that much. We all are very busy. As long as we can treat the patient, that is all right. We all are too busy to actually sit down and to have a deep conversation. Interview TCM 37.63

> Perhaps it is because we are all too busy. In our collaborations, they do their jobs, we do ours. Interview WMN 29.23

Therefore, due to the very limited time available, healthcare professionals are probably more concerned with solving the patient's immediate problems and have very limited time for interprofessional communication and KS.

6.3.2.6 Asymmetrical Decisional Powers

Additionally, it was also identified that TCM and WM healthcare professionals hold uneven decision-making powers, which could cause problems for sharing patient knowledge. For instance, when being interviewed, the head of the neurosurgical department stated:

> Before collaborative works, we need to inform TCM doctors what problem this patient has, what treatments have already been conducted, what we want you TCM doctors to do. All these details, they [TCM doctors] need to know. Interview WMD 2.140

This quotation, in particular the sentence "what we want you TCM doctors to do", shows a high degree of power over the processes of collaboration, the patient and TCM doctors. In this case, probably, TCM doctors can only perform patient treatments following the neurosurgical practitioners' instruction and command. Thus, they are most unlikely to communicate and share knowledge with WM professionals actively, voluntarily and spontaneously.

> In collaborative patient treatments, we of course have the decision making power, because the patient is in our department. We just need TCM doctors to help us. Interview WMD 8.31

As in the above quotation, this imbalance of decisional power is also reflected in statements of several interviewed TCM doctors, such as:

> If neurosurgical patients need acupuncture treatments, neurosurgeons would initiate a consultation note and telephone us. Then we go to treat patient with acupuncture. [...] In this process, we do not have decision power. For example, this patient clearly needs TCM treatment, but we cannot do anything about it, because neurosurgeons need to make this decision, not us. Interview TCM 16.17

As reflected in the above quotation, TCM doctors hold less power. Therefore, they are most likely to maintain a passive position, avoid any confrontations and to follow instructions, instead of actively and voluntarily proposing their ideas, opinions and suggestions. For them, even if they intend to share knowledge, they have very little power or influence to have their views recognised.

6.3.2.7 Absence of Hospital Requirement for Interprofessional Communication

> There is no specific requirement for WM and TCM collaboration, which mainly depends on problems we have found in our practice of medicine. We would voluntarily invite TCM doctors for collaboration. It in fact is for the benefit of patients. [...] In terms of communication, there is no such requirement from the central government. Moreover, in our hospital, there is no requirement that WM and TCM practitioners need to communicate with each other. Interview WMD 20.13

No requirements have been established by the hospital management which explicitly demand communication and KS between WM and TCM professionals. Therefore, professionals from both medical teams probably perceive that communication and KS are optional, not compulsory, and not important. Consequently, the absence of hospital requirements for interprofessional communication was considered as a KS barrier.

Furthermore, when discussing hospital policies, one of the hospital managers stated:

> Some hospitals have some kind of regulation that WM and TCM teams need to adequately communicate and collaborate. In this case, practitioners are forced to do this. But in our hospital, we do not have this requirement. It is like if you [a WM practitioner] do not communicate and collaborate with TCM doctors for ten years, no one would care about that and no one would criticise you. Therefore, there is no supervision on this. But in those hospitals that have this regulation, doctors have to collaborate. Interview WMD 1.83

According to the quotation above, it is perceived that if explicit hospital requirements can be established and implemented, these requirements could be strong motivators in encouraging, demanding and regulating the exchange of patient knowledge.

6.3.3 Section Summary

This section discusses the core category of the emerging theory, namely, the philosophical issues. More specifically, this section discusses two sub-categories: philosophical conflicts and professional conflicts.

In the discussion of the philosophical conflicts, it was found that the divergent conceptual systems of TCM and WM have resulted in substantial professional boundaries and a significant distance between the two medical communities. Moreover, these philosophical conflicts have formulated philosophical tensions, which not only reinforce the professional boundary and exacerbate the distance, but also create enormous difficulties for interprofessional communication and KS.

Furthermore, as discussed in Sect. 6.3.2, there are ongoing professional tensions between the neurosurgical and TCM medical teams, which have conflicting professional understandings and prejudices against each other's medical approach, and which compete for power and professional standing. Also, both philosophical and professional tensions have created distrust, disregard and even resentment between the two medical teams. Hence, healthcare professionals are not motivated and are unwilling to communicate with each other.

Furthermore, a very important finding presented and discussed in this section is that both philosophical conflicts and professional conflicts could have been caused by a lack of interprofessional common ground. In fact, the interprofessional common ground could be the key to reducing the philosophical and professional tensions, resolving the conflicts and improving KS between TCM and WM medical teams.

Finally, it is also discussed in this section that the interprofessional common ground needs to be established in both Chinese healthcare education and professional training programmes in the hospital environment. Therefore, the next Sect. (6.4) discusses the Chinese healthcare HE system and Sect. 6.5 presents and criticises KS barriers in the category of interprofessional training.

6.4 Chinese Healthcare Education

As discussed in Sect. 6.3 Philosophical Issues, a very important research finding is that there is a lack of interprofessional common ground to facilitate and to motivate the sharing of patient knowledge. It is also discussed in that section that some interprofessional common ground could be established in the Chinese healthcare education system, which emerged as one of the main categories.

This section aims at discussing the category of Chinese healthcare education and presenting KS barriers relating to this category. In more detail, this section discusses and criticises KS barriers in two sub-categories: lack of interprofessional education in healthcare HE and external influences on healthcare HE. Also, the final construct for this category is shown in Fig. 6.8.

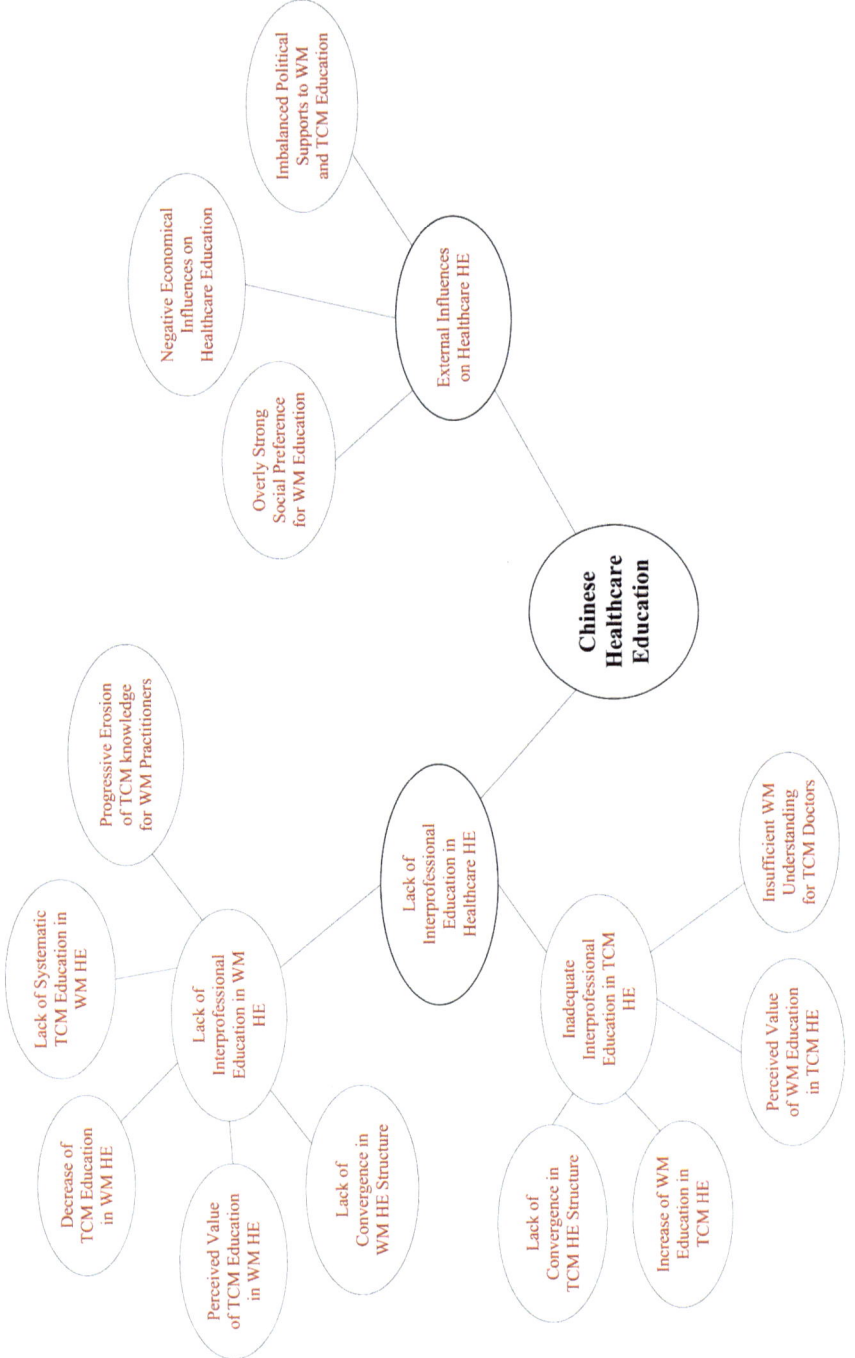

Fig. 6.8 Concept map for Chinese healthcare education

6.4.1 Lack of Interprofessional Education in Healthcare HE

As introduced by many WM and TCM informants, Chinese healthcare education consists of two parallel and almost insulated educational systems, one for TCM practitioners and the other for WM professionals. This section discusses KS barriers relating to the two educational systems, as shown in Fig. 6.9.

This section discusses two main issues: lack of interprofessional education in WM HE and lack of interprofessional education in TCM HE. It is also shown in the concept map that five barriers are going to be discussed in relation to the first issue: lack of convergence in WM HE structure, lack of systematic TCM education in WM HE, perceived value of TCM education in WM HE, decrease of TCM education in WM HE, progressive erosion of TCM knowledge for WM practitioners. Moreover, this section discusses four KS barriers relating to the second issue. These KS barriers are lack of convergence in TCM HE structure, perceived value of WM education in TCM HE, increase of WM education in TCM HE, and insufficient WM understanding for TCM doctors.

6.4.1.1 Lack of Interprofessional Education in WM HE

The application of coding and comparative analysis identified a lack of interprofessional education in Chinese WM HE, because of which WM professionals have very limited understandings about TCM, criticise and even have strong biases against some TCM theories and concepts, have insufficient interprofessional common ground, and therefore have enormous difficulties in communicating and sharing knowledge with TCM doctors.

This section discusses the WM HE system. Specifically, in this section, five KS barriers are discussed: lack of convergence in WM HE structure, decreasing value of TCM education in WM HE, lack of systematic TCM education in WM HE, decrease of TCM education in WM HE, and finally, progressive erosion of TCM knowledge for WM practitioners.

Lack of Convergence in WM HE Structure

> In China, WM education is a complete system. This system, because I have never been to Russia, I heard from some old practitioners, our education system imitated the Russian one in the 1950s. The current system has not changed too much. It is very similar as the healthcare systems in most Western countries. Interview WMD 1.09

As mentioned by some interviewed WM professionals, the current structure of WM education in China is very similar to the structure of medical education in Western countries.

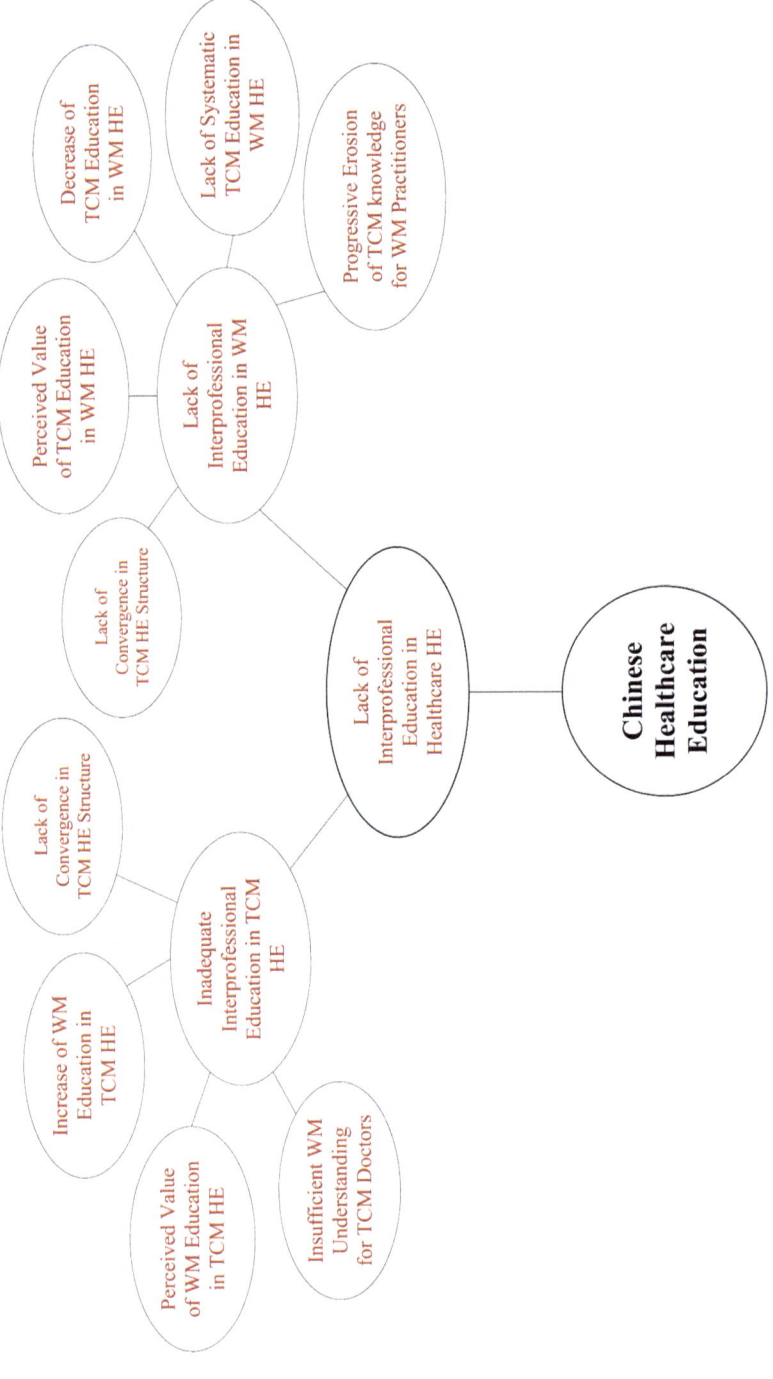

Fig. 6.9 Concept map for lack of interprofessional education in healthcare HE

More specifically, an interviewed neurosurgeon introduced the structure of Chinese WM education in more depth:

> (WM education consists of) bachelor, master, and doctoral levels of studies. WM education starts from the bachelor study, which can be further categorised into two stages. The first stage is the general foundation courses. Usually in the first year, students need to take modules like chemistry, physics, and biology. In the second year, they need to learn the medical foundations, such as anatomy, pathology. In third and fourth years, students learn clinical medicine, such as respiratory system, circulatory system. Students take the fifth year as an internship where they are actually practising medicine in a hospital. Postgraduate study includes two years of master's and three years of doctoral level studies. In the first year of the master's level study, students need to take fundamental courses, such as professional English and medical foundations. Then, students need to be involved in different kinds of medical research on various topics according to their supervisors. Then they need to prepare their thesis and viva. According to my knowledge, this education structure has existed since the 1950s. Interview WMD 2.21

As shown by the above quotation, throughout this educational structure, students can gain a good understanding of WM both in theory and in practice. However, as also shown by the above quotation, the WM education includes very limited teaching, training and practice in TCM.

Therefore, the lack of convergence in WM education was identified as a barrier to KS, since this structure has formed a clear professional boundary separating the communities of TCM and WM. This professional boundary distances the two medical communities, prevents activities of interprofessional collaboration, and hinders communication and the sharing of patient knowledge.

Moreover, this structure of WM education is incapable of establishing a sufficient interprofessional common ground to motivate and facilitate the interaction of patient knowledge between TCM and WM healthcare professionals. Specifically, the insufficient common ground is related to a lack of systematic TCM education in this WM education structure.

Lack of Systematic TCM Education in WM HE

Many interviewees claimed that, in WM universities, there is very limited TCM learning and practice available for students. For instance, the interviewed TCM lecturer, who is a coordinator of a TCM module in a local WM university, stated:

> The [TCM] module I am teaching includes [synthesises] about 20 modules that I learnt in my university [TCM education]. Therefore, it cannot be in much depth, just about some very basic theories. [Teaching of] things like acupuncture in some practical sessions is very superficial. It is impossible to include everything. Interview TCM Educator 47.13

Therefore, because they lack systematic TCM learning, WM students do not have a good understanding of TCM.

> We only have a basic understanding about TCM, actually very superficial. We only learnt something like the palpation, nothing else. Interview WMN 14.29

> In WM universities, they [WM students] learn some TCM, but it is very limited. It is just an optional module in one of the semesters. They are only required to have a general understanding. Interview TCM 17.65

Also, due to a lack of TCM knowledge, WM professionals "usually do not accept TCM" (Interview TCM 38.11) and do not have "a natural motivation to voluntarily collaborate with TCM colleagues" (Interview WMD 1.36).

Consequently, it was identified that the lack of systematic TCM education is a barrier to interprofessional communication and sharing patient knowledge, since the WM education system cannot establish a knowledge base for WM students that would provide sufficient interprofessional common ground for collaboration and communication with TCM doctors. Also, due to the lack of any appropriate interprofessional common ground, a number of WM professionals suspect and criticise TCM concepts and methods, and some of them even dismiss TCM and TCM practitioners (as discussed in Sect. 6.3.2.1). These suspicions, criticisms and dismissive attitudes not only could enhance philosophical and professional tensions, but also reinforce the untrusting relationship between the two types of healthcare professionals, and thus impede the necessary exchange of patient knowledge between professionals of TCM and WM.

Perceived Value of TCM Education in WM HE

In addition to the lack of systematic TCM education discussed in Section "Lack of Systematic TCM Education in WM HE", many interviewed practitioners claimed that TCM is considered as not important by WM students; for instance, an interviewed neurosurgeon stated:

> In our five-year bachelor education, we [WM practitioners] all need to learn TCM. We were required to have basic knowledge about TCM. We need to know what kind of system it is. But we do not understand TCM too much. Our learning was only aimed at passing the TCM module." Interview WMD 12.10

> "In WM education, the TCM module is not an important one. It is just an optional module. I reckon some people did not even read the book. Interview WMD 9.31

As reflected in the above quotations, not only do students consider TCM as optional and not important, but also the WM educational structure itself includes very limited TCM teaching and learning activities.

> We mainly learnt very basic TCM, only at the bachelor level. We did not have any TCM learning at master's and doctoral levels. WM higher education, in itself, did not pay attention to TCM teaching. TCM was just an optional module, which meant it was not necessary for us to take the module. Interview WMD 12.20

Similarly, the interviewed TCM lecturer stated:

> Now we [TCM module] are an optional module. To be honest, the teaching is not good, because the module is not important. Interview TCM Educator 47.11

According to the statement provided by the TCM lecturer, it is perceived that WM students may not take this module very seriously and thus do not have a holistic and thorough understanding of TCM.

The perceived value of TCM education in WM HE was identified as a barrier to the sharing of patient knowledge between TCM and WM healthcare professionals. It was identified that, because of this barrier, WM professionals do not have a sufficient interprofessional common ground with TCM and are not motivated to collaborate and communicate with TCM doctors. Moreover, the perceived value of TCM education implies that TCM is not important, is inferior and hence is not included in WM education. In this case, many interviewed WM professionals hold prejudices and dismissive attitudes against TCM and its professionals, even though they do not really know the traditional healing belief and methodology. Therefore, communication and KS with TCM doctors could be seen as not important and not necessary. Finally, the discussion above shows that the WM HE system exacerbates the philosophical and professional tensions between TCM and WM professionals, and reinforces the dominating position of WM in the hospital environment.

Decrease of TCM Education in WM HE

In addition to TCM being considered as not important (as discussed in Section "Perceived Value of TCM Education in WM HE"), the number of TCM teaching sessions and modules is decreasing. For instance, an interviewed neurosurgeon stated:

> There are some new WM graduates that I know of. They know very little about TCM, hardly ever studied TCM and only concentrated on WM learning. I think the current WM education is not like before, when we were at university. We had TCM modules and we were required to pass module exams. Interview WMD 21.17

As mentioned in the quotation above, TCM was probably evaluated as relatively more important when this neurosurgeon was a student in university. In contrast, nowadays, TCM is less important, and thus there is less TCM learning and training included in WM HE. Therefore, the amount of TCM education has been reduced.

> When I was a student [WM], we had a few TCM books and some lectures about TCM. But I heard people were saying that in recent years students have less and less TCM learning. Interview TCM 23.19

It was identified in the data collected that the decrease in TCM education augments the lack of interprofessional common ground between TCM and WM healthcare professionals, demotivates WM professionals from active interaction with TCM doctors, and reinforces the professional boundaries, the imbalance of professional standings in the hospital environment and the philosophical and professional tensions between the two medical communities. Therefore, the decrease in TCM education was considered as a barrier to interprofessional communication and KS.

Progressive Erosion of TCM Knowledge for WM Practitioners

An additional issue emerged during interviews with the neurosurgical interviewees. For instance, one of the interviewed neurosurgeons claimed:

> We learnt TCM. But we did not use TCM knowledge for a long time. We forget about it. Interview WMD 11.23

> In our [WM] bachelor level study, we had a TCM module. Because it was only one module, we have a low level understanding about TCM. But we still knew a little bit about TCM. After many years of practising WM, we forgot the majority of it. Interview WMD 11.33

Because neurosurgical practitioners do not use TCM knowledge in their daily practice of medicine, their limited TCM knowledge obtained in WM education is progressively forgotten.

The progressive erosion of TCM knowledge was identified as a barrier to sharing patient knowledge. This barrier reduces the interprofessional common ground for WM professionals and does not permit WM professionals to actively and spontaneously communicate and share knowledge when collaborating with TCM professionals.

6.4.1.2 Inadequate Interprofessional Education in TCM HE

Comparing to Sect. 6.4.1.1, which discuss the structure of WM education and related KS barriers, this section focuses on the structure of TCM education. Specifically, this section discusses four KS barriers: lack of convergence in the structure of TCM HE, perceived value of WM education in TCM HE, increase of WM education in TCM HE, and insufficient WM understanding for TCM doctors.

Lack of Convergence in TCM HE Structure

> [TCM education] is very similar to the general WM education structure, and includes bachelor level, master level and doctoral level of education. Interview TCM 15.46

As described by many TCM interviewees, the general structure for TCM education is very similar to that of WM, consisting of bachelor's, master's and doctorate levels of study. To be more specific, one of the TCM interviewees stated:

> There are many TCM-related modules in TCM universities, such as TCM basics, acupuncture, massage, TCM orthopaedics, and TCM herbal medicine. Apart from the TCM teachings, there are a number of WM modules. It is not like before, only concentrating on TCM. The current educational structure requires us to learn modern medical knowledge [WM]. Therefore, this education includes both TCM and WM. […] TCM modules were nearly two thirds, and the other one third is WM modules. Interview TCM 17.59

As shown in the above quotation, through this TCM education structure, students could be well trained as TCM practitioners. Moreover, students can also gain a relatively good understanding of WM.

This structure of TCM education could establish a WM knowledge base as an interprofessional common ground for students. Therefore, as discussed in Sect. 6.3, TCM doctors can understand some WM concepts and the terminology used by WM professionals. Also, this educational structure enables and motivates TCM doctors to voluntarily and spontaneously collaborate, communicate and share knowledge with WM professionals.

Nevertheless, the structure of TCM education was still considered as a barrier to the sharing of patient knowledge between TCM and WM healthcare professionals. It was identified that this educational structure could have further strengthen the philosophical tensions between the two types of healthcare professionals, since WM could be perceived as superior to TCM. Moreover, this structure could also form professional tensions, augment the imbalances in professional standing and power, encourage interprofessional competition and thus impede necessary interaction and KS.

Perceived Value of WM Education in TCM HE

At the beginning, it is necessary to recall that there is a very limited amount of TCM teaching and learning in WM HE, as discussed in Section "Perceived Value of TCM Education in WM HE". In contrast, it was revealed by many TCM interviewees that WM modules and sessions are considered as very important in TCM HE. For instance, two interviewed TCM doctors stated:

> In the TCM educational structure, we studied TCM theories for nearly one and a half years. We also learnt WM theories for one and a half year. They are almost half and half. We studied all TCM treatments and WM treatments in a compressed way. Interview TCM 6.20

> In my TCM education, we have nearly 40% WM modules, and 60% TCM modules. These two types of modules were both very important, since they influenced my practice of medicine after graduation. Interview TCM 5.32

These quotations reflect that TCM students may have a relatively good understanding of WM, and have some common ground, which is crucial for interprofessional collaboration and communication with TCM professionals.

Nevertheless, the value of WM education in TCM emerged as a KS barrier, since it not only compounds with the barrier of the structure of TCM HE, but also exacerbates the imbalances in professional standing and power between TCM and WM professionals, strengthens the philosophical and professional tensions, and demotivates TCM professionals from actively communicating and sharing patient knowledge with WM professionals.

Increase of WM Education in TCM HE

> Because WM is getting more and more advanced, it is more influential than TCM. Therefore, TCM seems relatively weak and small. I remember my thesis supervisor once mentioned to me that WM is almost equally important as TCM. Interview TCM 18.17

> Currently, the development of WM is better than the TCM development. Moreover, I feel that our government provides more support to WM. Therefore, TCM doctors must know WM. Interview TCM Educator 47.45

These two quotations indicate that WM is increasingly valued as important in TCM universities. Therefore, and as discussed by some TCM interviewees, the amount of WM teaching in TCM HE have been increased in recent years. For instance, an interviewed TCM doctor stated:

> Nowadays, students [TCM] need to learn more WM than we did. When they graduate from TCM universities it means they do not just know about TCM, but also to some extent they understand both TCM and WM. Interview TCM 17.59

At this point, it is important to compare the TCM education with the WM education. WM is treated as very important and a large amount of WM learning is included in TCM education, whereas TCM is considered as not important and is only optional to students in WM universities. These differences clearly reinforce philosophical tensions and conflicts between TCM and WM medical communities, augment professional tensions and competition, and develop untrusting, uncooperative relationships. Therefore, the increase in WM education not only emerged as an additional barrier to KS, but also compounds with the lack of convergence in TCM HE and the perceived value of TCM education discussed in Sections "Lack of Convergence in TCM HE Structure" and "Perceived Value of WM Education in TCM HE".

Insufficient WM Understanding for TCM Doctors

Even though there is a considerable amount of WM teaching and learning for TCM students in their HE, many interviewed TCM doctors claimed that they do not really have a deep and sufficient understanding of WM. For instance, a TCM doctor and a neurosurgeon stated:

> I can understand some WM terminology, but I think some WM theories and analysis are difficult to understand. After all, we did not learn WM as systematically as those WM doctors. Interview TCM 16.39

> TCM doctors need to extend their WM knowledge gained at universities. They need to know modern diagnosis methods, such as radiology, pathology, biology. They also need to know WM treatment methods. What are their underlying mechanisms? How effective are they? What are their defects? These defects are actually where they can help us. Interview WMD 2.137

Therefore, TCM education does not in fact effectively establish a sufficient interprofessional common ground for TCM doctors. This clearly is a barrier to interprofessional communication and creates great difficulties for sharing patient knowledge between TCM and WM healthcare professionals.

At this point, it is necessary to highlight that neither TCM HE nor WM HE can provide an adequate interprofessional common ground to students. Thus, both TCM and WM professionals have a limited understanding about each other's beliefs, have disagreements with the methodology used by the other medical team,

6.4 Chinese Healthcare Education   131

and have philosophical conflicts and professional tensions which prevent the sharing of patient knowledge.

6.4.2 External Influences on Healthcare HE

This section discusses external influences on healthcare HE in China. In more detail, three KS barriers emerged and are discussed in this section: overly strong social preference for WM education, negative economical influences on healthcare education, and imbalanced political supports to WM and TCM education. These barriers are shown in Fig. 6.10.

6.4.2.1 Overly Strong Social Preference for WM Education

As discussed in Sect. 6.2.3.1, an overly strong social preference for WM was identified as a barrier to KS. In addition to this barrier, the data gathered revealed a social preference for WM education.

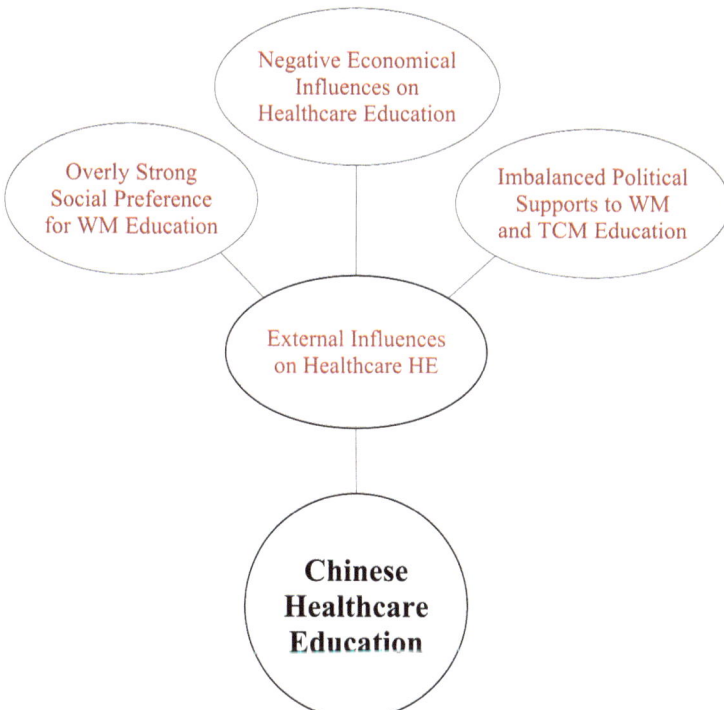

Fig. 6.10 Concept map for external influences on healthcare HE

> In the current environment, people think WM is more important. It is like only WM is scientific, because WM uses evidences. And the WM equipments are getting more and more advanced. We do not have this in TCM. But currently people like to use numbers to make a point. Therefore people think WM is more advanced and is more convincible. Therefore, WM students think learning TCM is useless and believe TCM is a deception. In this case, not only do they only have very limited TCM learning, but also they do not take TCM learning seriously. After graduation, they do something utterly different from TCM, for sure they will forget TCM knowledge. Although, in TCM education, students need to learn WM, the WM learning is not very deep. They only study basic things, like anatomy, etc. Interview TCM 38.45

As discussed in this quotation, because WM is much more popular, accepted and preferred by people, students in WM universities may not want to learn TCM, which could be seen as useless and as a deception.

Also, a few interviewed healthcare professionals claimed that, for instance:

> It is usually like this, a student would only think about applying to a TCM university in case they cannot make the entry requirements to a WM university. It is like this across the whole of China. There are a number of WM universities, but there are only a very few TCM universities. Moreover, there is a lack of attention to TCM teaching resources and staff qualification. Interview TCM 19.53

Many interviewed healthcare professionals asserted that, as shown for instance in the above quotation, a potential medical university applicant would most likely apply to a WM university. The student would only consider applying to a TCM university when the application to a WM university is rejected.

Both quotations above indicate a clear and strong social preference for WM education, which emerged as a barrier to sharing patient knowledge. The preference for WM education compounds the social preference for WM, augments imbalances in the professional standing and power of TCM and WM healthcare professionals, and enhances the philosophical and professional tensions between the two medical communities.

Moreover, the social preference for WM education could be related to the imbalanced political supports to WM and TCM universities. The next Sect. (6.4.2.2) discusses external political influences.

6.4.2.2 Imbalanced Political Supports to WM and TCM Education

> [In terms of education] personally, I think there is too much political emphasis on WM education and neglect for TCM education, which lacks political attention. Interview WMD 9.29

This quotation was provided by a neurosurgeon, who, like some other interviewed WM practitioners, pointed out that WM education receives stronger political support, whereas TCM education probably receives less political supports.

Similarly, many TCM practitioners provided very similar opinions. For instance, a TCM doctor stated:

> In terms of teaching, WM is much better. They have more teaching resources, because the government supports them more. For instance, Medical College [name] has very strong

6.4 Chinese Healthcare Education

teaching teams, outstanding teaching facilities. It is for sure they have better students with better futures. In comparison, TCM College [name] is a second class university. Students graduated from this college usually cannot easily get jobs. Therefore, they [this TCM university] have lower entry requirements, because fewer and fewer students apply for this college. If this college cannot get enough students, it has no money to operate. Interview TCM 21.23

Compared to WM universities, which receive strong political support and thus usually have much better teaching resources and facilities, as many TCM doctors pointed out, TCM universities are much less well supported. In this case, TCM universities usually do not have very good facilities and are not equipped with good teaching and research teams. Therefore, students usually are more interested in applying to WM universities.

The unequal political support to WM and TCM education emerged as a barrier to KS. This barrier indicates that the government consider WM is superior to and more important than TCM, and thus graduates from WM universities should have higher social status and higher professional standing and power in hospitals. This barrier evidently prevents activities of interprofessional communication and hinders processes of sharing patient knowledge, since it fuels philosophical conflicts and tensions, develops uncooperative and competing relationships and reinforces professional tensions between the two medical communities.

Finally, because they receive more political support, WM universities are usually more reputable than TCM universities and thus usually have more students of higher quality. Therefore, WM graduates usually have wider career opportunities after graduation. This issue is related to the Chinese economic environment.

6.4.2.3 Negative Economical Influences on Healthcare HE

When the strong social preference for WM education was being discussed with the interviewed healthcare politician, he stated:

I have never heard of this phenomenon. But I know that applicants for WM universities are much more numerous than those who apply to TCM universities. When a student is applying to a university, there are many issues that need to be taken into consideration. Besides personal interests, the student needs to think about how easy it is to find a good job after graduation. This is a problem. China not only has more WM universities, but also has more WM hospitals. Therefore, WM students can have wider career opportunities. Interview TCM Politician 34.19

This quotation is self-contradictory. On the one hand this politician denied that students prefer WM education, as "I have never heard of this phenomenon", which as perceived may not be entirely true. On the other hand, he stated that WM universities are much preferred, mainly because WM graduates "have wider career opportunities". Later on, in this interview, this politician added:

Doctors who select this profession, besides personal interests, they need to consider the career issues. […] The problem is that TCM is very cheap. In this case, a TCM doctor cannot make enough money for living. In other words, one should live a dignified and decent life based on being honest and hard-working. Interview TCM Politician 34.23

This quotation indicates that probably TCM doctors usually are less well paid and have lower social status, when compared with WM professionals. Therefore, students would prefer to go to WM universities, simply because after graduation they can have higher social standing and higher salary.

Many interviewed healthcare professionals provided similar views; for example, a neurosurgeon stated:

> I think our society is developing rapidly, everyone is pursuing materials and money [...] TCM is very cheap. In this case, TCM doctors cannot make a significant income to the hospital and therefore do not have valuable social standing. Therefore, fewer and fewer people want to learn TCM and want to practise TCM. Interview WMD 24.34

As shown in this quotation, because TCM doctors do not have "valuable social standing" and maybe do not have "satisfying personal income" (Interview TCM 15.43), students would prefer WM education.

To summarise the discussion above, due to these negative economical influences on Chinese healthcare education, TCM practitioners have relatively lower social standing and cannot survive in a hospital environment dominated by WM healthcare professionals (as discussed in Sect. 6.2.1). Also, as discussed in Sect. 6.3, this hospital environment does not permit active interprofessional communication and does not encourage the sharing of patient knowledge between TCM and WM healthcare professionals.

6.4.3 Section Summary

This section discusses Chinese healthcare education, which emerged as one of the main categories. Specifically, this section discusses two sub-categories in depth: lack of interprofessional education in WM HE and external influences on healthcare HE.

According to the discussion in this section, it became clear that the Chinese healthcare education system is unable to develop a sufficient interprofessional common ground to enable, encourage and motivate interprofessional communication and KS between TCM and WM healthcare professionals.

Also, due to the lack of a sufficient interprofessional common ground, TCM and WM healthcare professionals have very little understanding about each other's philosophical system, and thus have conflicting philosophical views and divergent conceptual systems and theoretical foundations for diagnosing and resolving patient problems and satisfying patient requirements. Thus, as discussed in Sect. 6.3, these philosophical issues result in philosophical tensions preventing the sharing of patient knowledge.

Moreover, the structures of WM HE and TCM HE reinforce imbalances of professional standing and power in hospitals, encourage interprofessional competition, and cause professional tensions, which can hinder processes of interprofessional collaboration and communication between TCM and WM healthcare professionals.

6.5 Interprofessional Training   135

Finally, the Chinese healthcare education is related to all four other categories: the contextual influence, philosophical issues, interprofessional training, and hospital management. It is necessary to note that the Chinese healthcare education system is closely linked to and has imposed its structure on interprofessional training programmes in hospitals.

6.5 Interprofessional Training

In addition to the KS barriers relating to the structure of Chinese healthcare education, KS is also prevented by an absence of interprofessional training schemes, sessions and programmes to bridge the gap in understanding between the professional communities of TCM and WM, and to develop an appropriate interprofessional common ground in order to enable, motivate and encourage interprofessional communication and KS.

This section discusses the interprofessional training issues, which emerged as one of the main categories. In more detail, this section discusses three main sub-categories: existing interprofessional training structure, absence of interprofessional training in the neurosurgery department, and absence of interprofessional training in the TCM department. Moreover, the final construct for this category is shown in Fig. 6.11.

6.5.1 Existing Professional Training Structure

This section discusses one of the sub-categories, namely, the existing professional training structure. The structure of this sub-category is shown in Fig. 6.12.

Specifically, and as shown in the concept map, this section discusses three barriers to sharing patient knowledge: lack of convergence in professional training structure in the neurosurgery department, lack of convergence in professional training structure in the TCM department, and lack of political emphasis on interprofessional training.

6.5.1.1 Lack of Convergence in Professional Training Structure in Neurosurgery Department

> We have an inner departmental professional training plan. Our department was evaluated as the Provincial Key Neurosurgery Department by the Hubei government, which requires that we need to have an annual departmental professional training plan. We need to make records for each training session, such as how many practitioners participated. It is a requirement by the provincial government. Interview WMD 20.39

A number of interviewed neurosurgical practitioners revealed that the neurosurgery department has a very systematic professional training plan. This plan is not just

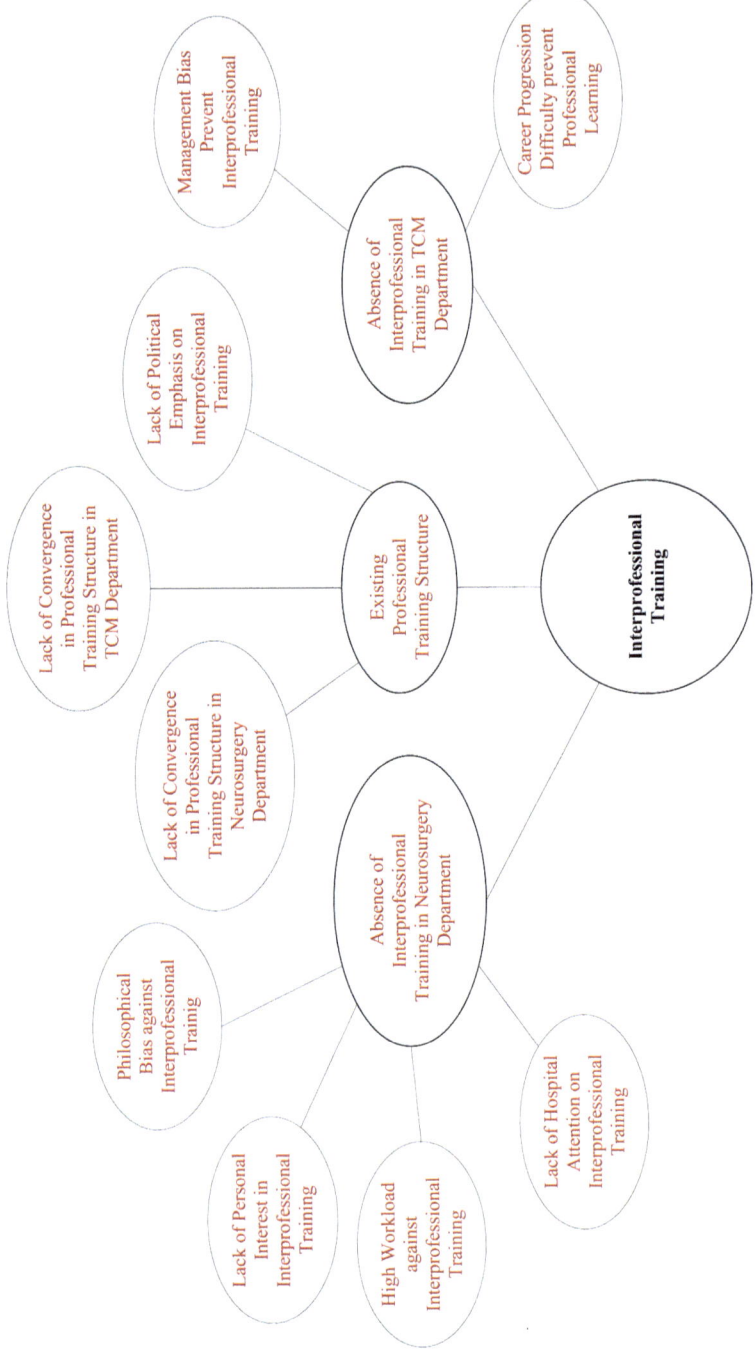

Fig. 6.11 Concept map for interprofessional training

6.5 Interprofessional Training

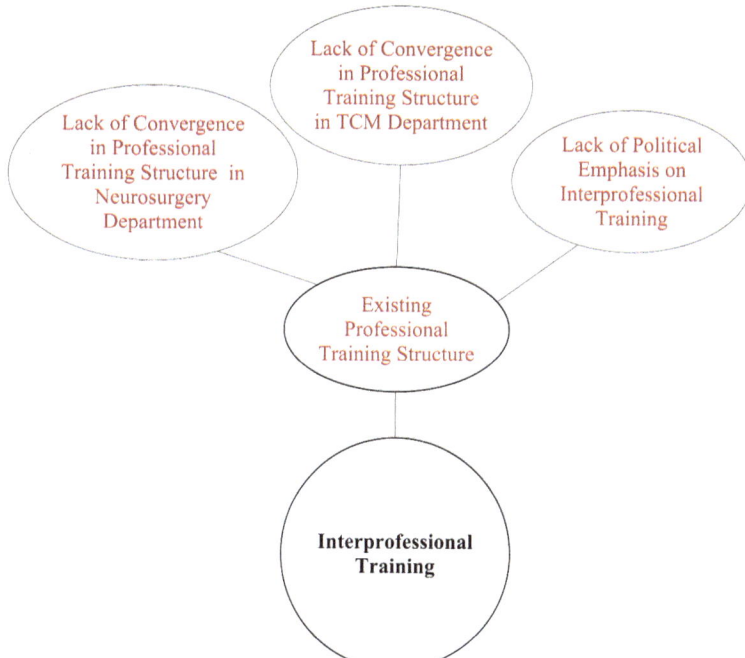

Fig. 6.12 Concept map for existing professional training structure

monitored by the hospital management, but also supervised by the provincial government.

More specifically, some interviewed neurosurgical professionals specified professional training strategies implemented in this department.

> Every practitioner is encouraged to take internship opportunities in better hospitals and better departments. In this way, they can learn professional knowledge. Interview WMD 11.41

> Nearly every week, or at least every month, we have lectures about medical law, or all kinds of medical knowledge. We neurosurgical practitioners also need to have knowledge about other departments, such as CT [computed tomography], clinical laboratory, anaesthesiology. Interview WMD 13.37

> We need to make enough credits from professional training annually. For instance, if I attend a national medical conference, I can make eight credits. If I attend a provincial conference, I can make four credits. If I attend a city level conference, I can make two credits. We are required to have 20 credits annually. Interview WMD 20.39

According to these quotations, there are generally four professional training strategies used in the neurosurgery department. Firstly, practitioners are encouraged to apply for internship opportunities in better neurosurgery departments in better hospitals in China. Secondly, there are well-organised lectures arranged within the hospital on a weekly basis. Thirdly, neurosurgical healthcare professionals are encouraged to conduct medical research studies, publish research results and attend medical conferences. Finally, professional training activities are related to the "annual year-end performance assessment" (Interview WMD 21.23) for individual healthcare professionals. Every neurosurgical practitioner must obtain 20 credits annually.

> Annually, the hospital management has an integral professional training plan. All hospital departments need to establish professional training plans. However, professional training is mostly limited to our specific subject. For example, I am a neurosurgeon, so my professional training would only focus on the area of neurosurgery, or focus on a specific disease [related to neurosurgery]. Interview WMD 20.41

However, the present professional training activities do not include learning on the overlapping areas of TCM and WM. Professional training in the neurosurgery department only concentrates on WM, particularly on subjects that can be immediately used by neurosurgical practitioners.

Therefore, neurosurgical professionals probably have a very limited understanding of TCM. Thus, these neurosurgeons and nurses do not have an adequate interprofessional common ground enabling them to communicate and share knowledge with TCM doctors.

6.5.1.2 Lack of Convergence in Professional Training Structure in TCM Department

Compared to the well-planned and well-implemented professional training in the neurosurgery department, professional training strategies and activities in the TCM department are neither systematically designed nor well implemented. For instance, an interviewed TCM doctor stated:

> All learning [sessions] are about WM, almost never focused on TCM. Hospital management pay more attentions on learning for WM practitioners. Interview TCM 37.49

The quotation above implies that TCM doctors are not required to engage in any professional training programmes. This could be due to a lack of attention, support and supervision from hospital management.

> I can publish papers and go to conferences that could make me enough professional training credits. We [TCM doctors] just do not need to do this anymore. Because we graduated from a TCM technical secondary school, originally we could be promoted to assistant professorship. But now it is impossible, if you want to get the assistant professorship, you need to have a bachelor degree. [...] We graduated from a TCM technical secondary school, so it is impossible for us, as we are not even qualified for the first requirement. Do you [the interviewer] think it is inappropriate? It is very very inappropriate. Interview TCM 37.53

Also, as reflected in the data collected, TCM doctors are not motivated to engage in professional training activities, since they claimed that they are never going "to get promoted" (Interview TCM 16.53). This implies a career progression difficulty for TCM doctors and a management bias against the TCM community, which demotivates TCM doctors from participating in professional training. Issues of career progression difficulty and management bias mentioned here will be further explored and discussed in Sect. 6.6.

6.5 Interprofessional Training

The present professional training in the TCM department was considered as a barrier to sharing patient knowledge with WM professionals, for two reasons. Firstly, the existing professional training strategy does not include any programmes and sessions focusing on the overlapping areas of TCM and WM, and thus cannot establish and develop a sufficient interprofessional common ground to enable and motivate interprofessional communication. Secondly, the lack of management support for the TCM department and the management bias against the TCM community, as discussed in this section, reinforce the professional boundaries, further distance the two medical communities, strengthen philosophical and professional tensions between the TCM and WM medical communities, and prevent individual professionals from actively and spontaneously sharing patient knowledge with each other.

6.5.1.3 Lack of Political Emphasis on Interprofessional Training

> In the 1970s and 1980s, there was a professional training strategy demanding that WM doctors learn TCM. Some of these people became very good and even leading doctors in some areas. This strategy, of course, was made mandatory by the central government. Interview WMD 8.27

As shown in the quotation above, in the 1970s and 1980s, there were "clear government requirements on TCM and WM mutual learning" (Interview WMN 10.51). However, nowadays, "the central government no longer require this [mutual learning] anymore" (Interview WMD 12.28), and hence activities of interprofessional learning are probably considered as not important by both hospital management and individual healthcare professionals.

> In the 1970s and 1980s, there was clear emphasis on the mutual learning. Now, gradually, there is no such emphasis anymore. Therefore, fewer and fewer people [WM doctors] know TCM. Interview WMD 2.47

Consequently, the lack of political emphasis emerged as a KS barrier, as there is a lack of effective governmental policies to regulate and encourage mutual learning aimed at increasing mutual understanding, building trust in each other's community, and stimulating interprofessional collaboration, communication and KS. Moreover, and specifically, the practice of coding identified two sets of KS barriers, one related to the neurosurgery department and the other to the TCM department. Therefore, the following two Sects. 6.5.2 and 6.5.3, discuss these KS barriers in both departments.

6.5.2 *Absence of Interprofessional Training in Neurosurgery Department*

This section discusses the absence of interprofessional training in the department of neurosurgery. This sub-category consists of four KS barriers, as shown in Fig. 6.13:

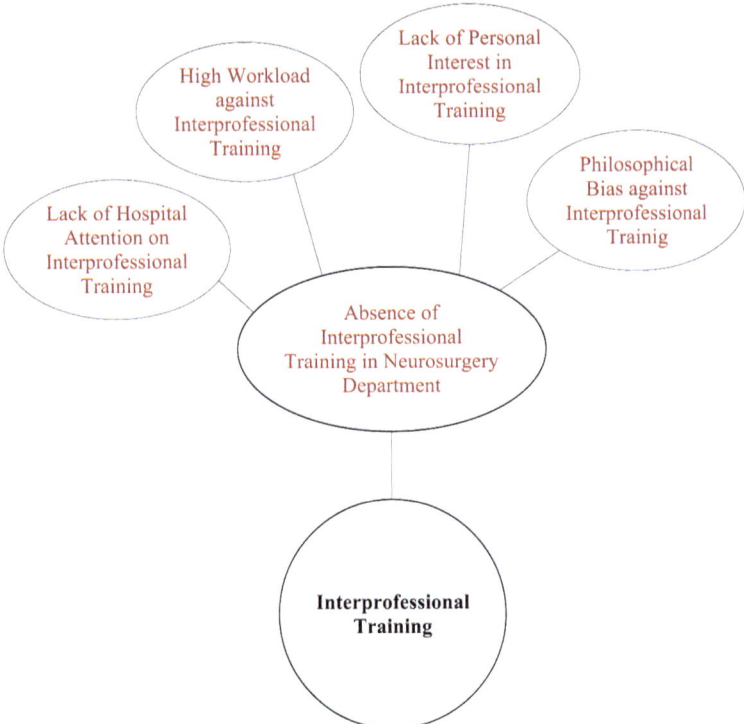

Fig. 6.13 Concept map for absence of interprofessional training in the neurosurgery department

This section discusses four KS barriers: philosophical bias against interprofessional training, lack of personal interest in interprofessional training, high workload against interprofessional training, and lack of hospital attention on interprofessional training.

6.5.2.1 Philosophical Bias Against Interprofessional Training

> There should be some learning strategies [about TCM]. But currently, in our hospital, TCM is in a secondary position. It is not in a leading position. Usually, it only shows up when we need it. Interview WMD 8.53

As stated by many interviewed neurosurgical practitioners, for instance the quotation above, WM professionals consider TCM as inferior and secondary, and therefore they do not want to learn TCM. Also, for instance, a TCM doctor stated:

> There are some WM practitioners who are interested in TCM and want to learn TCM. But some WM practitioners, I can say the majority of WM practitioners, think TCM is unscientific. Then, what is the point of learning TCM? Interview TCM 15.57

6.5 Interprofessional Training

Therefore, the philosophical bias against TCM prevents interprofessional learning and thus was considered as a barrier to sharing patient knowledge. This barrier not only prevents interprofessional training from being used as an approach to establish interprofessional common ground, but also strengthens philosophical conflicts and professional tensions, which could also hinder processes of KS.

Moreover, as shown in the previous quotation (Interview TCM 15.57), learning TCM is related to personal interest, which is discussed in the next Sect. (6.5.2.2).

6.5.2.2 Lack of Personal Interest in Interprofessional Training

> I think after my graduation from university, I haven't learnt any TCM. I think this is related to my personal attitude to accumulating medical knowledge. Interview WMD 11.37
> I think how much you know about TCM is related to personal interests. Interview WMD 39.27

A number of neurosurgical interview participants claimed that, as for instance in the two quotations above, learning TCM largely relies on the WM professional's personal interest in TCM.

> TCM is based upon thousand years of development. It can't easily be excluded. My understanding about TCM was formulated when I was young, as I was raised in this way. Naturally and unintentionally, we pass on this understanding to our children. This chain is unstoppable. Interview WMD 2.101

Some interviewed neurosurgical practitioners explained that personal interest in TCM is related to personal experience and family background. Moreover, several practitioners added that the personal interest is linked with "the living and working environment" (Interview WMD 48.35).

However, WM professionals are usually not really interested in learning TCM. Thus, due to a lack of personal interest, individual WM professionals are not motivated either to learn TCM or to interact with TCM professionals. Moreover, because of a lack of TCM learning, WM professionals usually do not have sufficient interprofessional common ground to enable and facilitate interprofessional communication and KS. Therefore, the lack of personal interest in interprofessional training was identified as a KS barrier.

6.5.2.3 High Workload against Interprofessional Training

As discussed in Sect. 6.3.2.5, neurosurgeons and nurses are suffering from overwhelmingly high workloads, which prevent them from necessary interprofessional communication and active KS. In addition, some interviewed neurosurgical professionals asserted that these extremely high workloads prevent them from participating in programmes and activities of interprofessional training; for example, two of them noted:

> We have limited TCM knowledge, because our workload is too high. Interview WMN 7.144
>
> It is already very difficult for us to learn neurosurgical knowledge. Interview WMN 32.19

As reflected in the above two quotations, neurosurgical practitioners are most likely to focus on learning WM methods and techniques, which could be immediately used in their daily work. In this case, interprofessional learning focusing on overlapping areas is most likely to be neglected.

Consequently, the high workload against interprofessional training emerged as a barrier to KS. This barrier prevents the establishment of an appropriate interprofessional common ground and hinders the sharing of patient knowledge between neurosurgical and TCM healthcare professionals.

6.5.2.4 Lack of Hospital Attention on Interprofessional Training

In addition, many interviewed neurosurgical interviewees pointed out that there are no explicit hospital requirements demanding interprofessional training. Thus, interprofessional learning could be seen as unimportant and unnecessary. For example, two of the interviewed neurosurgeons claimed:

> We have many training activities. But WM practitioners only learn WM. There is no requirement for WM practitioners to learn TCM. We are only required to learn professional knowledge in our subject. Interview WMD 19.06
>
> In our hospital, TCM is just TCM, and WM is just WM. The hospital does not have any requirement on mutual learning. Interview WMD 26.39

As reflected in the quotations above, the lack of hospital attention to interprofessional training is a barrier to KS. It was identified that, due to a lack of hospital attention, WM professionals are insufficiently motivated towards interprofessional learning and thus have very limited interprofessional common ground for sharing patient knowledge with TCM doctors. On the other hand, it is perceived that WM professionals could be better motivated if explicit requirements and systematic interprofessional training strategies can be effectively established by the hospital management.

6.5.3 Absence of Interprofessional Training in TCM Department

This section discusses the final sub-category, namely, the absence of interprofessional training in the TCM department. This sub-category consists of two KS barriers as shown in Fig. 6.14. These KS barriers are management bias prevents interprofessional training and career progression difficulty prevents professional training.

6.5 Interprofessional Training

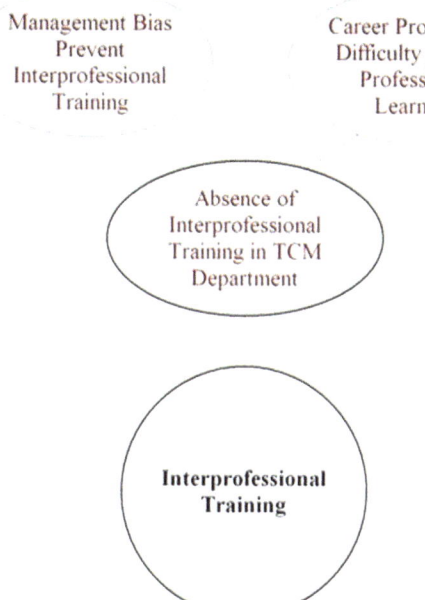

Fig. 6.14 Concept map for absence of interprofessional training in TCM department

6.5.3.1 Management Bias Prevents Interprofessional Training

> In terms of professional training, WM doctors are very dedicated. For us, it is not as good as for them, because there is no supervision. So just forget about it. Interview TCM 16.49

As shown in the quotation above, due to a management bias against the TCM department, all professional training activities are probably not very well implemented in this department. It is also reflected in the above quotation that TCM professionals are not motivated towards interprofessional training.

> WM doctors usually give lectures, for us TCM doctors, if we are interested we can go and listen. But it is not mandatory for us to be there. They [WM doctors] have many training schedules every week. We don't have any. Because we are considered not important [by the hospital management], since we cannot make a lot of profit. The entire hospital has been re-decorated, apart from our department. Interview TCM 16.51

As mentioned by a TCM doctor in the quotation above, the lack of motivation could not only be due to management biases, since TCM doctors are "considered as not important", but also be caused by the professional tensions between TCM and WM professionals.

Consequently, the management bias prevents TCM doctors from participating in activities of WM learning, so they have very limited interprofessional common ground to enable and to facilitate activities of interprofessional communication and KS. Moreover, the management bias enhances professional tensions and uncooperative relationships, which result in unwillingness to collaborate and communicate with WM professionals.

6.5.3.2 Career Progression Difficulty Prevents Professional Training

In addition to the management bias, the data gathered revealed a career progression difficulty, which prevents individual TCM professionals from participating in professional training programmes and sessions.

As discussed in Sect. 6.5.1.1, for individual healthcare professionals, their participation in professional training is evaluated by a year-end performance assessment, which is recorded and assessed in their career progression. However, several interviewed TCM practitioners claimed that "[there is] no need for professional training, [because we] cannot be promoted anyway" (Interview TCM 18.27). A very meaningful statement was provided by an interviewed TCM doctor:

> They [hospital management] do not let us, who graduated from a TCM technical secondary school, to get promoted. They put this limitation for us. Therefore, no one really try to make an effort [in professional training]. Interview TCM 16.53

Moreover, according to the quotation above, it became clear that the career progression difficulty for TCM doctors is related to the hospital management biases against the TCM department, which will be discussed in more detail in Sect. 6.6.1.3.

The career progression difficulty emerged as a KS barrier, since it demotivates TCM professionals from learning WM, constrains the development of interprofessional common ground for TCM doctors, and enhances professional tensions between TCM and WM medical communities.

6.5.4 Section Summary

This section discusses one of the main categories emerged from the comparative analysis, namely, the interprofessional training issues. Specifically, this section presents and discusses KS barriers relating to three sub-categories: existing professional training structure, absence of interprofessional training in the neurosurgery department, and absence of interprofessional training in the TCM department.

According to the discussion in this section, the existing professional training programmes are unable to establish an appropriate interprofessional common ground. In this way, TCM and WM professionals are not enabled, encouraged or motivated towards interprofessional communication and sharing patient knowledge.

Moreover, as discussed in this section, the existing professional training programmes reinforce the professional boundaries, enhance philosophical conflicts and strengthen philosophical tensions between the two medical communities. It is also reflected in the discussion that the existing professional training strategies augment imbalances of professional standing and power, reflect management bias in favour of WM departments, and reinforce philosophical and professional tensions, both of which could prevent processes of interprofessional communication and hinder the sharing of patient knowledge.

Moreover, the interprofessional training issues, as one of the main categories, interact with the categories of contextual issues, Chinese healthcare education, and philosophical issues. Furthermore, as reflected in the discussion in this section, the interprofessional training issues are closely related to hospital management and management strategies. The next Sect. (6.6) discusses KS barriers relating to hospital management.

6.6 Hospital Management

This section presents and discusses KS barriers relating to the final category, namely, hospital management. These barriers to sharing patient knowledge emerged from the data gathered and show that the management of this hospital has established management strategies and developed a hospital environment which are not conducive to and can even hinder the processes of sharing patient knowledge. The final construct for this category is shown in Fig. 6.15.

Specifically, and as shown in the concept map, this category of hospital management consists of two sub-categories: management bias against TCM and external influences on hospital management.

6.6.1 Management Bias Against TCM

The operation of open coding identified some areas in which the hospital management is biased against TCM and its practitioners, limiting their influence and power in the hospital environment. These biases were identified as barriers to communication and sharing patient knowledge between TCM and WM healthcare professionals. These barriers are shown in Fig. 6.16.

This section discusses six biases/barriers: management's philosophical bias against TCM, management financial bias against TCM, career progression inequality, recruitment inequality, investment inequality, and decrease of the TCM department.

6.6.1.1 Management Philosophical Bias Against TCM

In an interview with one of the hospital managers, he explicitly stated:

> In terms of the development of each department, we [hospital management] do not specifically support or discriminate against any departments. Interview WMD 1.28

This statement clearly claims that the hospital management treats all medical departments equally, with no preferences or biases, including the TCM department. Nevertheless, along with more in-depth discussion, this manager stated:

> It is entirely decided by the hospital manager's decision on how to develop the hospital, which can either be developed in a WM and TCM collaborative way, or depend on WM

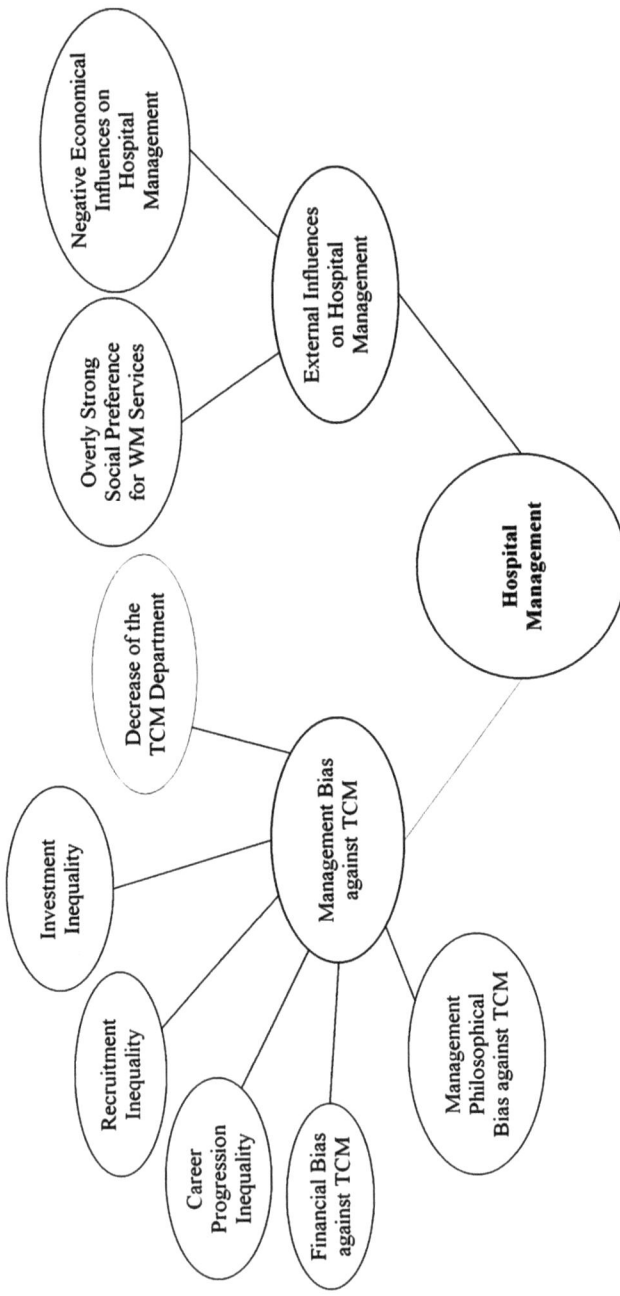

Fig. 6.15 : Concept map for hospital management

6.6 Hospital Management

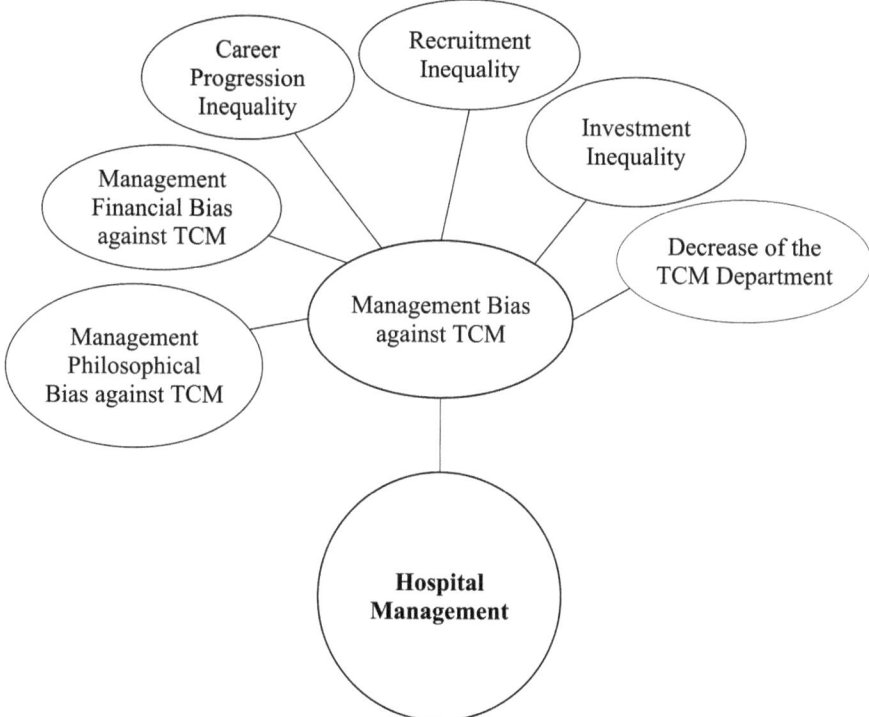

Fig. 6.16 Concept map for management bias against TCM

alone. We decided to develop the hospital in the WM way. So we do not support the TCM Department very much. Interview WMD 1.36

In fact, from the above quotation it became clear that managers in this hospital have decided to follow a "WM way", instead of relying on the collaboration of TCM and WM. In this case, the TCM department and professionals could be considered as not important and thus always receive less management support.

Many interviewed neurosurgical professionals also stated that TCM is less well supported by the hospital management. For instance, a neurosurgical nurse stated:

In our hospital, WM is taking the primary position, TCM is complementary. Everyone does not have enough understanding on TCM philosophy. Subconsciously, we think the TCM department is secondary. There are even some people who think this department may not be needed. […] It is decided by the high-up hospital management. There are some hospitals that I know of, and our hospital, which almost give up on the TCM Department. Interview WMN 14.15

As shown in this quotation, there is a strong management bias against the TCM department, since it is "complementary" (Interview WMD 23.17), in a "secondary" (Interview WMD 23.17) position, and thus almost given up by the hospital management.

More importantly, many TCM interviewees claimed that the TCM department is less well supported, probably because those managers do not really know the value of TCM.

> Support for TCM was mainly dependent on the hospital managers' understanding of TCM. Interview TCM 4.61

The hospital management may not have a good understanding of TCM. Therefore, they are most likely to give more support to the WM departments, which they can understand better and which they consider as more important. Furthermore, some TCM doctors claimed that the TCM department could be better supported if hospital managers have a better understanding of TCM.

In addition, a very interesting fact which should be noted here is that, according to the hospital website, all hospital managers are also WM healthcare professionals. Therefore, these managers/WM practitioners could consider that WM is superior to TCM and thus should receive more support.

Summarising the discussion above, a clear philosophical bias by management against TCM was revealed in data. This management bias could reinforce the dominant position of WM professionals, augment imbalances of power and professional standing between TCM and WM healthcare professionals, strengthen philosophical and professional tensions between the two types of healthcare professionals, and hence prevent active and spontaneous interprofessional communication and KS.

6.6.1.2 Financial Bias Against TCM

In addition to the philosophical bias discussed in Sect. 5.6.1.1, a number of interview participants repeatedly asserted that WM departments usually receive more management support, because they are more profitable than the TCM department.

> Hospital management would support those departments that can make a lot of profit. The hospital management would not support a WM department either, if it is not profitable. In terms of the TCM department, the hospital management neither say that TCM is scientific, nor say that TCM is not scientific. They also wouldn't say they are going to abolish the TCM department. They just do not provide any support, just let it be. Interview TCM 4.61

As shown in the above quotation, hospital management only support those medical departments, mostly in WM, which can make considerable financial profits. Therefore, because the TCM department is not a profitable medical department, it probably is unfairly treated and considered as less important and hence it is less well supported.

> Our hospital is currently operated under the Market Economy. Our [TCM] department is certainly operated under the Market Economy as well. […] The departmental income for us is kind of embarrassing for us. We are below the hospital average, although we have a very high workload. But we are less profitable, when compared with surgical departments or internal medicine departments. It is an undeniable truth, we can do nothing about it. Interview TCM 5.34

6.6 Hospital Management

As discussed in Sect. 6.2, the hospital management decisions and strategies are strongly influenced by the MEP. As explained and discussed in Sect. 6.2.1.3, the central government no longer gives financial support to all hospitals, as dictated by the implementation of MEP. Therefore, for hospital managers, it is more important to maximise the hospital's financial income and to increase profitability than to improve the quality of health services. Therefore, the TCM department is always "marginalised" (Interview TCM 15.17) and "discriminated" against (Interview TCM 4.63) by the hospital management.

The management's financial bias limits the power of TCM professionals in hospitals and has developed a pessimistic atmosphere among these practitioners. Therefore, TCM professionals are unlikely to actively communicate and spontaneously share knowledge with professionals of WM. On the other hand, the financial bias strengthens the WM dominance and enhances the power and standing of its professionals. Therefore, these WM professionals also would not voluntarily communicate and share knowledge with TCM practitioners, who are inferior in status, less powerful, and almost unable to survive in the competition between TCM and WM.

6.6.1.3 Career Progression Inequality

> I am a victim. I finished my TCM study and training in 1977. Since then, I have been practising TCM for all my life. But after all these years of hard work, I only have a middle level title because I don't have a bachelor degree. Interview TCM 21.21

When collecting data in the field, four out of seven TCM interviewees (the total number of TCM practitioners in this hospital) mentioned the difficulty of getting promoted. These TCM doctors had very similar characteristics in that they were aged approximately 50–60, graduated from TCM technical secondary school during the 1970s and 1980s and were very experienced in practising TCM. Moreover, it was observed that they were actually taking important positions in the provision of TCM services to patients.

> They would not let us, who graduated from TCM technical secondary schools, to get promoted. We are middle level titles now. They are restraining technical secondary school graduates from getting promotion. [...] Career progression is according to your graduation certificates; for example, one who has a bachelor degree can be promoted to a full professorship; one who has a college certificate can get an assistant professorship. They do not allow us to get promoted. Interview TCM 16.53

These TCM doctors may be well trained and very experienced after decades of practice, they find it very difficult to get promoted, because they do not have university degrees. As shown in the above quotation, this career progression difficulty has undeniably developed a pessimistic atmosphere among TCM doctors. A few TCM informants even explicitly expressed their resentment toward the hospital management.

It is worthwhile mentioning that, when being interviewed and discussing career progression issues, a TCM doctor stated that "career progression for TCM doctors is much slower [than for WM professionals], do not ask me why, and I do not want to say" (Interview TCM 5.25). After a little while, he requested the researchers to stop the digital recording. Then he started to complain about the unfair career progression and the hospital management, using some very strong language.

Therefore, the imbalance of career progressions causes resentment towards the hospital management among TCM practitioners. It is also pointed out that the imbalance augments the imbalances in the professional standing and power possessed by the two types of practitioners, reinforces the philosophical and professional tensions, and thus prevents the necessary exchange of patient knowledge when providing collaborative patient care.

However, very interestingly, one of the hospital managers, who participated this study, claimed that career progression is equal for all TCM and WM professionals.

> In terms of career progression, WM and TCM doctors are equal. Interview WMD 1.15

According to the comparative analysis applied on the data gathered, this statement is factually untrue, and this hospital manager was trying to protect his own *face*.

6.6.1.4 Recruitment Inequality

In addition to the career progression inequality, the data collected showed a recruitment inequality. For instance, an interviewed TCM practitioner asserted:

> The hospital management does not take TCM seriously. For example, it seems our hospital only recruits WM practitioners. We only had one new TCM postgraduate graduate [in recent years]. Interview TCM 17.85

As shown in the above quotation, since the hospital management does not consider the TCM department as an important one, managers focus more on recruiting new WM professionals.

Very similarly, the recruitment inequality was also reflected in several interviews with neurosurgical professionals; for example, a neurosurgeon stated:

> Our hospital needs development. Therefore, we only recruit WM professionals and the TCM community looks like it is moving backward. Interview WMD 23.15

As indicated in the above quotation, whilst the TCM community is declining, the community of WM is expanding rapidly. Thus, TCM professionals have considerably lower professional standing and much less power, receive less management attention and support, and almost cannot survive in a hospital environment dominated by an enormously large WM community. These imbalances enhance the philosophical and professional tensions and conflicts, and hinder the processes of sharing patient knowledge between the two types of practitioners.

6.6.1.5 Investment Inequality

Furthermore, the hospital management provides unequal investment in the TCM and WM departments. According to a number of interview participants, the neurosurgery department is one of the most profitable departments in this hospital. Therefore, the hospital management provides significant financial support to this department.

> I am not sure exactly how much income our department can make annually. But among all departments, we are in the top three." Interview WMD 26.9

> "Financially, the hospital is very supportive on the development of our department. We have just purchased a surgical microscope which costs over one million yuan [Chinese currency]. Interview WMD 2.58

When compared to the generous investment in the neurosurgery department, as discussed in the above quotation, the TCM department receives very little financial support from the hospital management. For instance, a TCM doctor stated:

> The income for our department is very low. In this case, the hospital management does not allow us to use more resources and purchase new equipment. The hospital definitely would not support us. Interview TCM 4.27

As reflected in the above quotation, the lack of financial support could be because of the management's financial bias against TCM, which has been discussed in Sect. 6.6.1.2.

The investment inequality was identified as a KS barrier, as it constrains the development of the TCM department and limits the power held by TCM professionals. This investment inequality compounds with the career progression inequality and the recruitment inequality, further strengthens the philosophical and professional tensions, causes uncooperative and competitive relationships between the two medical communities, and thus results in unwillingness to communicate and share patient knowledge.

6.6.1.6 Decrease of TCM Department

The present TCM community is a very small one in this hospital. For instance, a TCM doctor stated:

> TCM is a very small community. There are more than 300 doctors in our hospital. But there are only seven TCM doctors. We (TCM Department) are a rather small department. Interview TCM 4.30

As further pointed out by TCM interviewees, this very small community has been decreasing. This issue was discussed by some interviewed healthcare professionals. For instance, a TCM doctor and a neurosurgeon stated:

> The number of TCM doctors is actually decreasing. At present, we have seven doctors. Dr. [doctor name] and I are going to retire in the next year. We used to have a number of doctors, but some of them right now are practising WM. Interview TCM 3.30

> As soon as some TCM practitioners realise that they do not have a good future by practising TCM, they drop their career in TCM for some other more profitable business. Interview WMD 20.30

Many TCM doctors have quitted their career in TCM, because they do not have "satisfying personal income" (Interview TCM 15.43) and "valuable social standing" (Interview WMD 24.34), and probably because they face philosophical and financial biases and unequal treatments from the hospital management. As pointed out by a TCM interviewee, some of her colleagues are moving to "some other more profitable business" (Interview TCM 16.30).

> Some of my old colleagues decided not to practise TCM anymore. [For instance] Doctor [name] is a cosmetic surgeon now. It is a much more profitable business. Interview TCM 16.21

It is worthwhile to note that the researchers personally witnessed a reduction of the TCM community in this hospital. In the pilot study, there were seven TCM doctors working in the hospital. In the main study, the number had decreased to five, because two senior doctors had retired. In the follow-up study, the researchers were informed that the head of the TCM department (who was interviewed in the main study) had resigned his position and moved to another hospital in a different region (far away from Hubei) where the TCM profession is probably better paid and better supported by the hospital management.

The reduction of the TCM department was considered as a barrier to KS, as it reinforces the dominant position and power possessed by WM professionals, further exaggerates the imbalances in professional standings and power, strengthens the philosophical and professional tensions. Due to this barrier, interprofessional communication and the sharing of patient knowledge between TCM and WM professionals could be very difficult. For WM professionals, as a strong and very powerful community, they are probably unwilling to interact with TCM doctors, who are much less powerful, have lower standing and can barely survive in the hospital environment. On the other side, TCM professionals are not motivated to communicate and share knowledge with the more powerful WM professionals. For them, they are most likely to remain a passive position in TCM and WM collaboration, follow the instruction of WM professionals, and avoid direct confrontations.

6.6.2 *External Influences on Hospital Management*

From the statements provided by many informants, it was identified that the hospital management is influenced by the external social, political and economic environments, as shown in Fig. 6.17.

Two external influences are identified as KS barriers, namely, overly strong social preference for WM services and negative economic influences on hospital management. These two barriers are discussed in the following two Sects. 6.6.2.1 and 6.6.2.2.

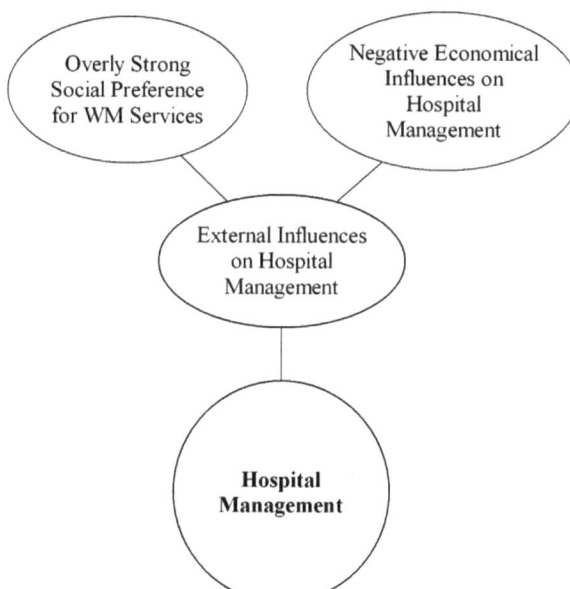

Fig. 6.17 : Concept map for external influences on hospital management

6.6.2.1 Overly Strong Social Preference for WM Services

Many statements from the interviewed healthcare professionals revealed a very strong social preference for WM services.

> Currently, in our hospital, the demand for TCM services [from patients] is significantly lower than the demand for WM. [The hospital] mainly relies on WM services. Interview WMD 20.13

> Patients have two choices, TCM or WM. Patients can come to the TCM Department directly. But the majority of them choose WM specialists and receive some basic WM treatments. After that, WM specialists may suggest to them to use some TCM treatments. We are at the receiving end. Interview TCM 15.69

Patients usually choose WM as their preferred approach. It was identified in data that this preference could be related to the social preference for WM, which is discussed in Sect. 6.2.3.1. It was also identified that the demand for WM services is much higher than for TCM.

When discussing this issue with the interviewed hospital manager, he pointed out that management strategies have been adjusted in accordance with the high demand for WM services.

> In our hospital, we are mainly WM oriented, which means we have very strong WM teams. TCM is only a partial complementary. Patients come to our hospital mainly for WM treatments. Therefore, in order to respond to the patients' needs, we need to continuously improve our WM service quality. Interview WMD 1.18

Therefore, hospital management needs to provide more support and more attention to those WM departments. Conversely, the TCM department receive less support and could be considered as less important.

Therefore, the social preference for WM services was identified as a barrier to sharing patient knowledge. As reflected in the discussion above, this barrier causes unequal hospital support to TCM and WM departments. This barrier could encourage competition between TCM and WM communities, reinforce the philosophical and professional tensions, demotivate both types of healthcare professional from active interprofessional collaboration and communication, and hinder the exchange of patient knowledge.

6.6.2.2 Negative Economical Influences on Hospital Management

As discussed in Sect. 6.6.1.2, the TCM department receives much less management support, because this department is considered as "less profitable" (Interview TCM 37.39). Many interviewed healthcare professionals further stated that this management issue is not only related to the implementation of MEP (as discussed in Sect. 6.2.1.3), but also caused by the external economic environment. For instance, the interviewed TCM educator stated:

> [...] it is related to the [national] economic policies and environment. Nowadays, profitability to a medical department [in hospitals] is very important. [...] Every department has an annual financial requirement [initiated by hospital management], which is related to not only the department, but also individual practitioners. TCM [medicine and treatments] is very cheap, therefore they [TCM doctors] usually cannot achieve this financial requirement. Interview TCM Educator 47.31

According to the above quotation, the hospital management and the hospital's internal environment are strongly influenced by the external economic environment. The data collected reflected that the management team probably has established strategies aimed at adapting the hospital's internal environment to the external environment.

However, as has been seen, these management strategies reinforce the philosophical and professional tensions between the TCM and WM professionals, alienate the two professional communities, and thus create problems for communication and the sharing of patient knowledge.

6.6.3 Section Summary

This section discusses the hospital management issues which emerged as one of the main categories. More specifically, this section discusses KS barriers relating to two sub-categories: management bias against TCM and external influences on hospital management.

According to the discussion, some existing strategies established and implemented by the hospital management have caused imbalances and inequalities between TCM and WM departments and their professionals. These management inequalities were identified as barriers to sharing patient knowledge, since they enhance the imbalances in the professional standing and power possessed by the two types of healthcare professionals, reinforce the professional boundary, and exacerbate the philosophical and professional tensions and conflicts between TCM and WM medical communities.

Also, it is reflected in the discussion in this section that the hospital's internal environment interacts with the external social, economic and political environments. These internal/external interactions have also resulted in problems for interprofessional communication and the sharing of patient knowledge between TCM and WM professionals. Moreover, the hospital management has initiated strategies aimed at adapting the internal environment in line with changes that have occurred in the external environments. As shown in the discussion, these hospital strategies may not always permit and encourage interprofessional communication, and in fact have reinforced the philosophical and professional tensions, preventing the sharing of patient knowledge.

Finally, at the end of this chapter, it is also important to conclude the discussion. This chapter presents the research findings and discusses individual barriers to KS. The discussion is conducted around the five main categories, namely, contextual influences, philosophical issues, Chinese healthcare education, interprofessional training, and hospital management. Finally, the discussion conducted in this chapter will be conceptualised and theorised into the final theory in Chap. 7.

Chapter 7
Discussion

Chapter 6 presented the research findings and discussed identified barriers to sharing patient knowledge between TCM and WM healthcare professionals. This chapter conceptualises the research findings and presents an integrated model of the final theory. Furthermore, this chapter compares the emerging model with existing KS models, elicits the implications of findings for the reality of practice and contributes to the body of knowledge in the field.

To be more specific, this chapter consists of four main sections: integration of findings, comparison with existing models, implications of findings for the reality of practice, and contribution of findings to the body of knowledge in the field.

7.1 Integration of Findings

As the result of data analysis, five main categories are saturated: contextual issues, philosophical issues, Chinese healthcare education, interprofessional training and hospital management. As emerged from the data, these five categories are mutually influential and merged into a final theory, which is shown in Fig. 7.1.

The diagram is separated into two parts, the hospital external environment and internal environment. The external environment includes Chinese healthcare education and contextual influences from the political, economic and social environments. The categories of interprofessional training and hospital management are categorised in the hospital internal environment.

Two types of arrow are shown the diagram, single-headed and double-headed arrows. Single-headed arrows represent unidirectional single relationships between categories. For instance, as discussed in Sect. 6.5, the category of hospital management can strongly influence the category of interprofessional training; however, the interprofessional training cannot affect hospital management decisions and strategies. Therefore, a single-headed arrow is used to link the two categories, from the hospital management to the interprofessional training. Double-headed arrows represent mutual and bi-directional relationships between categories. For example, the

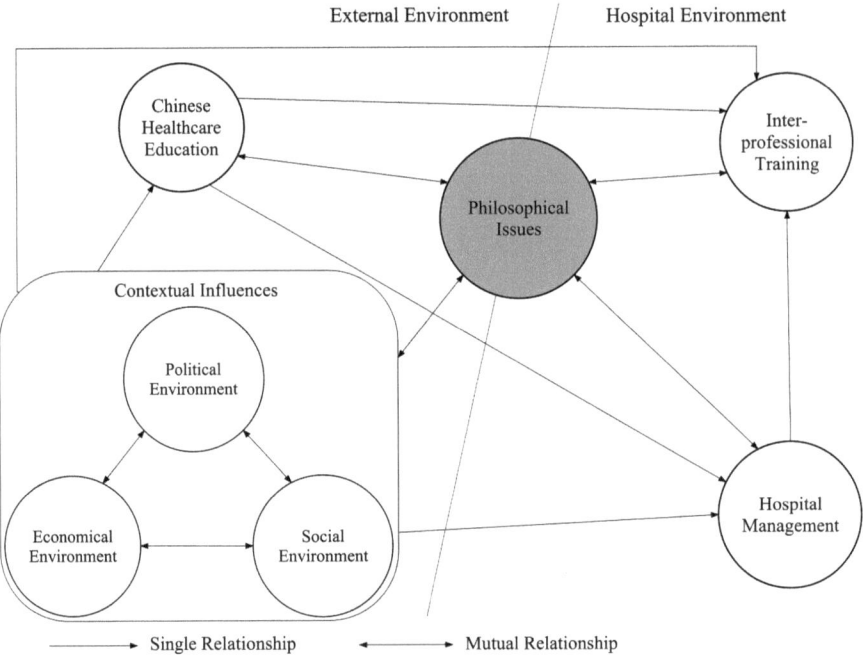

Fig. 7.1 Integrated model of research findings

categories of philosophical issues and interprofessional training are connected by a double-headed arrow, which means that the two categories mutually influence and reinforce each other.

Moreover, the category of philosophical issues was identified as the core category mutually connecting all other categories, and is placed at the centre of the diagram right over the external/internal boundary. The philosophical issues point to significant divergences of TCM and WM medical philosophies, conceptual systems and methodologies. These divergences result in philosophical and professional tensions between TCM and WM healthcare professionals. These two types of tensions emerged as the main barriers hindering communication and the sharing of patient knowledge between the two professional groups.

7.1.1 Philosophical Tensions

The research findings reveal that TCM and WM healthcare professionals showed a consistent lack of belief in each other's practices. Attitudes range from respectful disbelief to entire disregard of the other's role in the healthcare system. This latter attitude is more evident in WM practitioners, who often harshly criticise TCM beliefs and methodology, finding it useless "superstition" (Interview WMD 6.44) based exclusively on "personal experiences instead of scientific evidences" (Interview

7.1 Integration of Findings 159

WMD 2.96), which "lacks a scientific foundation" (Interview WMD 2.101). As asserted by many of the neurosurgical interviewees, WM is seen as purely scientific in its methodology and "superior" (Interview WMN 14.15) to TCM.

Conversely, many TCM doctors defended that their methodology is not only a "solid medical methodology" (Interview TCM 4.9), which consists of a systematic and consistent set of diagnostic and treatment methods, but also one which has a credibility and an understanding of the human body that has been revised through an evolution of thousands of years. Consequently, many TCM interviewees disagree with some of the WM beliefs and methods, which they find are not always appropriate and sometimes have adverse effects on patients' well-being.

The philosophical tensions are generated by a significant philosophical divergence between TCM and WM. This philosophical divergence leads to severe difficulties in understanding each other's diagnosis, clashes in indications for treatment, difficulties in interpreting requirements for complementarity of treatments and difficulties in understanding interpretations of patients' problems.

Also, as shown in the research findings, the philosophical tensions are caused by a lack of interprofessional common ground to facilitate communication and KS. This interprofessional common ground could be conceptualised as a knowledge base of overlapping interests and mutual conceptual understandings. The lack of interprofessional common ground exacerbates the philosophical divergence and results in conflicting understandings of patient symptoms and conditions.

As pointed out in the data analysis, the lack of interprofessional common ground is caused by the very limited number of interprofessional courses, lectures, and practical sessions in Chinese healthcare education which concentrate on the possible overlap of the healthcare systems. In this case, students from either system had very limited mutual knowledge and interprofessional common ground, and, more importantly, lacked motivation for interprofessional collaboration and communication.

In addition to the insufficient interprofessional teaching in the Chinese healthcare education system, the research also clearly identified a significant absence of interprofessional training schemes, sessions and programmes within the hospital environment to build understandings between the two professional communities and to develop an appropriate interprofessional common ground.

7.1.2 Professional Tensions

In addition to the philosophical tensions, the research findings illustrate professional tensions which result from substantial inequalities of power and status between TCM and WM healthcare professionals.

The research findings reveal that neurosurgeons have a higher professional standing and have almost dominant power over patients. Therefore, they often explicit instruct and regulate TCM doctors in what to do about the patient. In contrast, TCM doctors have a lower professional standing and hold less power. Therefore, TCM doctors are most likely to maintain a passive position, avoid any confrontations, and follow instructions, instead of actively, spontaneously, and voluntarily proposing their understandings and treatment suggestions. For them, even if they intend to share knowledge, they probably have very limited opportunities to do so and very little power to have their views recognised.

Therefore, professional tensions prevent KS, not only because these tensions reinforce the professional boundary and distance, but also because they create a hostile relationship between the two professional communities.

Moreover, the professional tensions are exaggerated and strengthened by the hospital management. It was shown that the hospital management provides evidently unequal managerial support to TCM and the neurosurgical department, has a philosophical bias against TCM and a financial bias against the TCM department.

Furthermore, the research findings show that management attitudes and hospital strategies are framed, influenced and constrained by the external political, economic and social environments. The data analysis identified evidence indicating that WM is preferred by patients, and thus WM professionals have a higher social standing in the current Chinese society. In comparison, TCM doctors are less respected and have lower social standing. This hospital external environment reinforces the professional tensions and results in competition and even resentment between TCM and WM professional teams in the hospital environment.

7.2 Comparison with Existing Models

After the emergence of the final theory, this section compares the emerging theory with KS models in the existing body of literature. This is the final process of Grounded Theory, as advocated by Strauss and Corbin (1998, p. 51): "The literature can be used to confirm findings and, just the reverse, findings can be used to illustrate where the literature is incorrect, is overly simplistic, or only partially explains phenomena."

Therefore, this section focuses on the comparison and discussion of models. Specifically, it discusses five models in two parts.

In the first part (Sect. 7.2.1), the integrated model is compared with the model of knowledge flow barriers developed by Lin et al. (2008), and Hall (2005)'s model for interprofessional teams. The discussion in this section is very detailed, since Lin et al. (2008) focus on KS in healthcare and Hall (2005) investigates healthcare interprofessional collaboration. Both issues are related to this study.

Discussion in the second part (Sect. 7.2.2) is relatively generic and less detailed. The emerging model is generally verified by comparing it to three existing models, namely, Lodhi (2005)'s culturally based KS model, the model of critical factors in KS proposed by Supar et al. (2005), and Ismail and Yusof (2008)'s KS model for public organisations.

7.2.1 Detailed Model Comparison

This section compares and discusses two models in detail. Firstly, Lin et al. (2008)'s model of knowledge flow barriers is discussed. This is the most comprehensive KS

7.2 Comparison with Existing Models   161

model identified by an extensive search of literature; it was systematically developed in a healthcare environment and social context very similar to China. Secondly, from the perspective of healthcare interprofessional collaboration, this section also compares Hall (2005)'s interprofessional teamwork model with the emerging model.

7.2.1.1 Lin et al. (2008)'s Model of Knowledge Flow Barriers

Lin et al. (2008) have developed a model of knowledge flow barriers on the basis of investigating seven hospitals in Taiwan. It is important to recall that this model has been discussed in Sect. 3.5 and rejected as a theoretical framework to guide data collection and analysis in this study, for two main reasons: (1) Lin et al. (2008)'s model investigates barriers to knowledge flow between homogeneous healthcare professionals; (2) the validity of this model is questioned, since several barriers are vaguely defined, as discussed in Sect. 3.5.

Nevertheless, Lin et al. (2008)'s model has been chosen to be compared with the model developed in this research project, mainly because Lin et al. (2008)'s model is the most comprehensive KS model identified by an extensive search of literature, and was systematically developed in Taiwan, a healthcare environment and social context very similar to mainland China.

In addition, it is necessary to mention that, in contrast to the adoption of GT in this research project, Lin and his colleagues used a very different research approach to develop an inductive exploratory theory. They used a complexity set of human behaviours, cultural historical activity theory (CHAT) and an *a priori* framework to guide their data collection and to frame data analysis. Finally, Lin et al. (2008) developed a framework of KS barriers (as shown in Sect. 3.5) and used a diagram to illustrate relationships between the identified KS barriers, as shown in Fig. 7.2.

Lin et al. (2008)'s model consists of five mutually related main categories: knowledge source barriers, knowledge flow context barriers, knowledge transferred barriers, organisational context barriers, and knowledge receiver barriers. These main categories are discussed in detail and are compared with the findings of this research project.

Knowledge Source Barriers

Lin et al. (2008) assert that KS can be impeded by the fear of losing ownership, the fear of losing privilege and positions of advantage, and the lack of trust toward the knowledge source. Therefore, Lin et al. (2008) propose three knowledge source barriers:

1. The knowledge source wants to maintain his prestige.
2. The knowledge source wants to maintain his competence.
3. The knowledge receiver doubts whether the knowledge is updated.

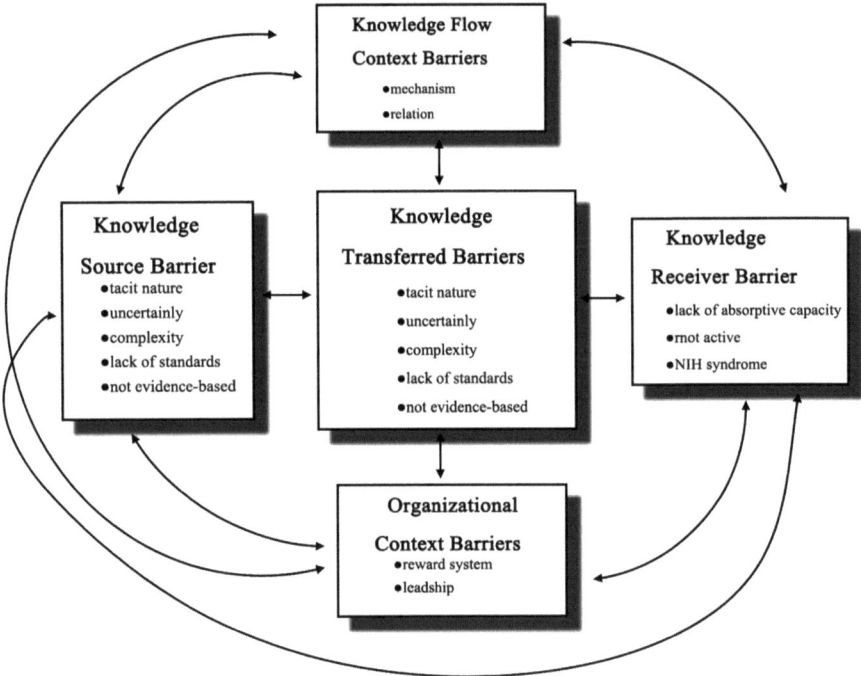

Fig. 7.2 Knowledge flow barriers model developed by Lin et al. (2008, p. 337)

Barriers one and two did not emerge in this research project. However, the third barrier indicates that trust is a critical issue for KS. In this project, the issue of trust emerged as a barrier to KS between TCM and WM healthcare professionals. Specifically, according to the research findings, philosophical and professional conflicts and tensions indicate a severe lack of trust between the two types of healthcare professionals.

Knowledge Receiver Barriers

Lin et al. (2008) identify three knowledge receiver barriers:

1. The knowledge receiver lacks absorptive capacity.

Lin et al. (2008) claim that the knowledge receiver should possess a sufficient knowledge base to assess and process knowledge shared by the knowledge source. This knowledge base is defined as absorptive capacity (Lin et al. 2008).

Very similarly, this research project identified an interprofessional common ground as a knowledge base of overlapping interests and mutual conceptual understandings between TCM and WM practitioners. As shown in the research findings, a lack of interprofessional common ground is a barrier to communication and KS, since it causes philosophical conflicts and reinforces philosophical and professional tensions. The interprofessional common ground is very similar to the absorptive capacity pointed out by Lin et al. (2008).

2. The knowledge receiver lacks a positive attitude.

This issue did not emerge as a KS barrier in this project. Moreover, Lin et al. (2008) fail to define and explain what "a positive attitude" is.

3. The NIH (not-invented-here) syndrome.

Lin et al. (2008) claim that doctors are often too egocentric to accept others' opinions. In this case, they are usually inactive, or even inclined to resist using material from outsiders (Lin et al. 2008). Lin et al. (2008) define this phenomenon as Not-Invented-Here (NIH) syndrome.

The NIH syndrome is not reflected in this study. However, as shown in the research findings, instead of the NIH syndrome, philosophical and professional tensions result in two egocentric medical communities and are considered as barriers to KS.

Knowledge Transferred Barriers

Some characteristics of knowledge (i.e. its tacit nature, uncertainty, complexity and lack of standards, and the fact that it is not evidence-based) become barriers to KS (Lin et al. 2008). More specifically, Lin et al. (2008) identify five KS barriers:

1. It is difficult to concretely express medical knowledge.
2. The uncertain nature of medical knowledge.
3. The complex nature of medical knowledge.
4. It is difficult to standardise medical knowledge.
5. The knowledge lacks evidence.

These KS barriers did not emerge in this study. This is because, unlike Lin et al. (2008)'s model, which focuses on all types of medical knowledge, this research project concentrates on sharing ethical and emotional knowledge and social and behavioural knowledge about individual patients. As explained in Sect. 3.2, both types of patient knowledge are not "difficult to concretely express", or overly "complex" or "uncertain" in nature, as described by Lin et al. (2008).

Knowledge Flow Context Barriers

Lin et al. (2008) assert that the lack of sufficient communication channels can become a barrier to KS. Therefore, Lin et al. (2008) point out five KS barriers:

1. Lack of sufficient mechanisms of knowledge flow.

This barrier is reflected in this research project. In this study, consultation meetings are identified as a communication channel for sharing patient knowledge. As shown in the research findings, these meetings can be considered as a good communication channel, since they allow practitioners from both TCM and WM teams to meet in person and to discuss patients' problems and conditions. Nevertheless, these consultation sessions and meetings are rather insufficient, since these meetings are in fact a formal handover of patients and not a vehicle for the interchange of knowledge and interprofessional communication.

2. Physicians lack time for knowledge flow.

The lack of time is also identified as a barrier to KS between TCM and WM healthcare professionals in this study. The research findings indicate that, due to overwhelmingly high workloads and very tight working schedules, both types of practitioners are very pressed for time and are more likely to deal with patient problems directly, usually without sufficient communication and exchange of knowledge about individual patients.

3. Poor relationships between the knowledge source and knowledge receiver.

Lin et al. (2008) assert that poor personal relationships could prevent knowledge flow. Similarly, in this research project, the philosophical and professional tensions have developed competitive, untrusting, and even resentful relationships between TCM and WM practitioners, and have caused difficulties for KS.

4. Lack of communications between the knowledge source and the knowledge receiver.
5. Knowledge sources/knowledge receiver don't know the other end of the knowledge flow.

The above two barriers are very vaguely defined and particularly confusing. Also, the description and explanation provided by Lin et al. (2008) are very limited. Therefore, it is decided not to discuss these two barriers in this book.

Organisational Context Barriers

Finally, for the category of organisational context barriers, Lin et al. (2008) identify six KS barriers:

1. Lack of a knowledge sharing culture among peers.

The research findings of this project reflect that there is a lack of KS culture in this hospital, for two reasons: (1) the hospital management cannot be considered as giving good KS leadership in establishing a suitable KS culture; (2) there is a lack of specific and strong hospital management requirements on the sharing of patient knowledge.

2. Lack of rewards and incentives toward knowledge flow.

The research findings of this study show that no reward plans and incentive strategies have been implemented for encouraging KS. As indicated by the findings, this is related to the lack of strong KS leadership and sufficient management attention to KS, as discussed above.

7.2 Comparison with Existing Models

3. Lack of performance appraisal concerning knowledge flow.

This research project did not identify any performance appraisal strategies and activities implemented for evaluating processes of sharing patient knowledge. Again, this is related to the lack of management attention to KS.

4. Lack of leadership for promoting knowledge flow.

The lack of leadership emerged as a barrier in this project. As shown in the research findings, the hospital management cannot be considered as giving good KS leadership, not just for failing to promote KS, but also because it has exacerbated conflicts and tensions between TCM and WM medical communities and created extra difficulties for KS.

5. The large distance between the echelons of knowledge sources and receivers.

Even though Lin et al. (2008) provide very limited explanation, it is presumed that "the large echelons of knowledge sources and receivers" refers to the imbalance of professional power and the gap in professional status. In this project, it was found that the imbalances of professional power and standing exacerbate philosophical and professional tensions and have become barriers to KS.

6. Too many medical specialties.

Lin et al. (2008) provide very little explanation of this issue, and, as shown above, definition of this barrier is particularly confusing. Therefore, this barrier is not discussed here.

Summary

Lin et al. (2008)'s model of knowledge flow barriers is different from the KS model developed in this research project. As shown in the discussion above, this could be mainly because Lin et al. (2008) studied KS among homogeneous healthcare professionals, whereas this research investigates KS between TCM and WM professionals, two very different types of healthcare practitioners.

However, the model proposed by Lin et al. (2008) partially verifies the research findings of this study. Moreover, despite differences in research aims, methodologies and findings, to a certain extent the two models complement each other. Also, the research findings of this project can extend Lin et al. (2008)'s model in the dimensions of knowledge source barriers, knowledge receiver barriers, knowledge flow context barriers, and organisational context barriers.

- Knowledge source barriers: As shown in the findings of this project, the lack of motivation is a barrier for KS and can be added to this dimension. The findings show that TCM and WM healthcare professionals are insufficiently motivated to engage in activities of sharing patient knowledge, mainly because of philosophical and professional tensions between the two professional teams, as well as the lack of management support.

- Knowledge receiver barriers: The research findings of this project show that differences in terminology should be considered as a knowledge receiver barrier. As shown in the research findings, TCM and WM healthcare professionals use two completely different terminological systems. The differences in terminology make the interprofessional communication and KS very difficult.
- Knowledge flow context barriers: The research findings show that issues of professional boundaries, conflicting philosophical beliefs and professional tensions can be added to this dimension. Firstly, it was found in this study that a substantial professional boundary separates and distances the TCM and WM professional communities, reinforces philosophical and professional tensions between the two communities and causes problems for KS. Secondly, it was identified that TCM and WM healthcare professionals adopt two completely different and sometimes conflicting medical philosophies. These conflicts in philosophical beliefs and values result in philosophical tensions and become substantial KS barriers. Finally, professional tensions reinforce the professional boundary, increase the distance between the two teams and add extra difficulties for interprofessional communication and KS.
- Organisational context barriers: These should include inequality of management support as a KS barrier. As shown in the findings of this project, the management of this hospital pays more attention and provides stronger managerial support to WM departments, whereas the TCM department is less well supported. According to the findings, unequal managerial support reinforces imbalances of professional standing and power, exacerbates philosophical and professional tensions, and discourages interprofessional communication and KS.

Finally, the research findings of this project indicate that influences from the external political, economic and social environments can be barriers to KS. Therefore, these external influences can also be added to Lin et al. (2008)'s model.

7.2.1.2 Hall (2005)'s Interprofessional Teamwork Model

Hall (2005) proposed a model for interprofessional teamwork in a Canadian healthcare environment. This model encompasses three main dimensions: "do you see what I see", values, and education systems.

"Do you see what I see"

Hall (2005) uses "do you see what I see" to represent different world-views possessed by different healthcare professional groups, who usually have very different experiences, values, problem-solving approaches and professional languages. Hall (2005) claims that these different world-views would result in difficulties for interprofessional collaboration and communication between healthcare professionals. As in this research project, it was found that the divergent world-views adopted by TCM and WM healthcare professionals have caused problems in understanding each other's values, diagnosis and treatment methods, and interpretation of patient problems and needs. These problems make communication and KS extremely difficult.

Values

Hall (2005) asserts that the difference in professional value systems is a barrier to collaboration and communication. Very similarly, as shown in the findings of this research project, TCM and WM healthcare professionals adopt very different medical philosophies, and thus have very different and sometimes conflicting professional values, which prevent necessary communication and KS.

Education Systems

Hall (2005) claims that healthcare education systems neglect the development of common philosophical understandings, shared professional values and collaborative relationships between students from different health disciplines. Hall (2005, p. 192) comments that this system for healthcare education "limits development of positive relationships between the learners of different professions and restricts understanding of and respect for others' roles". Very similarly, as shown in the research findings of this study, the almost insulated TCM and WM education systems result in a significant professional boundary between the two medical communities and a substantial divergence of philosophical views and values, and provide very little common ground for interprofessional collaboration and communication.

Summary

According to the above discussion, Hall (2005)'s model partially supports the research findings of this project. Moreover, the findings of this project extend Hall (2005)'s model. That is, in addition to the education systems, this research project found that interprofessional training strategies and activities in the hospital environment can also be used to develop common understandings, world-views and values between professional teams and to encourage communication and collaboration.

7.2.2 General Model Comparison

This section compares the emerging model with three existing KS models: Lodhi (2005)'s cultural based KS model, the model of critical factors in KS proposed by Supar et al. (2005), and Ismail and Yusof (2008)'s KS model for public organisations. In contrast with the comparison conducted in Sect. 7.2.1, discussion in this section is relatively general and less detailed, since these KS models are not related

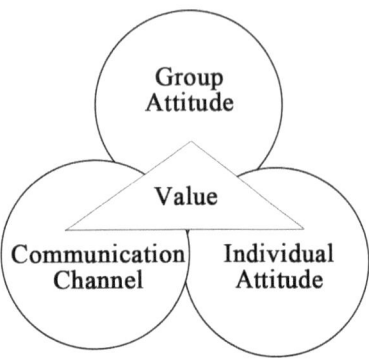

Fig. 7.3 Lodhi (2005, p. 70) cultural based KS model

to healthcare environments and are developed in very different social contexts. The discussion conducted here aims at supporting the emerging theory only in general terms.

7.2.2.1 Lodhi (2005)'s Cultural Based Model

Lodhi (2005) established a cultural based KS model based on the investigation of six postgraduate institutions in Pakistan. Findings of this research point to a KS model consisting of four main components, namely: communication channel, individual attitude, group attitude, and value. Lodhi (2005)'s model is shown in Fig. 7.3.

The model considers that, as discussed by Lodhi (2005), in addition to the issues of individual attitude, group attitude and communication channel which have been widely identified in KS literature and discussed in Sect. 7.2.1, the core to KS should be the shared values among KS participants.

All four components of Lodhi (2005)'s model are shown in the research findings of this project. Similarly to Lodhi (2005), this study also locates values at the centre of the model. That is, as shown in the research findings, the core problem of KS between TCM and WM healthcare professionals is the lack of overlapping interests, shared professional values and mutual conceptual understandings.

Also, as reflected in the research findings, these differences in values decide the attitudes of individual healthcare professionals and result in barriers to sharing patient knowledge with each other. Also, the research findings show that the attitudes of individual healthcare professionals form group attitudes and cause philosophical and professional tensions between TCM and WM professional groups. The two types of tensions are considered as barriers to sharing patient knowledge.

Finally, as one of the main components of Lodhi's (2005) model, the communication channel was identified as a KS barrier in this project. It is shown in the research findings that consultation meetings are used as the main communication channel for KS. However, these consultation meetings are merely used for handing over patients, not for interprofessional communication.

7.2 Comparison with Existing Models

Therefore, the model proposed by Lodhi (2005) partially supports the model developed in this study. In fact, the model developed in this study adds to Lodhi (2005)'s model, since it was found that the shared values of healthcare professionals can be increased and amplified by establishing an interprofessional common ground in the healthcare education systems and interprofessional training in the hospital environment. Moreover, this research project identified that the influences of the external political, economic and social environments as KS barriers. However, Lodhi (2005)'s model focuses on the organisational environment.

7.2.2.2 Supar et al. (2005)'s Model of KS Critical Factors

Supar et al. (2005) present a research study aimed at identifying critical factors influencing KS among academic staff in three higher education institutions in Malaysia. Their research findings point to four main categories, as shown in Fig. 7.4.

Supar et al. (2005)'s model consists of categories of cultural factors, technological factors, communication factors and organisational support factors. Among

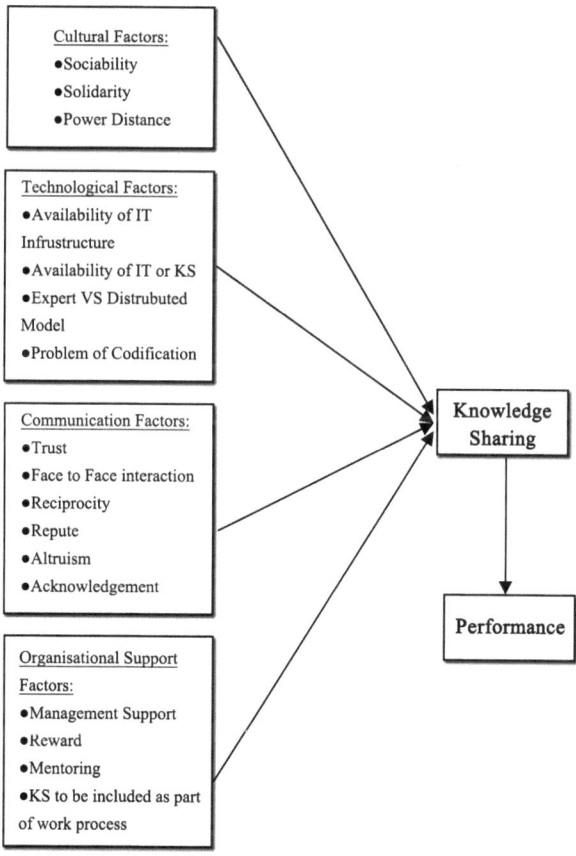

Fig. 7.4 Supar et al. (2005)'s model of KS critical factors

these categories, the technological factors are not reflected in this research project, because no information systems had been implemented in this hospital for the purpose of facilitating communication and KS. However, cultural factors, communication factors and organisational support factors are reflected in the findings of this project.

- Cultural factors: Supar et al. (2005) point out three cultural factors: sociability, solidarity and power distance. Sociability is not presented in this study, since healthcare professionals do not need to socialise in order to provide collaborative patient-centred care. On the other hand, as shown in the research findings, solidarity of TCM and WM healthcare professionals is the basis of the provision of patient-centred care. Finally, power distance is clearly presented as a barrier, which not only causes difficulties for KS and interprofessional communication, but also results in professional tensions and competition between the two professional groups.
- Communication factors: Six communication factors are identified by Supar et al. (2005): trust, face-to-face interaction, reciprocity, repute, altruism and acknowledgement. Among these factors, the repute factor is not presented in this study, since KS is important for the provision of patient-centred services, rather than for individual healthcare professionals to enhance their repute. However, the other five factors are reflected in this study. Firstly, there is a clear lack of trust between TCM and WM healthcare professionals. As reflected in the findings, the lack of trust does not necessarily mean a lack of personal trust, but represents a lack of trust in each other's philosophical beliefs and methodological systems. Secondly, face-to-face interaction is adopted by TCM and WM healthcare professionals when providing collaborative health services to patients in consultation sessions. But the face-to-face interaction is very limited, since these consultation meetings are very short (usually lasting no more than 20 min), which is clearly not conducive for in-depth and meaningful interprofessional communication. Thirdly, as shown in the research findings, there is a lack of reciprocity in sharing patient knowledge between TCM and WM healthcare professionals. The research findings show that the lack of reciprocity in interprofessional communication and KS is mainly caused by philosophical and professional tensions between the two medical communities. Fourthly, as shown in the research findings, for altruism purposes, TCM and WM healthcare professionals are collaborating for the purpose of providing the best possible health services to the patient. However, altruism is not presented in the processes of interprofessional communication and KS. Therefore, sharing knowledge about individual patients is largely overlooked in the processes of interprofessional collaboration. Finally, Supar et al. (2005) claim that acknowledgement can be considered as an incentive for KS. However, the element of acknowledgement is missing in KS between TCM and WM healthcare professionals, due to the lack of reciprocity, as well as philosophical and professional tensions.
- Organisational support factors: This category consists of four factors: management support, rewards, mentoring, and the inclusion of KS as part of the

7.2 Comparison with Existing Models

work process. The factor of mentoring is not relevant to KS between TCM and WM healthcare professionals, and there are no mentoring activities between the two professional teams. Therefore, mentoring is not reflected in the findings of this research project. Moreover, management support emerged as a KS barrier in this project. More precisely, due to a lack of specific and strong management support, interprofessional communication and KS are largely neglected by professionals from both teams. In addition, and again due to lack of management support, no rewards or incentive strategies have been implemented to encourage the sharing of patient knowledge. Finally, the sharing of patient knowledge is less prioritised, since KS activities are not clearly defined and regulated as part of the work process. Once again, this is due to a lack of management attention and support.

Consequently, according to the discussion above, Supar et al. (2005)'s model partially supports the model developed in this research project. Moreover, the research findings of this project also extends Supar et al. (2005)'s model in cultural, communication and organisational support factors.

1. Cultural factors: According to the findings of this study, factors relating to culture and tensions between professional groups should be added in this category. Firstly, the research findings reflect that there was a lack of KS culture, due to the absence of specific and strong hospital management requirements on the sharing of patient knowledge. Secondly, the research findings show that philosophical and professional tensions between TCM and WM medical teams resulted in great difficulties for KS.
2. Communication factors: Factors relating to the lack of motivation, common ground and time should be considered as communication factors. Firstly, the research findings of this study show that there is a lack of motivation for KS, caused by strong philosophical and professional tensions, as well as a lack of management support for KS. Secondly, as shown in the research findings, interprofessional common ground is an important element for the interprofessional communication and collaboration of TCM and WM healthcare professionals. This is because the lack of interprofessional common ground results in conflicting understandings of patient symptoms and conditions, disagreement with each other's approach and methods, and professional tensions. Finally, the research findings show that time is essential for KS. Because both TCM and WM healthcare professionals are extremely pressed for time, interprofessional communication and the sharing of patient knowledge are usually not prioritised in the collaborative provision of health services to patients.
3. Organisational Support Factors: According to the findings of this project, unequal management support should be added to the organisational support factors. As shown in the research findings, hospital management provides unequal managerial support to the TCM and WM communities. The unequal management support exaggerates professional tensions between the two communities and results in barriers to KS.

In addition to the discussion above, it should also be noted that Supar et al. (2005)'s model concentrates on the organisation's internal environment. According to the findings of this project, influences from the external political, economic and social environments can result in barriers to KS. Therefore, these types of external influences can also be added to Supar et al. (2005)'s model.

7.2.2.3 Ismail and Yusof (2008)'s KS Model for Public Organisations

On the basis of a wide search of literature, Ismail and Yusof (2008) propose a KS model for public organisations. As shown in Fig. 7.5, this model consists of three dimensions, technological, organisational and individual. When the above model is compared with the research findings of this study, the technological dimension is not identified in this research, because ICT infrastructure has not been implemented to facilitate communication and KS in this hospital. However, the individual dimension and the organisational dimension are reflected in this project.

- The individual dimension consists of four factors: awareness, trust, personality and job satisfaction. Among these issues, personality and job satisfaction are not presented in this study. As perceived, for ethical reasons, the personality and job satisfaction of individual healthcare professionals are not obstacles to the provision of patient-centred services. However, issues of awareness and trust are reflected in the findings of this research project. Firstly, as shown in the

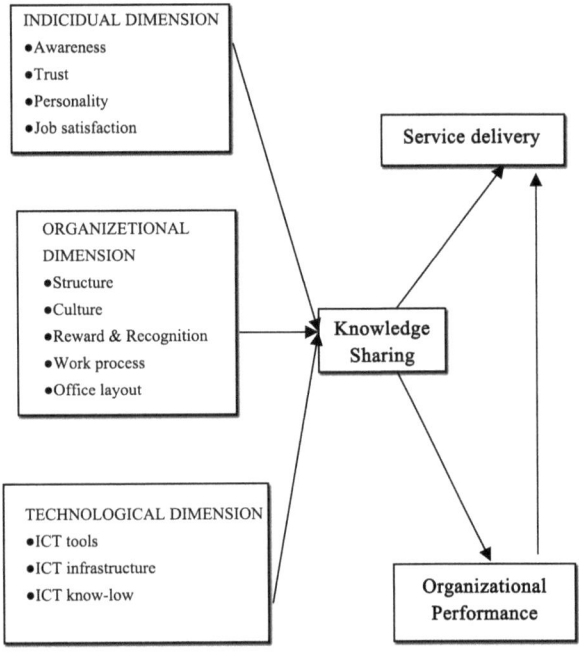

Fig. 7.5 Ismail and Yusof (2008)'s KS model for public organisations

findings, healthcare professionals are lacking in KS awareness, not only because of the lack of hospital management support, but also due to philosophical and professional tensions between TCM and WM professional teams. Secondly, KS is impeded by the lack of trust in each other's philosophical beliefs and methodological systems.

- The organisational dimension includes five issues: structure, culture, reward & recognition, work process and office layout. Among these issues, office layout is not reflected in this study. This is because KS is required by the provision of collaborative healthcare to patients, whereas in some business organisations it is voluntary and spontaneous and can be encouraged by appropriate office layout. Apart from the office layout, the issues of structure, culture, rewards & recognition and work process are reflected in this research project. Firstly, the structure of this hospital is designed to favour WM. This structure undeniably exacerbates philosophical and professional tensions between the TCM and WM healthcare professionals. Secondly, as shown in the research findings, there is a lack of KS culture, caused by the absence of specific and strong hospital management requirements on KS. Thirdly, due to a lack of hospital management attention and support, rewards and recognition are not offered in the process of sharing patient knowledge. Finally, because KS activities are not clearly defined and regulated as part of the work process, the process of sharing patient knowledge is less prioritised.

Also, as shown on the right hand side of Ismail and Yusof (2008)'s model, KS is capable of improving organisational performance and service delivery. It is shown in this study that KS can substantially increase the quality of patient service provision, and therefore this hospital could have higher customer satisfaction as a strong advantage when competing with other hospitals.

The above discussion shows that Ismail and Yusof (2008)'s KS model for public organisations partially supports the model developed in this study. In addition, the research findings of this study can extend Ismail and Yusof (2008)'s model in both the individual dimension and the organisational dimension.

- Individual dimension: The findings of this study can add six issues to this dimension: motivation, lack of common ground, time, professional tensions, terminology, and imbalance of professional power and standing. Firstly, according to the research findings, individual healthcare professionals from both TCM and WM medical teams showed inadequate motivation for sharing patient knowledge, because of a lack of management support and substantial philosophical and professional tensions between the two groups of healthcare professionals. Secondly, the lack of common ground between individual practitioners results in conflicts of philosophical understanding and beliefs, as well as causing great difficulty for the exchange of patient knowledge. Thirdly, the research findings show that healthcare professionals give a low priority to communication and KS, because they are pressed for time. Fourthly, professional tensions between individual healthcare professionals, including competition and imbalance of power and standing, could prevent the sharing of knowledge. Fifthly, according to the findings, different professional terminologies used by individual practitioners cause difficulties in interprofessional interaction and KS. Finally, the research findings show that the imbalances of professional power and standing results in professional tensions and exacerbates philosophical tensions. Therefore, the imbalance of professional power and standing is considered as a barrier to the sharing of patient knowledge.

- Organisational dimension: According to the research findings, three issues can be added to this dimension: management support, insufficient communication channels and management inequity. Firstly, this research project points out that activities of sharing patient knowledge are not prioritised and are even considered as not important by professionals from both teams, because of the lack of management support. Secondly, the findings of this project show that consultation meetings as a communication channel for KS are insufficient. In fact, these meetings have become a formal handover of patients and usually last no longer than 20 min. These conditions are clearly not conducive to interprofessional communication and KS. Finally, the research findings show an inequality in the managerial support provided to the TCM and WM departments. This management inequality, as illustrated in the findings, has substantially exacerbated philosophical and professional tensions between the two professional teams.

Moreover, an additional dimension can be added to Ismail and Yusof (2008)'s model. That is, the findings of this research project show that influences of the external political, economic, and social environments can be considered as barriers to KS.

7.2.2.4 Summary

Discussion in this section shows that the integrated model which emerged in this research project can be verified and supported by KS models developed by Lodhi (2005), Supar et al. (2005) and Ismail and Yusof (2008).

Both Sects. 7.1 and 7.2 in this chapter are aimed at conceptualising the research findings and making discussion at a conceptual level. In contrast, the rest of this chapter elicits implications for the reality of practice and contributions to knowledge.

7.3 Implication of Findings for the Reality of Practice

The research findings have important implications for the reality of practice. This section discusses these implications from the following four perspectives: communication and collaboration issues, education and professional training, hospital management and external influences on KS.

7.3.1 Communication and Collaboration Issues

As implied in the research findings, in order to improve KS between TCM and WM healthcare professionals, efforts could be made on seven issues: severe philosophical divergence, interprofessional common ground, substantial professional boundary, dissonance of professional terminology, inequality in professional standing and power, communication in interprofessional consultations, and the participation of nurses.

7.3.1.1 Severe Philosophical Divergence

Collaboration in a healthcare environment requires healthcare professionals to work cooperatively. Very often, these healthcare professionals are from different backgrounds and have different philosophies, values and basic perspectives, which are potential sources of conflict and could hinder collaboration and KS (San Martin-Rodriguez et al. 2005).

As shown in this project, WM and TCM healthcare professionals adopt two completely different philosophical stances and methodological approaches. That is, TCM doctors adopt a holistic perspective, in which patients are diagnosed and treated as an integral entity (Zhu 2010; Zhang 2010), whereas WM professionals usually employ a micro approach, in which practitioners are more interested in localising a disease in a specific part of the human body than in looking at the patient with the problem (Efferth et al. 2007; Zhang 2010). Moreover, TCM is based on 2300 years of evolution and accumulation of experience. On the other side, WM is based on scientific paradigms and evidence-based research (Cheng 2000). In addition, the two medical systems have entirely different diagnosis and treatment methods and techniques (Liu 2003; Sherman et al. 2005). These differences discussed above are rooted in the basic philosophies of TCM and WM, result in very different philosophical lenses for viewing and resolving patient problems, and cause problems in the exchange of patient knowledge.

To mitigate this philosophical divergence, the research findings point out that it is important to establish an interprofessional common ground, which is discussed in the following Sect. (7.3.1.2).

7.3.1.2 Interprofessional Common Ground

As shown in the data, KS between TCM and WM professionals is very difficult due to a lack of interprofessional common ground to facilitate and motivate necessary communication. This interprofessional common ground was identified as a knowledge base of overlapping interests and mutual conceptual understandings. The lack of interprofessional common ground exacerbates the philosophical divergence, results in conflicting understandings of patient symptoms and conditions, and reinforces the professional boundary and distance.

As reflected in the literature, many researchers propose that communication needs some common ground as a communication platform (e.g. Grice 1975; Horton and Keysar 1996). Without common ground, Frank (1961, p. 1801) asserts that "members of each discipline come together and talk at each other but do not communicate, even when they earnestly try to make themselves clear and avoid undue technical terminology". This is because, as further discussed by Frank (1961), an individual usually talks to him/herself and is unaware that the message may have limited meaning to the others, who have different frames of concepts and assumptions.

Therefore, it is essential to put in place an appropriate interprofessional common ground between TCM and WM healthcare professionals. Moreover, as shown in the data, and advocated by a number of studies (e.g. Hall 2005; Zwarenstein and Reeves 2006; Reeves et al. 2007), an interprofessional common ground could be established in healthcare education and in interprofessional programmes and sessions in the hospital environment.

7.3.1.3 Substantial Professional Boundary

This study identified a clear and substantial professional boundary, which has formulated two very distinctive professional communities, and which prevents communication and KS between the two communities.

It is well reported in the literature that a strong professional boundary hinders KS (Nicolini et al. 2008; Ferlie et al. 2005). Zwarenstein and Reeves (2006) assert that practitioners are more likely to communicate internally and within the community, but rarely across the professional boundary. This is because, as explained by Currie and Suhomlinova (2006), professionals belonging to the same professional groups have more commonalities in meanings and knowledge patterns, which are necessary foundations for meaningful communication and KS. Moreover, professionals from different medical fields often have very different philosophies, values, and basic theoretical perspectives, which are inhibitors to collaboration and KS (San Martin-Rodriguez et al. 2005).

In this case, it is important to soften the boundary separating the TCM and WM communities within the hospital environment. This can be achieved by increasing commonalities in communication and by establishing and enhancing the interprofessional common ground.

7.3.1.4 Dissonance of Professional Terminologies

Differences in professional terminologies have long been recognised as a problem for KS (Davenport et al. 1998; Alavi and Leidner 2001; Stenmark 2002). For instance, Hollenberg (2006) presents the research findings of a project conducted in a Canadian healthcare environment and points out that differences in professional terminology are significant barriers to communication in healthcare collaborations.

7.3 Implication of Findings for the Reality of Practice

Similarly, as pointed out by the research findings of this project, TCM and neurosurgical professionals use completely different professional terminologies. Also as shown in the findings, the terminological difference makes the process of sharing patient knowledge extremely difficult. Often, knowledge shared by one party cannot be properly received and correctly comprehended by the other party.

The research findings indicate that the terminological gap between TCM and WM professionals can be reduced by increasing understanding of each other's philosophy and terminology.

7.3.1.5 Inequalities in Professional Standing and Power

The data analysis identified that, when compared with TCM doctors, neurosurgical professionals have a higher professional standing and hold more power. Therefore, as reflected in the findings, neurosurgeons usually explicitly instruct and regulate TCM doctors in what they should do about the patient. In contrast, TCM doctors are most likely to maintain a passive position, avoid any confrontations, and to follow instructions, instead of actively, spontaneously and voluntarily putting forward their understandings and treatment suggestions.

Currie and Suhomlinova (2006) present very similar research findings based on studying hospitals in the NHS in England. They point out that the status and power imbalances of different healthcare professions are barriers to KS. They claim that hospital doctors usually possess more power in hospitals, so "other professionals were expected to accept the higher status knowledge of hospital doctors, following which they would represent hospital doctors' interests in other decision-making arenas" (Currie and Suhomlinova 2006, p. 21).

As implied by the findings of this study, strategies need to be implemented aiming at balancing professional status, maintaining equality of TCM and WM communities and resolving tensions resulted by the competition for professional power and status.

7.3.1.6 Communication in Interprofessional Consultations

As discussed in the research findings, communication and collaboration usually occur in consultation sessions, which are also the main vehicle for the sharing of patient knowledge. However, these consultation sessions are aimed almost exclusively at resolving patient problems at hand, and are hardly a good communication channel for KS. In reality, as expressed by a number of informants, the meetings usually last no more than 20 min, during which the diagnosis of the patient is presented by the WM professional and a brief discussion occurs between all participants. This is of course not conducive to in-depth interprofessional discussion.

Therefore, it is important to explore and develop the use of the consultation meetings as a channel for sharing patient knowledge. It is also necessary to explicitly define and regulate processes and activities of KS during these meetings.

7.3.1.7 The Participation of Nurses

As reflected by many neurosurgical nurses interviewed in this study, they are the healthcare professionals closest to patients, the ones who interact with patients regularly and take care of patients daily. Therefore, these nurses have a better understanding of the needs, requirements and expectations of patients, and possess more of the ethical and emotional knowledge and the social and behavioural knowledge about patients on which this study focuses.

As discussed in Sect. 6.1.3, nurses, although present in those consultation meetings, may not truly participate in the processes of interprofessional collaboration and may not freely exchange patient knowledge with their counterparts on the other side. Men (2008) reports that, in the Chinese culture, nurses usually do not have a respected social status. In addition, Zhou (2008) asserts that, in hospitals, nurses are responsible for making up-to-date reports on patients' conditions to doctors, but do not have the power to make any decisions or take any actions without obtaining the doctor's consent. Thus, as also found in this study, neurosurgical nurses, although present in those consultation meetings, are usually mere spectators and very rarely intervene or propose ideas and suggestions. In this case, all the patient knowledge obtained by nurses is most probably lost, never transmitted to TCM doctors, and the requirements of patients can hardly be achieved or their satisfaction guaranteed.

Consequently, it is important to increase the participation of nurses in interprofessional consultation, and empower nurses to protect the benefits and rights of patients during the processes of collaboration. Nurses can also play a leading role in initiating interprofessional communication and mediating the exchange of patient knowledge.

7.3.2 Education and Professional Training

A very important finding of this study is that there is a lack of interprofessional common ground for communication and KS. As discussed in Sect. 6.2.1.2, the lack of interprofessional common ground reinforces the professional boundary, exacerbates philosophical and professional conflicts and creates difficulties for communication and KS between TCM and WM professionals. Also, as emerged from data, the interprofessional common ground can be established in healthcare HE and in interprofessional programmes in healthcare organisations.

Many research studies (e.g. Lary et al. 1997; Hall 2005; San Martin-Rodriguez et al. 2005) identified an increasing specialisation in subjects and medical areas in medical education, resulting in fragmentation of health services. Members of each medical area have very limited knowledge regarding the practices, expertise, responsibilities, skills, values, and theoretical foundations of other professions (Hall 2005; Rodriguez et al. 2005). In this case, healthcare professionals do not have a common ground and thus often have difficulties in collaboration and communication with others from different medical disciplines. Therefore, it is important to prepare individual healthcare professionals to know more about the overlapping areas of practice and the potential areas of collaboration at two levels: firstly, pre-licensure level in medical universities and institutions; secondly, at post-licensure level, through strategies and activities of interprofessional training in hospitals (Freeth et al. 2002; Zwarenstein 2006).

At the pre-licensure level, and as reported in the research findings, the Chinese healthcare education system consists of two almost isolated sub-systems, one for WM and one for TCM. This educational system includes very few interprofessional modules, lectures, and practical sessions concentrating on the possible overlap of the healthcare systems. There is, therefore, virtually no education to support interprofessional collaboration and communication. In this case, students from either system have very limited mutual knowledge and interprofessional common ground, and, more importantly, lack motivation for interprofessional collaboration and communication. Therefore, it is clear that it is important to embed and increase interprofessional education programmes in both TCM and WM universities and educational institutions.

Furthermore, at the post-licensure level, it was found that there is an absence of interprofessional training schemes, sessions and programmes in the hospital environment. The existing professional training programmes mostly focus on their respective professional subjects and methods; rarely on the interprofessional areas. This reflects a perception that hospital management and leadership place very little importance on communication and professional co-operation between the two groups, thus reinforcing philosophical divergence and educational problems. In this case, healthcare professionals not only begin with very limited common ground to facilitate KS, but also are actively demotivated to engage in interprofessional activities and the sharing of patient "real needs" (Interview WMN 14.35). Therefore, the communication and KS problems can be resolved by establishing very specific interprofessional training schemes and activities in the hospital environment aimed at increasing mutual understanding and developing an appropriate interprofessional common ground.

7.3.3 Hospital Management

Organisational management is the key to the success of any knowledge management programme in any type of organisation (DeTienne et al. 2004). In addition, DeTienne et al. (2004) and Singh (2008) further claim that organisational management should be able to identify potential conflicts which might prevent the process of KS and to resolve these conflicts when they occur.

However, as revealed by the research findings, the management of this hospital not only neglects the existence of philosophical and professional tensions between TCM and WM healthcare professionals, but also further strengthens the conflicts and tensions by evidently treating the two communities unequally and providing more managerial support to WM departments. Clearly, current hospital management strategies result in imbalances of professional standing and power between TCM and WM healthcare professionals, reinforce the professional boundary and tensions, and develop untrusting and even resentful relationships.

In order to improve KS between TCM and WM healthcare professionals, hospital management must provide equal managerial support to TCM and WM departments, establish strategies to balance the positions of the two medical communities, and create trusting relationships and mutual recognition between TCM and WM practitioners in the hospital environment.

7.3.4 *External Influences on KS*

The data analysis identified some influences on KS from the external political, economic and social environments. According to the research findings, the hospital's external environment not only interacts with the internal environment and influences the establishment of hospital management strategies, but also can be considered as barriers to sharing patient knowledge in the collaboration of TCM and WM professionals. This section discusses the political, economical and social influences which emerged from the data analysis.

7.3.4.1 Political Influences

Even though it was virtually impossible to interview healthcare politicians in relatively high-level government positions, it emerged from the data analysis, and was pointed out by Liu (2003) and Zhu and Liu (2009), that TCM and WM medical communities, as two existing components of the Chinese healthcare system, receive very unequal political support, even though the central government explicitly requires the two communities to be equally supported.

As revealed by the research findings and confirmed by Liu (2003) and Zhu and Liu (2009), there is no specific strategy and no actual plan of implementation established by the central government to guide and evaluate the implementation of these health policies. In this case, these policies are not well implemented in hospitals and not properly enforced and supervised by local government (Liu 2003). Liu et al. (2008) argue that those healthcare policies are "sentences without meaning".

Due to the lack of strong political action maintaining the equality of the two communities, hospital management evaluates each department on the basis of 'profitability' (Liu 2003). Therefore, TCM departments are always less well supported and considered as less important, since they are usually not as profitable as the WM ones (Liu et al. 2008).

The existence and development of TCM needs political support from the central government (Zeng 2008). As implied by the findings of this research project, the Chinese central government must reinforce the existing healthcare policies, which need to be assisted by clear implementation plans and evaluation strategies.

7.3.4.2 Economical Influences

In the mid-1980s, the Chinese government implemented the Market Economy Policy (MEP), which aimed at reforming a planned economy into a market economy in various industries and services, including the healthcare services and the healthcare organisations (Hsiao 1995; Fruehauf 1999; Liu et al. 1999). Generally speaking, China's reforms have been very successful and have significantly boosted the Chinese economy (McMillan and Naughton 1992).

However, since the implementation of MEP, the central government no longer fully fund any types of public healthcare services (Hsiao 1995). Instead, hospitals and health organisations have to rely on user fees to support medical and operational expenditures (Hsiao and Yip 2009). This has created enormous problems in the Chinese healthcare system. Liu et al. (1999) report that hospitals arbitrarily increase patient care fees, which has caused "sky high" charges after simple medical procedures.

Moreover, the implementation of MEP has encouraged a social materialism, in which people's ideology and behaviour are more money-oriented; this includes healthcare professionals in healthcare sectors (Xie 2006). It has been reported that many doctors only aim at pursuing higher personal income, rather than practising medicine ethically to treat patients and save lives (Xie 2006). For instance, Liu (2006) reveals that many doctors seek bribes from patients and relatives. To control this serious and unethical behaviour of healthcare professionals, the Chinese central government had to establish legislation to define bribery in hospitals is criminal behaviour, so that, once identified, the doctor would be prosecuted (Liu 2006). Moreover, Hu (2006) reports that some doctors refuse to treat patients unless the patient fees are fully paid. Therefore, patients have very little power to make their opinions and requirements recognised when receiving health services.

In addition to the above problems reported in the literature, this project found that the implementation of MEP forces the hospital management to maximise hospital income and profitability. Thus, the hospital management usually supports only the WM departments that can make a lot of profit. TCM departments are usually less profitable, and hence receive less support, and are even "marginalised" (Interview TCM 19.19) and "discriminated" (Interview TCM 4.27) by the management. As shown by the data analysis, the unequal management support to WM and TCM departments reinforces philosophical and professional tensions and demotivates healthcare professionals to engage in necessary communication and KS about individual patients.

Consequently, as reflected in the research findings, it is necessary to reduce the effects of MEP on Chinese healthcare organisations, reinforce the implementation of the patient-centred healthcare approach, and promote the power and position of patients in the processes of healthcare.

7.3.4.3 Social Influences

Liu (2003), who is a professor in a TCM university in China, claims that Chinese people believe WM is a product of state-of-the-art scientific technologies and thus have more trust in the methods of WM. Comparably, people show less trust in TCM, and some people consider TCM as unscientific and a superstition (Zhang 2007). Sometimes, TCM doctors are even criticised as 'liars' (Wang 2006a).

More seriously, the existing literature points to several social incidents appearing to exclude TCM out of the national healthcare system (Fan 2003; Fang 2005, 2006, 2007, 2010; Zhang 2006; Wang 2006b). Even though these incidents did not have any real impact on the existence of TCM in the Chinese healthcare system, they imply a severe lack of trust toward the traditional medical philosophy and therapy. Moreover, as shown in the data collected in this study, these social incidents exacerbate the imbalances in professional standing, strengthen philosophical and professional tensions between TCM and WM communities, and increase the lack of trust within the hospital environment.

Consequently, strategies need to be established by the government which aim at reinstalling confidence in TCM. Also, it is necessary to propagate knowledge of TCM and WM to the public, to encourage a proper understanding of the advantages and disadvantages of both types of medicine.

7.4 Contribution of Findings to the Body of Knowledge in the Field

This research project reported in this book investigates communication and KS problems between TCM and WM healthcare professionals in their collaborative and complementary provision of healthcare services to patients in Chinese hospitals. In addition, this project contributes to the body of knowledge by providing a first theory consisting of a number of barriers hindering the sharing of patient knowledge between the two types of healthcare professionals. In more detail, this research project contributes to two fields: health informatics, and knowledge management and sharing.

7.4.1 Health Informatics

The theory established in this study contributes to the field of health informatics in China. This is a field which is relatively under-developed and which has recently received increasing attention from academic researchers and healthcare professionals (Zheng 2010). However, the existing body of literature mostly concentrates on implementing hospital information systems to assist hospital management, computerising patient histories and records, and providing solutions to optimise patient flow in hospitals (Song 2010; Chui 2010; Sun 2010; Li 2010; Zheng 2010). On the basis of an extensive search of literature, it was recognised that not much existing research investigates communication between individual healthcare professionals and the existing problems of interaction in Chinese hospitals.

The communication and KS problems investigated in this research project have not been studied previously. This research project therefore provides a first set of insights into the communication problems between WM and TCM healthcare professionals, and proposes a framework of KS barriers causing the communication problems existing in the collaboration between TCM and WM professionals.

7.4.2 Knowledge Management and Sharing

Knowledge management and sharing have been increasingly recognised as important to the provision of patient services in healthcare organisations (Dobbins et al. 2010). However, and despite the attempts made by Chinese hospitals to implement KM strategies and encourage KS activities (Li et al. 2010), KM and KS implementation in reality is not well studied and reported, and existing problems have not been identified and resolved (Bian et al. 2010). In fact, the existing body of literature consists mostly of conceptual works without sufficient support based on empirical investigation and data collected in context.

This research project provides a perspective on the context of KS in Chinese healthcare organisations. Furthermore, this research project establishes a theory which consists of a number of barriers to communication and KS between TCM and WM healthcare professionals in Chinese hospitals.

The theory developed in this study can be used by hospital management and information professionals in Chinese hospitals to resolve the KS problems, to mitigate the effects of identified KS barriers, and to improve communication between TCM and WM medical communities. Moreover, the theory can provide useful indications and can be used as a theoretical foundation for KM and KS research studies in healthcare organisations in different contexts in different countries.

7.5 Conclusion

This chapter integrates the research findings, which are presented and discussed in Chap. 5, into an integrated model. Additionally, this chapter conceptualises the research findings and identifies that the sharing of patient knowledge between TCM and WM healthcare professionals is mainly hindered by philosophical and professional tensions.

Moreover, in this chapter, the integrated model emerged in this research project is compared with existing KS models in the literature. Also, this chapter identifies contributions to the existing body of knowledge and links the research findings to the reality of practice by eliciting implications.

The next chapter, Chap. 7, concludes the research project. Specifically, the next chapter provides a brief summary of the research findings, answers the research question and points out limitations and future work.

Chapter 8
Conclusion

This book reports on a PhD research project aimed at identifying barriers to sharing patient knowledge in the collaboration of TCM and WM healthcare professionals in the context of Chinese hospitals. This chapter concludes this book. More specifically, this conclusion chapter discusses the following issues: summary of research findings, responding research questions, practical implications, limitation of this study and future works.

8.1 Summary of Research Findings

As discussed in Chap. 6, the data collected point to five main categories of KS barriers, namely:

- The contextual influences: The data analysis identified some contextual influences from the hospital external environment, constraining and impeding activities of sharing patient knowledge between TCM and WM healthcare professionals within the hospital environment. Specifically, the research findings point to three types of contextual influences, namely, political, economical and social influences. As revealed by the research findings, these contextual influences have created imbalances of professional standings and power in hospital, in which WM professionals possess relatively higher professional standings and hold considerably stronger power. These imbalances have formed professional tensions between the two medical communities, demotivating and preventing individual professional from active and spontaneous interprofessional communication and KS of patient knowledge.
- Philosophical issues: The research findings reveal significant divergences of conceptual systems, theoretical ground, diagnostic and treatment methods, and professional terminologies used by the professionals of TCM and WM. These philosophical divergences have created ongoing philosophical tensions between the two groups, have resulted in conflicts of opinions and perspectives and a climate of distrust, disregard, and unwillingness to communicate in the two

communities. Also as shown in the research findings, the philosophical tensions could be the result of a lack of interprofessional common ground to enable, facilitate and motivate communication and KS. The lack of interprofessional common ground is caused by the inadequate interprofessional education in the Chinese healthcare education and an absence of interprofessional training programmes in the hospital environment.

- Chinese healthcare education: The data collected revealed that the Chinese healthcare education consists of two almost insulated educational systems, one for TCM and one for WM. Students from both systems have limited knowledge and understandings about the other system. Thus, this national healthcare education system is incapable of establishing and developing an adequate interprofessional common ground to enable and facilitate the interaction of patient knowledge between TCM and WM professionals. Also, this national healthcare education system has failed to build a foundation of trust and a collaborative and cooperative relationship between the two types of practitioners, and is not motivating or permitting voluntary and spontaneous interprofessional collaboration and communication.
- Interprofessional training: As shown in the research findings, professional training programmes, sessions and activities for TCM and WM practitioners in the hospital environment also are insulated in their respective fields. Therefore, the hospital professional training reinforces the lack of interprofessional common ground caused by the healthcare education and thus prevents active and voluntary interprofessional communication and the interaction of patient knowledge.
- Hospital management: The research findings point out that the hospital management provides more attention and support to WM departments, whereas the TCM Department is not only less supported, but also could be discriminated by the hospital management. As reflected in data collected, the hospital management has exacerbated the philosophical and professional tensions between communities of TCM and WM, encouraged interprofessional competition, augmented imbalances of power and professional standings. Thus, professionals from both communities are not motivated and even unwilling to communicate and share knowledge with each other.

Conceptualising and synthesizing the research findings, it was identified that KS is mainly hindered by two types of interprofessional tensions: philosophical tensions and professional tensions.

The philosophical tensions are caused by the substantial divergence in philosophies, theoretical grounds and conceptual systems of TCM and WM. These tensions have resulted in conflicts of opinions and perspectives, which in turn have created a climate of distrust, disregard, and unwillingness to communicate in the two communities. Additionally, the philosophical tensions are resulted by a lack of interprofessional common ground to facilitate communication and KS. The lack of interprofessional common ground is caused by lacking of interprofessional education in the Chinese healthcare education and by lacking of interprofessional training in the hospital environment.

The professional tensions are resulted by substantial asymmetries of power and professional standings between the two medical communities. The data analysis clearly revealed that neurosurgeons have relatively higher professional standings and have almost dominant power over patients. Therefore, they often explicitly instruct and regulate TCM doctors on what to do on the patient. Comparably, TCM doctors have lower professional standings and hold relatively less power. Therefore, TCM doctors are most likely to maintain a passive position when collaborating with neurosurgical practitioners, avoid any confrontations and to follow instructions, instead of actively and voluntarily proposing their ideas, understandings and suggestions. Finally, there also seem to be an absence of influence by a third professional group that is fundamental in KS of patient knowledge: the nurses.

8.2 Responding Research Questions

In the introduction of this book, Chap. 1, the main research question for this research project is presented. The main research question is:

> What are the barriers for sharing patient knowledge between healthcare professionals from traditional and Western medicines in their patient-centred interprofessional collaborations?

In order to respond to this main research question, it is more effective to answer the two more specified research questions, which are decomposed from the main research question.

1. What are the barriers that hindering the sharing of patient knowledge between TCM and WM healthcare professionals?

   The research project identifies in total forty-six barriers for sharing patient knowledge. These KS barriers have emerged from the five main categories mentioned above and synthesised into the two main tensions also discussed above.

2. What are the relationships between these barriers?

   As emerged from data, the five main categories are closely related and interact with each other. To be more specific, and as shown in Fig. 7.1, the category of philosophical issues, as the core category of the final theory, is related to all other four categories. Similarly, the category of contextual influences is also mutually related to all four categories. Moreover, the category of Chinese healthcare education is not only influenced by the contextual influences, but also affects categories of philosophical issues, hospital management, and interprofessional training. Finally, the category of interprofessional training receives influences from categories of contextual influences, Chinese healthcare education and hospital management and is mutually related to the philosophical issues.

8.3 Practical Implications

As reflected from the research findings, in order to improve KS and mitigate barriers, efforts need to be made aiming at resolving the philosophical and professional tensions existing between TCM and WM healthcare professionals. Specifically, actions need to be made from both inside and outside of the hospital environment.

8.3.1 Internal Actions

Firstly, within the hospital environment, there is a need to formalise the process of interprofessional collaboration and formally demand and regulate activities of interprofessional communication and sharing patient knowledge. Moreover, it is necessary to encourage nurses to be more participative to consultation meetings, where TCM and WM collaboration and KS occur, and to initiate and mediate activities of sharing patient knowledge.

Secondly, the hospital management should establish very specific interprofessional training schemes and programmes. For both types of healthcare professionals, these programmes and sessions could increase mutual understanding, acceptance of each other's philosophy and beliefs, could enhance a better understanding of each other's professional terminology and, more importantly, effectively put in place an interprofessional common ground to enable, facilitate and motivate interprofessional communication and KS.

Thirdly, in order to reduce and resolve the professional tensions, the hospital management needs to effectively establish and implement explicit strategies aiming at equally support TCM and WM departments, eliminate imbalances of power and professional standings and foster a harmonious hospital environment, which could be more conducive for interprofessional collaboration and communication.

Finally, it is important to emphasise that these solutions must be supported by the hospital managers and leaders in both medical communities, who should realise that the collaboration of TCM and WM is not just politically imperative, but may bring tangible benefits through mutual trust aiming at maximising the patient welfare.

8.3.2 External Actions

In addition, as shown in the findings, these internal actions implemented within the hospital environment may not be adequate. Strategies and actions need to be initiated and implemented at the national strategic level. Specifically, four implications are elicited from the research findings and are presented as follows.

Firstly, the Chinese central government should realise that the existing national healthcare policies, which are established aiming at maintaining the equity and the coexistence of TCM and WM medical communities in the national healthcare system, are not effective and not fully implemented. Thus, more specific, clear and strong national policies should be formulated.

Secondly, the central government should recognise that the Market Economy Policy (MEP) has had a negative impact on the national healthcare system, the operation of healthcare organisations in the country and has diluted the centre of patient. Therefore, strategies need to be made aiming at reducing the negative effects of MEP and re-emphasise the centre of patient in the national healthcare service.

Thirdly, the Chinese government has the mission of educating people. This should include educating health professionals and the public on advantages and disadvantages of Traditional Chinese Medicine and Western Medicine. In this case, the two types of healthcare professionals could have more balanced social standings and could be equally respected by the public.

Finally, it is critically important to embed and increase interprofessional education programmes in both TCM and WM universities and educational institutions. Therefore, graduates from both healthcare education systems can have a foundation of trust, formulate more cooperative and collaborative relationships, an interprofessional common ground collaboration, communication and KS.

8.4 Limitations of This Study and Mitigation Strategy Adopted

The main limitation of this study lies in the selected research methods. As discussed in this book, this research project adopted GT as the overarching research methodology to guide the analysis of data collected in a single case-study design. The problem is, as discussed by Yin (2003), the single case-study design provides little basis for scientific generalisation. Therefore, a frequently heard question is "how can you generalize from a single case?" (Yin 2003, p. 10). Similarly, like some other qualitative research methodologies, GT is often criticised as limited in generalisability (Morse 1999). Strauss and Corbin (1998) defend that usually a GT research study aims at developing a substantive theory, which is "developed from the study of one small area of investigation and from one specific population" (Strauss and Corbin 1998, p. 267). A substantive theory can explain "specifically for the populations from which it was derived and to apply back to them" (Strauss and Corbin 1998, p. 267). This research project aims at generating a substantive theory applicable to the case-study only, not aiming at generalising a theory to a broader population. Nevertheless, and certainly, the generalisability can be achieved by future studies in the purpose of generalising the substantive theory established in this project.

Another limitation is that the lead researcher himself grew up in a social environment very similar to the research site. Therefore, even though the personal experience helped enhancing the contextual sensitivity, it was very difficult for the researcher to be completely immersed in data, without receiving any influences from the past experience. In this case, the researchers adopted the coding definition list, quotation list and concept map to assist the practice of data analysis as well as to maintain an objective stance. The use of these analytical tools has been discussed in-depth in Chap. 4.

Furthermore, in this research, the identification of KS barriers is relying on the researchers' own interpretation and dependent on the theoretical and contextual sensitivities of the researchers. Nevertheless, and considering this project is the first inductive qualitative research conducted by the lead researcher, his own interpretation, evaluation and judgement of the data collected may not always have been the best. In order to effectively minimise this limitation, three strategies were used. Firstly, the researchers actively participated international academic conferences, which provided opportunities to discuss the research operation and the latest findings with world-leading researchers. Secondly, for several times, the findings of this research project have been presented and discussed openly among academics and colleague in Wuhan University as well as the University of Sheffield. In addition, the research processes and findings are reported in several papers authored by the researchers and are published in peer-reviewed international conferences and academic journals.

Finally, since the aim of this project is to identify KS barriers impeding the sharing of patient knowledge, the cause and consequence relationships, which could exist between individual barriers, is not included in this study. This could be considered as an additional limitation to this study and can be explored by future works.

8.5 Future Works

This research project points to seven potential areas, which should be further explored and studied by future work.

Firstly, future work could aim at continuing the progress made in this study. That is, future work can explore the cause and consequence relationships between individual KS barriers and thus gain deeper understandings to the communication problems between TCM and WM healthcare professionals.

Secondly, the substantive theory generated in the study can be expanded and generalised by investigating other medical fields (e.g., cardiology and orthopaedics). Also, the theory generalisation can be achieved by studying other hospitals in other geographical regions in China. It is also important to mention that this study can be used as a source and a starting point for further investigations on KS in interprofessional healthcare collaborations throughout the world.

Thirdly, future work can focus on identifying and creating opportunities and channels for TCM and WM healthcare professionals to interact and share patient knowledge, both during the patient consultation meeting and in general processes of diagnosis and treatment provision.

Fourthly, in order to improve communication and KS between TCM and WM healthcare professionals, future works can be conducted aiming at exploring and formulating specific and practical hospital management strategies, on the basis of the identification of barriers to sharing patient knowledge.

Fifthly, as revealed by the data collected, the hospital investigated in this study does not have any information systems implemented aiming at facilitating interprofessional communication and the externalisation, storage and transmission of patient knowledge. Therefore, future studies could be conducted to design this type of computerised communication platform connecting individual practitioners of WM and TCM, to observe problems occurred in the system implementation, and to evaluate the utilisation and effect of this system in the real life context.

Sixthly, this research study concentrates on the exchange of patient knowledge between TCM and WM practitioners. However, this study does not attempt to

8.5 Future Works

understand the behaviour and pattern of sharing patient knowledge within teams of TCM and WM. Therefore, future work can investigate the activities, processes and barriers of sharing patient knowledge within each medical team and examine how these internal KS behaviours affect interprofessional communication and KS.

Finally, according to the research findings, consultation notes and patient records, which are currently used in interprofessional collaboration, only include technical knowledge of patient. Thus, future works can explore the utilisation of these tools to facilitate the externalisation and transmission of patient knowledge in the processes of TCM and WM collaboration. Moreover, it is perceived that implementing ICT infrastructure and digitising these two documentations could create a more effective, efficient and convenient communication and KS platform. This could also be explored in the future.

Appendices

To support the description of research processes and the discussion of research findings in this book, three appendices are attached.

Appendix 1 is a sample of interview scripts used for interviewing neurosurgical professionals at the very beginning of the main study. Appendix 2 is a sample of coding definition list, which was used interactively with a quotation list, a sample of which is shown in appendix 3. These three tools have been discussed extensively in Chap. 4 Research Methodology and Design.

Appendix 1: A Sample of Interview Script for Neurosurgical Practitioners

Section 1: General Research Context

1. What is your role in the hospital?
   您在医院担任什么样的工作?
   Trigger Question:
   What does it involve?
   工作具体包括哪些内容？

Appendices

2. Could you please generally introduce your department?
   请您大概地介绍一下您的科室?
   Trigger Questions:
   What is the role of your department in this hospital?
   您的科室在医院担任什么角色？地位是怎样的呢？
   How many doctors are there in your department?
   科室有多少医生?
   What about your annual patient number and income?
   科室每年收治多少个病人?年收入大概是多少?

3. Do you think there is a need for TCM in your treatments?
   您认为在病人治疗的过程中需要中医的帮助吗？

   Trigger Questions:

   In your practice of medicine, which areas do you think you need TCM collaboration?
   有哪些地方需要中医的帮助？

   What reasons do you think that you need TCM involvement?
   有哪些原因使您想使用中医？

4. What do you think of this collaboration?
   您怎样看待中西医的合作?
   Trigger Question:
   Do you think this kind of collaboration valuable?
   您觉得这种合作有价值吗?
   What do patients think?
   病人是如何看待中西医合作的?

5. Are there any political emphasises on TCM and WM communication and collaboration?

国家有没有相关的政策强调中西医的沟通与合作呢?

Trigger Questions:

How these political emphasises effect your practice of medicine?

这些政策对您的日常诊疗有什么影响?

Appendices 199

6. In terms of communication, how do you usually communicate with TCM doctors?
在沟通渠道的运用上,您通常是如何与中医进行交流的？

Trigger Questions:

What communication channels you are using both formally and informally?
在这种沟通当中,正式的和非正式的沟通渠道有哪些?

What do you think about these communication channels?
您如何评价这些沟通渠道?

Follow-up Questions:

Are there any limitations on consultation as formal communication channel?
会诊作为主要的沟通渠道有什么局限性?

What strategy do you think can improve the communication across these two communities?
有哪些策略能够加强中西医之间的沟通?

Section 2: Exploration of KS Barriers

7. What are the philosophical differences between TCM and WM?
   中医和西医的理论有哪些区别?
   Trigger Questions:
   How do these differences impact on interaction about individual patients when you are working with TCM doctors?
   这些理论上的区别是否会影响必要的信息和知识交流?

Appendices

8. Certainly that WM and TCM professionals use rather different professional terminologies, how do these differences effect your communications and KS about patient?
中西医理论上的差别当然也造成了中西医术语体系的不同。这些不同是否会影响知识共享与传递？

Follow-up Questions:
What would you do when you find out you can't understand each other's language?
在沟通过程中如果遇到不太明白的专业术语,您会如何处理？
What strategies you use in order to overcome these terminological differences?
您使用哪些方法来减小专业术语的不同给知识共享带来的障碍？

9. There were two movements in history intended to eliminate TCM, what do you think of these movements?
   在中国的近代史上有两次针对中医的政治运动。您是怎样看待这两次运动的?

   Follow-up Questions:
   What are the impacts caused by these two movements to the current situation?
   这两次运动对现在有什么样的影响?

10. Can you generally introduce WM and TCM education systems in China?
    您能不能大概的介绍一下西医和中医的教育?
    Trigger Questions:
    What do you think of this education structure in terms of supporting WM and TCM communication?
    从支持西医和中医交流的角度出发,您如何看待中国的医疗教育体系?
    Why did the government design educational structure in this way?
    从支持西医和中医交流的角度出发,政府为何构建当前的教育体系和结构

11. What professional learning strategies have been implemented in your hospital?
现在您们医院有没有一些策略来促进医生的学习?

    Follow-up Questions:

    What do you think of these learning strategies in supporting TCM and WM communication and collaboration?
    这些策略对中西医的合作有没有一些帮助?

12. Can you generally introduce doctors' and nurses' career progression in your department?
    您能不能介绍您们科室医生晋升的情况?
    Follow-up Questions:
    Do TCM doctors have the same career progression structure?
    中医的医生是不是大致也是这样一个情况?

13. What is the role of hospital management in encouraging knowledge sharing and communication between TCM and WM?
   在支持中西医交流和知识共享方面,医院的管理者充当什么样的角色?
   Follow-up Questions:
   Is there any inequality in management support between TCM and WM departments?
   管理者在对中西医科室的扶持上,会不会有偏差?
   Any reason for this?
   您觉得原因是什么?
   What do you think about the market economy? Is it a strong impact to TCM?
   您是怎样看待市场经济的?是不是对中医有比较大的打击?

Appendix 2: A Sample of Code Definition List

Category of philosophical issues

Sub-categories	3rd level categories	Concepts	Codes	Definition
Philosophical conflicts	Different conceptual systems	Holistic VS localised approach to practice	[TCM took holistic view, whereas WM took micro view of patients' problem]	TCM doctors take a holistic view to see patient, where WM doctors use a micro view
		Different diagnostic methods	[TCM and WM have very different diagnosis methods]	TCM and WM professionals use very different diagnostic methods
		Different treatment methods	[TCM and WM have different treatments]	TCM and WM professionals use very different treatment methods to resolve patient problems
		Divergent theoretical grounds	[Non-quantify of TCM WM]	From WM professionals' perspective, WM is based on accurate quantification, whereas TCM is not quantifiable
			[None-quantify of TCM TCM]	From TCM professionals' perspective, WM is based on accurate quantification, whereas TCM is not quantifiable
		Terminology discrepancies	[Terminology difference]	From WM professionals' perspective, terminologies of TCM and WM are entirely different
			[Terminology difference TCM]	From TCM professionals' perspective, terminologies of TCM and WM are entirely different
		Conflicts of philosophical beliefs	[Disagree WM]	TCM doctors do not agree with WM methods and beliefs
			[Don't believe TCM TCM]	TCM doctor provided that WM doctors do not believe TCM philosophy
			[Feel discriminated]	Due to WM doctors do not believe TCM philosophy, TCM doctors felt discriminated, pessimistic, and sad
		Inadequate interprofessional common ground	[Communication needs basic knowledge]	KS and communication needs mutual and common knowledge

Appendix 3: A Sample of Quotation List

Category of philosophical issues

Sub-Categories	3rd level categories	Concepts	Codes	Quotations
Philosophical conflicts	Different conceptual systems	Holistic VS localised approach to practice	[TCM took holistic view, whereas WM took micro view of patients' problem]	*TCM 6.72* 这些有迷信色彩,但是涉及到宏观世界,微观世界觉得是一种迷信。这是观念和学术理论的不同的体系。如果不采取了解和包容的态度很可能认为是迷信。你说阴阳五行,从这个自然观念来看,排除迷信色彩,还是一环扣一环,跟这个生物链一样的。
				TCM 18.07 基本上不可能把中医和西医完全结合在一起,因为中医采用的是宏观的角度看病人。这个是最基本的理论基础 [*Translation*] "It is almost impossible to integrate both TCM and WM methods into one medical procedure. It is because TCM takes a holistic view of human body, which is the philosophical foundation for TCM." Interview TCM 18.7
				WMD 24.9 西医总是很微观的看身体具体的某一个部位。你如果头有问题就医头,如果脚有问题就医脚。但是中医是把病人看作一个整体。他们不光是看那一个病症,所以西医是从微观的角度,中医呢是从一个整体的角度。

Sub-Cat-egories	3rd level categories	Concepts	Codes	Quotations
				[Translation] "WM always localises diseases into particular parts of human body. If you have a head problem, then treat the head. If you have problems with your feet, then treat the feet. However, TCM treats a patient as a whole. They [TCM doctors] are not just dealing with the disease itself. Therefore, WM is from a micro perspective, TCM is holistic". Interview WMD 24.9
				TCM Politician 34.3 中医讲的是整体的治疗,讲宏观讲经验,或者说它是个模糊科学。西医就是来自于实验室的,它是一个精密科学。或者就是叫做数字科学。这两个体系要融合,融合起来不容易。

References

Abidi S (2007) Healthcare knowledge sharing: purpose, practices, and prospects. In: Bali R, Dwivedi A (eds) Healthcare knowledge management: issues, advances, and successes. Springer, New York, pp 67–86
Alavi M, Carlson P (1992) A review of MIS research and disciplinary development. J Manage Inf Syst 8(4):45–62
Alavi M, Leidner D (2001) Review: knowledge management and knowledge management systems: conceptual foundations and research issues. MIS Q 25(1):107–136
Al-Hawamdeh S (2003) Knowledge management: cultivating knowledge professionals. Chandos, Oxford
Allan G (2003) A critique of using grounded theory as a research method. Electronic J Bus Res Methods 2(1):1–10
American Educational Research Association (1992) Ethical standards of the American Educational Research Association. American Educational Research Association, Washington, DC
American Psychological Association (1992) Ethical principles of psychologists and code of conduct. Am Psychol 47(12):1597–1611
American Sociological Association (1989) Code of Ethics. American Sociological Association, Washington, DC
Andrews J et al (2006) Information-seeking behaviours of practitioners in a primary care practice-based research network (PBRN). J Med Libr Assoc 93(2):206–212
Ayyub B (2001). Elicitation of expert opinions for uncertainty and risks. Taylor & Francis, Boca Raton
Beach M (2001) Blood heads and AIDS haunt China's countryside. Lancet 357(9249):49
Benbasat I et al (1987) The case research strategy in studies of information systems. MIS Q 11(3):369–386
Bian Y, Zhou S, Li X, Bing T (2008) Break barriers and promote knowledge management in hospitals. Military Med J South Ch 22(4):61–62
Blackler F (1995) Knowledge, knowledge work and organisations: an overview and interpretation. Organization Stud 16(6):1021–1046
Boisot M (1995) Information space: a framework for learning in organizations, institutions and culture. Routledge, London
Bouthillier F, Shearer K (2005) Knowledge management and information management: review of empirical evidence. In: Maceviciute E, Wilson TD (eds) Introducing information management: an information research reader. Facet, London, pp 139–150
Brice A, Gray M (2003) Knowledge is the enemy of disease. Library Inf Update 2(3):36–37
Bryman A (2001) Social research methods. Oxford University Press, Bath
Bryman A (2002) Research methods and organisation studies. Routledge, London
Bryman A (2008) Social research methods, 3rd edn. Oxford University Press, Oxford
Bryman A, Bell E (2003) Business research methods. Oxford University Press, Oxford

Cai Y, Ju F (2009) Waiting for the spring of traditional Chinese medicine: a public statement by Chen Zhu, the Minister of Health. Chin J Pract Chin Mod Med 22(16):F0002 (in Chinese)

Cao G, Sun Y (2009) Respect requirements of in-patient and finalising nursing service culture. Clin J 18(10):108–109 (in Chinese)

Carlson ED (2000) A case study in translation methodology using the health-promotion lifestyle profile II. Pub Health Nurs 17(1):61–70

Cassell J, Jacobs S (1987) Handbook on ethical issues in anthropology. American Anthropological Association, Washington, DC

Chen C (1989) Medicine in rural China. University of California Press, Los Angeles

Chen M (2008) Research on knowledge management methods based on hospital process. Chin Hosp Manage 28(11):30–32 (in Chinese)

Chen H et al. (2009). The implementation of electronic records management in facilitating knowledge sharing at software development projects. In: Proceedings of the 11th International Conference on Informatics and Semiotics in Organisations, 11–12 April, 2009, Beijing, China.

Chen LJ et al (1999) Brief introduction on development of Chinese medicine in new China. Mag Chin Med Manage 9(5):7–8 (in Chinese)

Chen S et al (2009) Strategy of development of hospital human resources based on knowledge management. Mod Hosp 9(6):1–2 (in Chinese)

Cheng J (2000) Review: drug therapy in Chinese traditional medicine. J Clin Pharmacol 40(5):445–450

Chen Y (2009) Exploring for hospital's management of medical knowledge. Mod Hosp 9(10):1–3 (in Chinese)

Chi C (1994) Integrating traditional medicine into modern health care systems: examing the role of Chinese medicine in Taiwan. Soc Sci Med 39(3):307–321

Chinese Government (2012). Economic system. http://english.gov.cn/about/economy.htm. Accessed 1 Aug 2014

Choo C (2000) Working with knowledge: how information professionals help organizations manage what they know. Library Manage 21(8):395–403

Choo CW (1998) Information management for the Intelligent Organization: the art of scanning the environment. Information Today, Medford

Chui L (2010). Designing hospital management system. Manage Observer 22:269–270 (in Chinese)

Collis J, Hussey R (2003). Business research: a practical guide for undergraduates and postgraduate students. Palgrave McMillan, Hampshire

Cook S, Brown J (1999) Bridging epistemologies: the generative dance between organizational knowledge and organizational knowing. Organ Sci 10(4):381–400

Copeland G (2005) A practical handbook for clinical audit. http:// citeseerx.ist.psu.edu/viewdoc/download?doi=10.1.1.131.4403&rep=rep1&type=pdf. Accessed 1 Aug 2014

Corbin J, Strauss A (1990) Grounded theory research: procedures, canons, and evaluative criteria. Qual Sociol 13(1):3–21

Currie G, Suhomlinova O (2006) The impact of institutional forces upon knowledge sharing in the UK NHS: the triumph of professional power and the inconsistency of policy. Pub Adm 84(1):1–30

Currie G et al (2007) Spanning boundaries in pursuit of effective knowledge sahring within networks in the NHS. J Health Organ Manage 21(4–5):406–417

Dally A (2003) The trouble with doctors: fashions motives and mistakes. Robson Books, London

Davernport TH, Prusak L (1998) Working knowledge: how organization manage what they know. Harvard Business School Press, Boston

Davidson P et al (2003) Traditional Chinese medicine and heart disease: what does western medicine and nursing science know about It? Eur J Cardiovasc Nurs 2(3):171–181

De Brún C (2007) Knowledge management and the national health service in England. In: Bali R, Dwivedi A (eds) Healthcare knowledge management: issues, advances, and successes. Springer, New York, pp 179–188

References

de Lusignan S et al (2002) A knowledge-management model for clinical practice. J Postgrad Med 48(4):297–303
Delva D et al (2008) A new model for collaborative continuing professional development. J Interprofessional Car 22(S1):91–100
Department of Health (1998) Information for health: an information strategy for the modern NHS 1998–2005. NHS Executive. http://webarchive.nationalarchives.gov.uk/+/www.dh.gov.uk/en/Publicationsandstatistics/Publications/PublicationsPolicyAndGuidance/DH_4002944. Accessed 1 Aug 2014
DeTienne K et al (2004) Toward a model of effective knowledge management and directions for future research: culture, leadership, and ckos. J Leadersh Organ Stud 10(4):26–43
Ding H, Yu H (2010) Neurosurgery in Chinese specialised hospitals. J Tradit Chin Med Manage 18(7):654–655 (in Chinese)
Dobbins M et al. (2010) A knowledge management tool for public health: health-evidence.ca. BMC Pub Health 10:496
Dwivedi A et al (2007) Building new healthcare management paradigms: a case for healthcare knowledge management. In: Bali R, Dwivedi A (eds) Healthcare knowledge management: issues, advances, and successes. Springer, New York, pp 3–10
Du F, Sun Z (2005) Investigating hospital knowledge management system implementation. J Inf 5:55–57 (in Chinese)
Eardley A, Czerwinski A (2007) Knowledge management for primary healthcare services. In: Bali R, Dwivedi A (eds) Healthcare knowledge management: issues, advances, and successes. Springer, New York, pp 201–220
Efferth T et al (2007) From traditional Chinese medicine to rational cancer therapy. Trends Mol Med 13(8):353–361
Eisenhardt K (1989) Building theories from case study research. Acad Manage Rev 14(4):532–550
Elden M, Chisholm R (1993) Emerging varieties of action research: introduction to the special Issue. Hum Relat 46(2):121–142
Esposito N (2001) From meaning to meaning: the influence of translation techniques on non-English focus group research. Qual Health Res 1(4):568–579
Fan R (2003) Modern western science as a standard for traditional Chinese medicine: a critical appraisal. J Law Med Eth 31(2):213–221 (in Chinese)
Fang H (2006) Abolishing traditional Chinese medicine: ignorant or salvation? Natl Med Front China 6:77–80 (in Chinese)
Fang Z (2005) How should we evaluate traditional Chinese medicine. Dig Sci Technol 6:76–78 (in Chinese)
Fang Z (2007) Zhongyixinshiji Dalunzhan: PipingZhongyi. Peking Union Medical College Press, Beijing
Fang Z (2010). Health promotion: how can it convince the public. Pub Health 8:16–17 (in Chinese)
Fennessy G, Burstein F (2007) Role of information professionals as intermediaries for knowledge management in evidence-based healthcare. In: Bali R, Dwivedi A (eds) Healthcare knowledge management: issues, advances, and successes. Springer, New York, pp 28–40
Ferlie E et al (2005) The diffusion of innovations: the mediating role of professional groups. Acad Manage J 48(1):117–134
Fernández W (2004) The grounded theory method and case study data in is research: issues and design. In: Proceedings of Information Systems Foundation Workshop: Constructing and Criticising Australian National University
Fitzgerald F (1990) Physical diagnosis versus modern technology—a review. West J Med 152:377–382
Ford D, Chan Y (2003) Knowledge sharing in a multi-cultural setting: a case study. Knowl Manage Res Pract 1(1):11–27
Frank L (1961) Interprofessional communication. Am J Pub Health 51(12):1798–1804
Freeth D et al (2002) A critical review of evaluations of interprofessional education: occasional paper no. 2. The Higher Education Academy, London. http://www.health.heacademy.ac.uk/lenses/occasionalpapers/m10123.html.[Accessed 1 Aug 2014

Fruehauf H (1999) Chinese medicine in crisis. J Chin Med (61):1–9
Gabbay J, le May A (2004) Evidence based guidelines or collectively constructed "mindlines?": ethnographic study of knowledge management in primary care. Br Med J 329:1013–1017
Glaser B (1978) Advances in the methodology of grounded theory: theoretical sensitivity. Sociology, Mill Valley
Glaser B (1992). Basics of grounded theory analysis: emergence vs forcing. Sociology, Mill Valley
Glaser B, Strauss A (1967) The discovery of grounded theory: strategies for qualitative research. Aldine Transaction, London
Goldman L, Ausiello D (2008) Cecil medicine: an expert consult title online + print, 23rd edn. Saunders Elsevier, Philadelphia
Gorman G, Clayton P (2005) Qualitative research for the information professional: a practical handbook. Facet, London
Gorman P, Helfand M (1995) Information seeking in primary care: how physicians choose which clinical questions to pursue and which to leave unanswered. Med Decis Mak 15(2):113–119
Goulding C (2007) Grounded theory: a practical guide for management, business and market researchers. Sage, Los Angeles
Gourlay S (2003) The SECI model of knowledge creation: some empirical shortcomings. http://eprints.kingston.ac.uk/2291/1/Gourlay%202004%20SECI.pdf. Accessed 1 Aug 2014.
Grant A (2007) Tacit knowledge revisited—we can still learn from polanyi. Electronic J Knowl Manage 5(2):173–180
Gray J (1998) Where's the chief knowledge officer? To manage the most precious resource of all. Br Med J 317:832
Gray J, de Lusignan S (1999) National electronic library for health (NeLH). Br Med J 319(7223):1476–1479
Grice HP (1975) Logic and conversation. In: Cole P, Morgan J (eds) Syntax and semantics 3. Academic, New York, pp 41–58
Guo F (2006) Discussion of the theories of the integration of traditional Chinese medicine and western medicine. J Clinical Exp Med 5(4):408–409 (in Chinese)
Guo M et al (2007) Challenges and management of traditional Chinese medicines in health services in urban China. J Manage Chin Med 15(2):77–79 (in Chinese)
Guo T (2010) Evaluating traditional Chinese medicine. J Part Sch CPC Hangzhou Munic Comm 1:18–24 (in Chinese)
Guo Z (2005) Establishing hospital knowledge management system. Chin J Hosp Adm 21(11):775–776 (in Chinese)
Hall P (2005) Interprofessional teamwork: professional cultures as barriers. J Interprofessional Car 19(Suppl 1):188–196
Hammond S, Glenn L (2004) The ancient practice of Chinese social networking; guanxi and social network theory. E:CO 6(1-2):24–31
Han F (2006) The start of traditional Chinese medicine and western medicine collaboration movement. Ch Newsweek 44:95 (in Chinese)
Harkness JA, Schoua-Glusberg A (1998) Questionnaires in translation. Zuma-Nachrichten Spezial vol. 3, (pp. 87-125).
Herbert C (2005) Changing the culture: interprofessional education for collaborative patient-centred practice in Canada. J Interprofessional Car 19(Supplement 1):1–4
Herdman M et al (1997) 'Equivalence' and the translation and adaptation of health-related quality of life questionnaires. Qual Life Res 6(3):237–247
Hesketh T, Zhu W (1997). Health in China: the healthcare market. Br Med J 314:1616
Hillier S, Jewell J (1983) Health Care and traditional medicine in China, 1800–1982. Routledge & Kegan Paul, London
Hofstede G (1994) The business of international business is culture. Int Bus Rev 3(1):1–14
Hofstede G, Hofstede GJ (2005) Culture and organizations: software of the mind, 2nd edn. McGraw-Hill, New York

References

Hollenberg D (2006) Uncharted ground: patterns of professional interaction among complementary/alternative and biomedical practitioners in integrative health care settings. Soc Sci Med 62(3):731–744

Holm S (1997). Ethical problems in clinical practice: the ethical reasoning of health care professionals. Bell & Bain, Glasgow

Horton W, Keysar B (1996) When do speakers take into account common ground? Cognition 59(1):91–117

Hsiao W (1995) The Chinese health care system: lessons for other nations. Soc Sci Med 41(8):1047–1055

Hsiao W, Yip W (2009) China's health care reform: a tentative assessment. Ch Econ Rev 20(4):613–619

Hu G (2009) Take patient as the centre and provide premium services. Jiangsu Healthc Ind Manage 20(3):49–50 (in Chinese)

Hu Y (2006) Talk about the diathesis of 21 century surgeon. Mod Hosp 6(4):92 (in Chinese)

Huang X, Huang Y (2009) Communication skills in community nursing services. Chin Community Dr 11(18):219 (in Chinese)

Hubei G. (2014). Introduction to Hubei. http://en.hubei.gov.cn/hubei_info/ introduction. Accessed 1 Aug 2014

Hussain F et al (2004) Managing knowledge effectively. J Knowl Manage Pract. May 2004. http://www.tlainc.com/articl66.htm. Accessed 1 Aug 2014.

Hyatt R (1978) Chinese herbal medicine: ancient art and modern science. Wildwood House, London

Hyde K (2000) Recognising deductive process in qualitative research. Qual Mark: Res: Int J 3(2):82–89

Ipe M (2003) Knowledge sharing in organisations: a conceptual framework. Hum Resour Dev Rev 2(4):337–359

Ismail MB, Yusof ZM (2008) Knowledge sharing models: do they really fit public organizations. In: *ITSim2008*. Proceedings of International Symposium on Information Technology. 26–28 August, 2008, Kuala Lumpur, Malaysia

Ju Q (2009) Communication skills for nurses in outpatient paediatric infusion room. Chin Community Dr 11(18):246–247 (in Chinese)

Kaptchuk TJ (2000) The web that has no weaver: understanding Chinese medicine. McGraw Hill, New York

King N (2010) Interviews in qualitative research. Sage, London

Koepsell D (1999) Introduction to applied ontology: the philosophical analyses of everyday objects. Amer J Econ Sociol 58(2):217–220

Lam TP (2001) Strengths and weakness of traditional Chinese medicine and western medicine in the eyes of some Hong Kong Chinese. J Epidemiol Community Health 55:762–765

Lary M et al (1997) Breaking down barriers: multidisciplinary educational model. J Allied Health 26:63–69

Lee J (2001) The impact of knowledge sharing, organizational capability and partnership quality on is outsourcing success. Inf Manage 38(5):323–335

Li D et al (2008) Research on hospital knowledge management strategies. Chin Health Serv Manage 235(1):15–16 (in Chinese)

Li J et al (2009) Establishing and finalising assessment criteria for individual healthcare professionals. Hosp Manage Forum 11(26):20–24 (in Chinese)

Li L (2010) Applying information technologies in hospital management. Med Inf 23(16):2509–2510 (in Chinese)

Li Z (2009) Scientific definition of TCM—science, philosophy, human,name and reality. Ch J Tradit Chin Med Pharm 24(4):410-418 (in Chinese)

Li P, Wang Z (2008) Using knowledge management to propel healthcare informatic strategy innovation. Chongqing Med Sci 37(9):995–1000

Li R, Liu X (1992) A commentary on modern history of traditional Chinese medicine. Chin J Med Hist 22(1):1–6 (in Chinese)

Li S et al (2010) Research of knowledge management in hospitals: a literature review. Chin J Med Library Inf Sc 19(5):36–39

Li Y (2005) 6C strategy for hospital knowledge management. China Contemp Med 11(1):21 (in Chinese)

Li Y et al (2008) Research on knowledge management for establishing research—oriented hospital. Hosp Adm J PLA 15(4):314–315 (in Chinese)

Liebowitz J (1999). Knowledge management handbook. CRC, London

Lin C et al (2008) An exploratory model of knowledge Flow barriers within healthcare organizations. Inf Manage 45(5):331–339

Liu G (2006) Doctors accepting bribery can be convicted. Hosp Manage Forum 6:15–16 (in Chinese)

Liu H et al (2008) Market economy policy and the development of traditional Chinese medicine in china. Health Econ Res 4:20–21 (in Chinese)

Liu J et al (2006) Core contents of knowledge management in hospital libraries. Chin J Med Library Inf Sci 15(5):1–4 (in Chinese)

Liu J et al (2007) Tacit knowledge management of hospital libraries. Chin J Med Library Inf Sci 16(3):32–34 (in Chinese)

Liu L (2003). The consideration of traditional Chinese medicine (in Chinese). Guangxi Normal University Press, Guilin.

Liu S (2010). Opportunities for traditional Chinese medicine in the healthcare reformation. China Invest 6:66–67 (in Chinese)

Liu Y (2005) Traditional Chinese medicine in modern time: research and strategies. J US-China Med Sci 2(2):55–62 (in Chinese)

Liu Y et al (1999) Equity in health and health care: the Chinese experience. Soc Sci Med 49(10):1349–1356

Lodhi S (2005). Culture based knowledge sharing model. PhD, National College of Business Administration & Economics, Lahore, Pakistan

Lomas J (2007) The in-between world of knowledge brokering. Br Med J 334:129–132

Lv WB (2005) Integration of Chinese and western medicine and westernisation of Chinese medicine. Chin J Integr Tradit West Med 25(1):6–7 (in Chinese)

Ma M (2009). The influence of fuxi culture on Chinese medicine. Tribute Educ C 2:60–63 (in Chinese)

Ma XQ (1999) Between two worlds: the use of traditional and western health service by Chinese immigrants. J Community Health 24(6):421–437

Maciocia G (1989) The foundations of Chinese medicine: a comprehensive text for acupuncturists and herbalists. Churchill Livingstone, London

Maizes V et al (2009) Integrative medicine and patient-centred care. Explor: J Sci Heal 5(5):277–289

Marshall S, White A (1994) Interviewing respondents who have English as a second language: challenges encountered and suggestions for other researchers. J Adv Nurs 19(3):566–571

Mason R et al (1997) An historical method for MIS research: steps and assumptions. MIS Q 21(3):307–320

Matsuo M, Easterby-Smith M (2008) Beyond the knowledge sharing dilemma: the role of customisation. J Knowl Manage 12(4):30–43

Maylor H, Blackmon K (2005) Researching business and management. Palgrave Macmillan, Basingstoke

McEvily S et al (2000) Avoiding competence substitution through knowledge sharing. Acad Manage Rev 25(2):296–311

McGrath P et al (2006) Patient-centred care: qualitative findings on health professionals' understanding of ethics in acute medicine. Bioethical Inq 3(3):149–160

McMillan J, Naughton B (1992) How to reform a planned economy: lesson from china. Oxf Rev Econ Pol 8(1):130–143

Mertins K et al (2003) Knowledge management—concepts and best practices. Springer, New York

Men Y (2008) Resources of pressure for nurses: an analysis of the present situation. Chin J Urban Rural Ind Hyg 4(2):64–65 (in Chinese)
Meng J (2007). Knowledge management strategy retaining hospitals advantage in competition. Mod Hosp 7:160–161 (in Chinese)
Mohamed M (2008) The "continuumization" of knowledge management technology. VINE: J Inf Knowl Manage Syst 38(2):167–173
Moghaddam A (2006) Coding issues in grounded theory. Issues Educ Res 16(1):52–66
Morse J (1999) Qualitative generalizability. Q Health Res 9(1):5–6
Myers M (1997) Qualitative research in information systems. MIS Q 21(2):241–242
Myers M (1999) Investigating information systems with ethnographic research. Commun Assoc Inf Syst 2(23):2–20
Myers M, Newman M (2007) The qualitative interview in is research: examing the craft. Inf Organ 17(1):2–26
National Bureau of Statistics of China (2005). Chinese statistical yearbook of Chinese medicine. National Bureau of Statistics of China, Beijing. http://www.moh.gov.cn/mohbgt/s8274/200805/35286.shtml. Accessed 1 Aug 2014.
National Bureau of Statistics of China (2013) China health and family planning statistical yearbook. http://www.nhfpc.gov.cn/mohwsbwstjxxzx/s79 67/201404/6a76c0e465684c2b97e9e0b-c1f0eb2d3.shtml. Accessed 1 Aug 2014.
New China News Agency (1950) National Healthcare Conference. New China News Agency, 22 Aug 1950
NHS (2002) Principles for best practice in clinical audit . Radcliffe Medical Press, Oxon. http://evidencebasednursing.it/secretroom/audic_clini co.pdf. Accessed 1 Aug 2014
Nicolini D et al (2008) Managing knowledge in the healthcare sector. A review. Int J Manage Rev 10(3):245–263
Nonaka I (1994) A dynamic theory of organizational knowledge creation. Organ Sci 5(1):14–37
Nonaka I, Takeuchi H (1995) The knowledge-creating company: how Japanese companies create the dynamics of innovation. Oxford University Press, Oxford
Nonaka I et al (2000) SECI, Ba and leadership: a unified model of dynamic knowledge creation. Long Range Plan 33:5–34
O'Connor A et al (2003) Risk communication in practice: the contribution of decision aids. Br Med J 327(7417):736–740
Onions P (2006) Grounded theory applications in reviewing knowledge management literature. In: Proceedings of Postgraduate Research Conference, Methodological Issues and Ethical Consideration, 24th May 2006, Leeds Metropolitan University, UK
Orlikowski W, Baroudi J (1991) Studying information technology in organizations: research approaches and assumptions. Inf Syst Res 2(1):1–28
Pandit N (1996) The creation of theory: a recent application of the grounded theory method. Qual Rep 2(4). http://www.nova.edu/ssss/QR/QR2-4/pandit.html. Accessed 1 Aug 2014
Patton M (2002) Qualitative research and evaluation methods. Sage, London
Pavia L (2001) The era of knowledge in health care. Health Car Strateg Manage 19(2):12–13
Peng G, Nunes M (2008) Issues and difficulties in doing participative research in China: lessons learned from a survey in information systems research. In: Proceedings of The European Conference on Research Methodology for Business and Management Studies (ECRM 2008), 19–20 June 2008, Regent's College, London, UK
Peng W, Littlejohn D (2001) Organisational communication and strategy implementation—a primary Inquiry. J Contemp Hosp Manage 13(7):360–363
Petrides L (2002) Organizational learning and the case for knowledge-based systems. New Dir Inst Res 2002(113):69–84
Pickard A (2007) Research methods in information. Facet, London
Polanyi M (1966) The tacit dimension. Garden City, New York
Pratt DD (1991) Conceptions of self within China and the United States: contrasting foundations for adult education. Int J Intercul Relats 15(3):285–310
Probst G et al (2000) Managing knowledge: building blocks for success. Wiley, Chichester

Punch K (2005) Introduction to social research: quantitative and qualitative approaches. Sage, London

Qian Y, Wu J (2003) China's transition to a market economy: how far across the river? In: Hope N, Yang D, Li M (eds) How far across the river. Stanford University Press, Stanford

Qiu F (2010) The orientation for healthcare reformation is the "macro government" and "macro economy. Bus Financ Rev 12:32–33 (in Chinese)

Rapoport R (1970) Three dilemmas of action research. Hum Relats 23(4):499–513

Reeves S et al (2007) Key factors in planning and implementing interprofessional education in health care settings. J Allied Health 36(4):231–235

Remenyi D et al (1998) Doing research in business and management: an introduction to process and method. Sage, London

Ren Y (2010) Viewpoint—one year anniversary of healthcare reformation. New Financ Econ Mon 6:8 (in Chinese)

Riege A (2005) Three-dozen knowledge-sharing barriers managers must consider. J Knowl Manage 9(3):18–35

Rodon J, Pastor J (2007) Applying grounded theory to study the implementation of an inter-organizational information system. Electron J Bus Res Methods 5(2):71–82

Rong Z et al (2005) Discuss knowledge management and hospital knowledge management. J Mil Surg Southwest China 7(2):59–62 (in Chinese)

Rosenberg W, Donald A (1995) Evidence based medicine: an approach to clinical problem-solving. Br Med J 310:1122

Ryu S et al (2003) Knowledge sharing behavior of physicians in hospitals. Expert Syst Appl 25(1):113–122

Salmador M, Bueno E (2007) Knowledge creation in strategy-making: implications for theory and practice. Eur J Innov Manage 10(3):367–390

San Martín-Rodríguez L et al (2005) The determinants of successful collaboration: a review of theoretical and empirical studies. J Interprofessional Car 19(Suppl 1):132–147

Saunders M et al (2007) Research methods for business students. Prentice Hall, New York

Sawhney M, Prandelli E (2000) Communities of creation: managing distributed innovation in turbulent markets. Calif Manage Rev 42(4):24–54

Schubert P et al. (1998) A global knowledge medium as a virtual community: the NetAcademy Concept. In: Proceedings of the 4th Americas Conference on Information Systems. Baltimore, MD

Servin G (2005) ABC of knowledge management. NHS National Library for Health: Knowledge Management Specialist Library. http://research.fraserhealth.ca/media/ABC_of_KM.PDF

Shao K (2007) Existence and development of private traditional Chinese medicine specialised hospital in the new era. Chin J Clin Pract Med 8(7):84–86 (in Chinese)

Sharif M et al (2005) Facilitating knowledge sharing through lessons learned system. J Knowl Manage Pract. http://www.tlainc.com/articl82.htm. Accessed 1 Aug 2014.

Sheffield J (2008) Inquiry in health knowledge management. J Knowl Manage 12(4):160–172

Sherman K et al (2005) The practice of acupuncture: who are the providers and what do they do? Ann Fam Med 3(2):151–158

Singh S (2008) Role of leadership in knowledge management: a study. J Knowl Manage 12(4):3–15

Smith R (1996) What clinical information do doctors need? Br Med J 313:1062–1068

Song J (2010) Discussing hospital information systems and strategies of improvement. Med Inf 23(9):3065–3066 (in Chinese)

Song Y et al (2006) Development and strategies of hospital knowledge management. Soft Sci Health 20(4):366–367 (in Chinese)

Sperber A (2004) Translation and validation of study instruments for cross-cultural research. Gastroenterology 126(Supplement 1):124–128

Srikantaiah T, Koenig M (2000) The evolution of knowledge management. In: Knowledge management for the information professional. Information Today, Medford

Stenmark D (2002) Information vs. knowledge: the role of intranets in knowledge management. In: Proceedings of the 35th Hawaii International Conference on System Sciences, Hawaii, USA

Steward M (2001) Towards a global definition of patient centred care: the patient should be the judge of patient centred care. Br Med J 322:444–445

Strauss A, Corbin J (1990) Basics of qualitative research: grounded theory procedures and techniques. Sage, London

Strauss A, Corbin J (1998) Basic of qualitative research: techniques and procedures for developing grounded theory, 2nd edn. Sage, London

Sun B (2010) Analysing key issues when upgrading hospital information system. Med Inf 23(8):26 (in Chinese)

Sun C (2003) Research in communication of traditional Chinese medicien and western medicine doctors. J Nanjing Univ Tradi Chin Med 4(1):6–9 (in Chinese)

Supar N et al (2005) Factors affecting knowledge sharing and its effects on performance: a study of three selected higher academic institutions. In: Proceedings of the International Conference on Knowledge Management (ICKM), 7–9 July, 2005, Kuala Lumpur, Malaysia

Tao B et al (2005) Current situation of traditional Chinese medicine in regions in poverty. J Chin Med Manage 5(5):30–31 (in Chinese)

Taylor K (2004) Divergent interests and cultivated misunderstanding: the influence of the west on modern Chinese medicine. Soc Hist Med 17(1):93–111

Tellis W (1997) Introduction to case study. Qual Rep 3(2). http://www.nova.edu/ssss/QR/QR3-2/tellis1.html. Accessed 1 Aug 2014

Temple B, Young A (2004) Qualitative research translation dilemmas. Qual Res 4(2):161–178

The University of Sheffield (2012) Ethics policy for research involving human participants, data and tissue. The University of Sheffield, Sheffield. http://www.sheffield.ac.uk/ris/other/gov-ethics/ethicspolicy. Accessed 1 Aug 2014.

Tian Y (2003) Differences between Chinese and western medical theories and modernization of TCM. Chin J Basic Med Tradit Chin Med 9(7):3–4 (in Chinese)

Tong J, Mitra A (2009) Chinese cultural influences on knowledge management practice. J Knowl Manage 13(2):49–62

Trochim M (2006) Deductive and inductive thinking. http://www. socialresearchmethods.net/kb/dedind.htm. Accessed 1 Aug 2014.

Tuomi I (1999) Implications of the reversed knowledge hierarchy for knowledge management and organizational memory. J Manage Inf Syst 16(3):107–121

Twinn S (1997) An exploratory study examing the influence of translation on the validity and reliability of qualitative data in nursing research. J Adv Nurs 26(2):418–423

Twinn S (2000) The analysis of focus group data: a challenge to the rigour of qualitative research. NT Res 5(2):140–146

United Nations Health Partners Group in China (2005). A health situation assessment of the people's republic of China. United Nations Health Partners Group in China, Beijing

Unschuld P (1985) Medicine in China: a history of ideas. University of California Press, Los Angeles

Van Beveren J (2003) Does health care for knowledge management? J Knowl Manage 7(1):90–95

Van Niekerk J, Roode J (2009). Glaserian and straussian grounded theory: similar or completely different? In: Proceedings of South African Institute for Computer Scientists and Information Technologists. Riverside, Vanderbijlpark, South Africa.

Vasconcelos A (2008) Dilemmas in knowledge management. Library Manage 29(4–5):422–443

Veal A (2005) Business research methods: a managerial approach. Pearson Addison Wesley, Frenchs Forest

Vogt W (1993) Dictionary of statistics and methodology: a nontechnical guide for the social sciences. Sage, Thousand Oaks

Wang B (2006b) On the past, present and future of traditional Chinese medicine from the history of abolition traditional Chinese medicine. Med Philos: Humanist Soc Med Ed 27(12):19–20 (in Chinese)

Wang C (2008) The great reformation from the plan economy to the market socialism. Xinxiang Forum 11:29–31

Wang LD (2000) Purposes and methods in intensive and critical care with integrated Chinese and western medicine. Chin J Integr Tradit West Med Intensive Crit Care 7(6):323–325 (in Chinese)

Wang N (2006a) Approaching traditional Chinese medicine. China Today 55(8):61 (in Chinese)

Wang S (2010) Fifteen relationships need to be managed in integrated traditional and western medicine hospitals. Zhong Guo Bao Jian Ying Yang Za Zhi 3:115–117 (in Chinese)

Wang X et al (2004) A self-learning expert system for diagnosis in traditional Chinese medicine. Expert Syst Appl 26(4):557–566

Warrell D et al (2005) Oxford textbook of medicine. Oxford University Press, New York

Weber R (2004) The rhetoric of positivism versus interpretivism: a personal view. MIS Q 28(1):3–12.

Wong TW et al (1993) Traditional Chinese medicine and western medicine in Hong Kong: a comparison of the consultation processes and side effects. J Hong Kong Med Assoc 45(4):278–284

Wu Z (1991) Applying traditional Chinese medicine after brain surgery. J Chin Physician 6:42–45 (in Chinese)

Xie W (2006) Problems and solutions for hospital managements under the new economical situation. Li Lun Yu Shi Jian 9:57–58 (in Chinese)

Xu J (2009) Zhu-Zi-Bai-Jia and the culture of traditional Chinese medicine. Health Horiz 24:124–125 (in Chinese)

Yan Q (2009) Development of hospital knowledge management. Med Soc 22(1):45–46

Yan Y (2006) Generally discuss innovative methodologies in integrated Chinese and western medicine research. Chin Med Mod Distance Educ Ch 4(8):11–12 (in Chinese)

Yang H (2010) Healthcare reformation in progress—steady steps. Chin Invest 6:38–41 (in Chinese)

Yang L (2009) Hospital knowledge management evaluation system base on ANP. Chin J Health Stat 26(5):509–511 (in Chinese)

Yang T et al (2006) Discuss the implementation of knowledge management in hospital management. J Yunyang Med Coll 25(5):320 (in Chinese)

Yang Y (2005) Discussion of the integration of traditional Chinese medicine and western medicine. Chin Foreign Med J 3(1):84–86 (in Chinese)

Yang Y (2009) Finalising healthcare insurance and stimulate hospital development harmoniously. Jiangsu Healthc Ind Manage 20(4):27–28 (in Chinese)

Yao L (2009) Recognise "taking patient as the centre". Mod Hosp 9(9):3–5 (in Chinese)

Yin R (1994) Case study research, design and methods, 2nd edn. Sage, Newbury Park

Yin R (2003) Case study research: design and methods, 3rd edn. Sage, London

Zeng S (2008) Strong supports to the development of traditional Chinese medicine. Qian Jin Lun Tan 2:64 (in Chinese)

Zhang B, Cang S (2009) Establishing "Patient-Centred" assessment modes in hospitals by using the scientific development perspective. Chin J Curr Hosp Manag 7(11):39–41

Zhang B, Li C (2005) Construction of knowledge sharing model in hospital management. Chin Rural Health Serv Adm 25(10):35–37 (in Chinese)

Zhang B, Li C (2006) Hospital management oriented knowledge-sharing mechanisms. Ind Eng J 9(6):15–17 (in Chinese)

Zhang C (2010). Evaluating western medicine from the perspective of traditional Chinese medicine. Med Philos: Humanist Soc Med Ed 5:53–55 (in Chinese)

Zhang F et al (2009) Establishing premium registration patient services. Jiangsu Healthc Ind Manage 20(5):73–74 (in Chinese)

Zhang G (2006) Farewell to traditional Chinese medicine and remedies. Med Philos: Humanist Soc Med Ed 27(4):14–17 (in Chinese)

Zhang G (2007) The function of philosophy of science in counter attack the receding of anti-science. Stud Dialect Nat 23(10):82–86 (in Chinese)

References

Zhang Q et al (2007) Discuss traditional Chinese medicine in new cooperative medical schemes. Chin Rural Health Serv Adm 27(3):228–229 (in Chinese)

Zheng X (2010) Clinical informatics: improve health care through information sharing. Inf Med Equip 3:70–72 (in Chinese)

Zhong H (2009) The patient-centred care and hospital marketing strategies. Manage Obs 30:234–235 (in Chinese).

Zhou D, Liu X (2007) Modes of knowledge management based upon hospital technical innovation system. Forum Sci Technol China 11(11):111–115 (in Chinese)

Zhou L et al. (2007) Knowledge sharing in complementary healthcare communities of practice: the coexistence of traditional and western medicine in China. In: proceedings of the 2nd Annual South East European Doctoral Student Conference, June 2007, Thessaloniki, Greece

Zhou L et al (2008) Supporting decision making in risk management through an evidence-based information systems project risk checklist. Inf Manage Comput Secur 16(2):166–186

Zhou L et al. (2010) Identifying knowledge sharing barriers in interprofessional healthcare collaboration of traditional and western medicine in China. In: Proceedings of IADIS International Conference Information Systems 2010, 18–20 March, 2010, Porto, Portugal.

Zhou X (2008) The status of nurse in conducting clinical decision. J Fuzhou Gen Hosp 6(15):96 (in Chinese)

Zhu X, Liu X (2009) Traditional Chinese medicine specialised hospitals expect to be treated equally as western healthcare organisations. Chin J Pract Chin Mod Med 22(1):3–4

Zhu Y (2010) Discussing the holistic view of traditional Chinese medicine. J Tradit Chin Med Lit 4:35–36 (in Chinese)

Zwarenstein M, Reeves S (2006) Knowledge translation and interprofessional collaboration: where the rubber of evidence-based care hits the road of teamwork. J Contin Educ Health Prof 26(1):46–54

If you have any concerns about our products,
you can contact us on
ProductSafety@springernature.com

In case Publisher is established outside the EU,
the EU authorized representative is:
**Springer Nature Customer Service Center GmbH
Europaplatz 3, 69115 Heidelberg, Germany**

Printed by Libri Plureos GmbH
in Hamburg, Germany